Contemporary Biomedical Ethical Issues and Jewish Law

Contemporary Biomedical Ethical Issues and Jewish Law

Fred Rosner, M.D., M.A.C.P.

KTAV PUBLISHING HOUSE, INC.

JERSEY CITY, NEW JERSEY

Library of Congress Cataloging-in-Publication Data

Rosner, Fred.
  Contemporary biomedical ethical issues and Jewish law / Fred Rosner.
      p. cm.
  Includes bibliographical references.
  ISBN 978-0-88125-946-9
  1. Medical laws and legislation (Jewish law) 2. Medical ethics—Religious
aspects—Judaism. I. Title.
  KBM3098.R664 2007
  296.3'642—dc22

                                                                    2006102422

Table of Contents

Preface

I have been writing and lecturing on Jewish Medical Ethics since graduating medical school in 1959 at which time I received a copy of Rabbi Lord Emmanuel Jakobovits; now classic book *Jewish Medical Ethics* as a gift. Rabbi Jakobovits, who did pioneering work in the field, is known as the father of Jewish Medical Ethics. He actually coined the phrase "Jewish Medical Ethics."

The current volume entitled *Contemporary Biomedical Ethical Issues and Jewish Law* is a compilation of both secular and Jewish ethical dilemmas in the modern practice of medicine.

I am indebted to Mrs. Sophie Falk, Mrs. Wendy Fein, Mrs. Miriam Rodriguez and Mrs. Jackie Engracia for typing the manuscript. I also acknowledge permission from the editors of *The Mount Sinai Journal of Medicine and The Einstein Journal of Biology and Medicine* for permission to reprint several essays which originally appeared in those journals.

Finally, I wish to express my gratitude to Mr. Bernard Scharfstein, publisher of KTAV Publishing House, Inc., and his staff for their dedication and commitment to the production of this handsome new volume on Jewish Medical Ethics.

Fred Rosner, M.D.,
New York, December 2006

Introduction

Contemporary Biomedical Ethical Issues and Jewish Law

In the beginning of Jewish history, religion and healing were inseparable because priest and physician were one and the same person, administering healing with divine sanction. The advent of scientific medicine in the middle of the nineteenth century nearly completely separated medicine from religion. Nevertheless, Jewish physicians traditionally consider their vocation to be spiritually endowed and not merely an ordinary profession. Ethical standards for the practice of medicine among Jews have always been high. Jews have always held physicians in great esteem.

Throughout history, Jews have exerted a tremendous influence on the development of medical science. They have always excelled in medical practice, teaching, administration, and research, and they continue to do so. More than 20 percent of all Nobel Prize winners for medicine are Jewish.

The importance of medicine among the Jews is best seen in the long line of rabbi-physicians that began in the talmudic period (Mar Samuel being the most famous example) and continued through the Middle Ages (examples include Maimonides, Nachmanides, and Judah Halevi). Various factors were responsible for this combination of professions which continues to this day. Medicine was sanctioned by biblical and talmudic law and had an important bearing upon religious matters. Teaching or studying the Torah or word of

God for reward was not considered ethical, because God taught Torah to Moses and the Israelites for nothing, and we should emulate God by not accepting a fee for teaching Torah. Therefore, the practice of medicine was most often chosen as a means of livelihood. This trend was further strengthened by the fact that during the greater part of the Middle Ages, Jews were excluded from almost all other occupations, including public office, and medicine was one of the few dignified occupations by which they could earn their living [1].

Jewish Medical Ethics

The emergence of Jewish medical ethics as a distinct subspecialty within Jewish thought and Jewish law is a relatively recent phenomenon. The late Rabbi Lord Immanuel Jakobovits's doctoral thesis entitled "Jewish Medical Ethics," submitted to London University in 1955 and published by New York's Philosophical Library in 1959, was the first use of the phrase. This landmark monograph was perhaps a revolutionary publication, not merely because the term or concept of Jewish medical ethics was unknown at that time, but because the subject itself had been entirely unexplored and left without any literary or scholarly expression in any Western language. Physicians, medical students, and other interested parties had no writings to consult to familiarize themselves with Jewish views even on such elementary subjects as abortion, contraception, euthanasia, autopsy, and the like. Only a handful of people, mostly rabbis, could consult the original Hebrew and/or Aramaic sources scattered in rabbinic writings, often in highly technical terminology, covering many centuries of legal casuistry and creativity.

Yet we are reminded that the study of Jewish medical ethics is not a twentieth-century phenomenon. The Jewish people have been studying, writing about, and practicing Jewish medical ethics for thousands of years. The Jewish tradition, which dates back to Sinai, is perhaps the longest unbroken tradition in bioethics that is still followed by its adherents.

Throughout the millennia, Judaism and medicine have marched hand-in-hand as allies, not as rivals. The mainstream of Jewish tradition has placed an enormous value on human life and health, has given human beings an obligation to preserve life and health, and has pursued a dual track of encouraging recognized medical therapy together with faith in the Almighty. Judaism has also, for the most part, rejected all varieties of dualism and rivalries between the body and the spirit, maintaining rather that spiritual progress can be enhanced by a healthy body. Our ancients already had insights, as well, into preventive medicine and behavioral medicine [2].

Because Judaism and medicine enjoy a historical and intellectual kinship, it is only natural that Jewish law is best qualified to apply its reasoned pragmatic rules of morality to the practice of medicine. In the words of Rabbi Jakobovits,

For many centuries, rabbis and physicians, often merging their professions into one, were intimate partners in a common effort for the betterment of life. The perplexities of our age challenge them to renew their association in the service of human life, health and dignity. Indeed, they challenge Judaism itself to reassert its place as a potent force in the moral advancement of humanity" [3].

Jews, to whom questions of medical ethics are a quest not only for applicable humanitarian principles but also for divine guidance, must, of necessity, seek answers in the teachings of the Torah. *The Torah of God is perfect* (Psalms 19:8), and in its teachings the discerning student can find eternally valid answers even to newly formulated queries. As physicians and patients turn to rabbinic authorities for answers, Jewish scholars seek to elucidate and expound the teaching of the Torah in these areas of profound concern.

Judaism is guided by the concept of the supreme sanctity of human life and the dignity of man created in the image of God. The preservation of human life in Judaism is a divine commandment. Jewish law requires physicians to do everything in their power to prolong life but prohibits the use of measures that prolong the act of dying. Far greater value is attached to human life in Judaism than in the Christian tradition or in Anglo-Saxon common law. In order save a life, all Jewish religious laws are automatically suspended; the only exceptions are those prohibiting idolatry, murder, and forbidden sexual relations such as incest.

In Judaism, the practice of medicine by a physician does not constitute an interference with the deliberate designs of Divine Providence. A physician does not play God when he practices medicine. In fact, a physician not only has divine license to heal but he is obligated to heal. A physician in Judaism is prohibited from withholding his healing skills.

Judaism is a "right-to-life" religion. This obligation to save lives is not only individual but communal. Certainly a physician, who has knowledge and expertise far greater than that of a layperson, is obligated to use his medical skills to heal the sick and thereby prolong and preserve life. It is erroneous to suppose that having recourse to medicine shows lack of trust and confidence in God, the healer. The Bible takes for granted the use of medical therapy and actually demands it. Although it is not mandatory in Jewish law to study medicine, once a person becomes a physician, he is obliged to use his skills and knowledge to heal the sick.

In Judaism, not only is a physician obligated to heal, but a patient is obligated to seek healing from physicians rather than rely on faith healing. The Talmud states that a wise person should not reside in a city that does not have a physician. The twelfth-century Jewish scholar and physician Moses Maimonides ruled that one is obliged to accustom oneself to a regimen that will preserve the body's health and heal and fortify it when it is ailing.

The extreme concerns in Judaism about the preservation of health and the prolongation of life require that a woman's pregnancy be terminated if her life is endangered by the pregnancy, that a woman use contraception if her life would be threatened by pregnancy, that an organ transplant be performed if it can save or prolong the life of a patient dying of organ failure, and that a postmortem examination be performed if the results of the autopsy may provide immediate information to rescue another dying patient. Judaism prohibits cruelty to animals, but it sanctions experimentation on animals to find cures for human illnesses as long as the animal experiences no pain and suffering.

Judaism also allows patients to accept experimental medical or surgical treatments when no standard therapy is available and the experimental therapy is administered by the most experienced physicians whose intent is to help the patient and not just to satisfy their academic curiosity.

In Judaism, the infinite value of human life prohibits euthanasia or mercy killing in any form. Handicapped newborns, mentally retarded persons, psychotic persons, and patients dying of any illness or cause have the same right to life as anyone else, and nothing may be done to hasten their death. On the other hand, there are times when specific medical or surgical therapies are no longer indicated, appropriate, or desirable for a patient who is irreversibly, terminally ill. Under no circumstances, however, can general supportive care, including food and water, be withheld or withdrawn to hasten a patient's death.

Thus, in Judaism every human being is considered to be of supreme and infinite value. It is the obligation of individuals and society to preserve, hallow, and dignify human life to care for the total needs of all persons so that they can be healthy and productive members of society. This fundamental principle of the sanctity of life and the dignity of man as a creation of God is the underlying axiom upon which all medical ethical decisions are based [4].

The Physician's Mandate to Heal

The basic principles in Judaism governing the practice of medicine, whether in the doctor's office or over the telephone or on the Internet, are based on the premise that in Jewish tradition a physician is given specific divine license to practice medicine. The biblical verse *and heal he shall heal* (Exodus 21:19) is interpreted by the talmudic sages (Baba Kamma 85a) to teach us that authorization to heal is granted by God to the physician. In Jewish law, a physician is not merely allowed to practice medicine but is in fact commanded to do so if he has chosen to become a physician. This biblical mandate is based upon two scriptural precepts. *And thou shalt restore it to him* (Deuteronomy 22:2) refers to the restoration of lost property. Moses Maimonides, in his Commentary on the Mishnah (Nedarim 4:4), states that "it is obligatory from the Torah for the physician to heal the sick, and this is included in the explanation of the scriptural phrase *and thou shalt restore it to him,* meaning to heal his body." Thus, Maimonides, like the Talmud (Nedarim 38b), states that the law of restoration includes the restoration of the health of one's fellowman. If a person has "lost his health" and the physician is able to restore it, he is obligated to do so.

The second scriptural mandate for the physician to heal is based on the phrase *neither shalt thou stand idly by the blood of thy neighbor* (Leviticus 19:16). The passage refers to the duties of human beings to their fellow men and the moral principles which the sages expound and apply to every phase of civil and criminal law. If one stands idly by and allows one's fellow man to die without offering help, one is guilty of transgressing this precept. A physician who refuses to heal, thereby resulting in suffering and/or death of the patient, is also guilty of transgressing this commandment.

If one asks why God granted physicians license and even mandate to heal the sick, one can offer the following explanation. As already mentioned, a cardinal principle of Judaism is that human life is of infinite value. The preservation of human life takes precedence over all commandments in the Bible except three: adultery, murder, and forbidden sexual relations. Life's value is nearly absolute and supreme. In order to preserve a human life, the Sabbath and even the Day of Atonement may be desecrated, and all other rules and laws save the aforementioned three are suspended for the overriding consideration of saving a human life. He who saves one life is as if he saved a whole world (Sanhedrin 37a). Even a few moments of life are worthwhile.

Jewish law also requires a physician to be well trained and licensed by the local authorities [5]. An unlicensed physician is liable to pay compensation to the patient for unintentional errors or side effects. A negligent physician is obviously culpable even if licensed. However, he is not liable for misjudgments or side effects or a bad outcome if he acted responsibly. This topic is discussed extensively elsewhere [6]. Judaism protects physicians from undeserved liability but stresses that the physician must recognize the limits of his ability and demands that physicians consult with more experienced colleagues in situations of doubt.

A physician is entitled to reasonable fees and compensation for his services [7]. In talmudic times, when physicians, rabbis, teachers, and judges served the community on a part-time basis only and had other occupations and trades, their compensation was limited to lost time and effort. Nowadays, however, when physicians have no other occupation, they can charge for their expert medical knowledge and receive full compensation. Excessive fees are discouraged but are not prohibited if the patient agrees to the fee in advance. Indigent patients should be treated for reduced fees or no fee at all. These principles are applicable both to a salaried physician and to a physician in private practice who charges fee-for-service.

These Judaic principles require that physicians place the interests of the patient first and advocate for any care they believe will materially benefit the patient. Physicians must practice good medicine, eliminate whatever is unnecessary, and be conscious of the need to contain costs. Physicians must also practice within the areas in which they are credentialed and must do so in the best interests of their patients.

The Patient's Responsibility to Stay Healthy

The prevention of illness and the avoidance of dangers to life are mandated in Jewish law. The maintenance of one's health requires Jews to avoid harmful foods and activities and to prevent danger wherever possible. Preventive medicine has been the centerpiece of the Jewish system for more than two thousand years. The Jewish view emphasizes prevention over treatment.

An entire chapter in Moses Maimonides' famous code of Jewish law [8] is devoted to hygienic and medical prescriptions for healthy living and for the prevention of illness. Among the many subjects discussed are normal bodily excretory functions, recommended times for eating, amounts and types of food to be consumed, beverage imbibition, exercise, sleep habits, cathartics, climatic and weather effects on eating habits, detrimental and beneficial foods, fruits, meats, vegetables, bathing, bloodletting, sexual intercourse, and domicile.

One must also be concerned about ecological and environmental factors, such as clean air and sunshine, which may have an impact upon one's health. One must observe rules of personal hygiene, such as hand washing before eating. Diet, exercise, sex, and bodily functions must all be tended to as outlined by Maimonides. He concludes his exposition as follows:

> I guarantee that anyone who conducts himself according to the directions we have laid down will not be afflicted with illness all the days of his life, until he ages greatly and expires. He will not require a physician, and his body will be complete and remain healthy all his life unless his body was defective from the beginning of his creation, or unless he became accustomed to one of the bad habits from the onset of his youth, or unless the plague of pestilence or the plague of drought comes onto the world [8].

Maimonides cites exceptions to the goal of preventing rather than treating illness. Genetic diseases and certain epidemics of diseases cannot be prevented. For this reason, the final paragraph in Maimonides' chapter on the regimen of health states that a person should not reside in a city that does not have a physician. A similar pronouncement is found in the Talmud (Sanhedrin 17b).

Maimonides supports the adage "An ounce of prevention is more valuable than a pound of cure." More evidence for this thesis is found in his medical writings [9].

The Patient's Responsibility to Seek Healing When Ill

The Bible tells us to *take heed to thyself, and take care of thy life* (Deuteronomy 4:9) and *take good care of your lives* (ibid. 4:15). These biblical mandates make it clear that patients are obligated to care for their health and life. Man does not have full title over his body and life. He must eat and drink to sustain himself and must seek healing when sick.

In the Western world, citizens are endowed with a variety of legal rights. People have the right to die, the right to refuse treatment, the right not to be resuscitated, the right to abortion, and many other rights. Rarely does one hear about responsibilities and obligations of citizens. Judaism requires everyone to do what is proper in order to be healthy. It is an obligation in Judaism to be healthy. Hence one should accept appropriate medical advice, whether given in person, over the telephone, by fax, e-mail, or over the Internet. One should not smoke, one should eat properly and not excessively, one should exercise regularly, sleep adequately, only engage in proper and legitimate sexual activities, and lead an overall healthy life style. There are more obligations and legal imperatives in Judaism.

Thus, while much of the modern secular ethical system is based on rights, Judaism is an ethical system based on duties and responsibilities. The late Rabbi Lord Immanuel Jakobovits eloquently articulated the Jewish view as follows:

> *Now in Judaism we know of no intrinsic rights. Indeed there is no word for rights in the very language of the Hebrew Bible and of the classic sources of Jewish law. In the moral vocabulary of the Jewish discipline of life we speak of human duties, not of human rights, of obligations, not entitlement. The Decalogue is a list of Ten Commandments, not a Bill of Human Rights [10].* •

Medicine on the Internet

A new bioethical issue in the field of medicine is the Internet, which is a magnificent scientific tool to provide health education of high quality to masses of people. It is an unparalleled information source whose use Judaism supports because of its potential to inform people about healthy living to prevent or to mitigate illness. Primary prevention activities can deter the occurrence of a disease or adverse event. Smoking cessation reduces the risk of lung cancer. A variety of prevention strategies (e.g., aspirin, exercise, control of weight, blood pressure, and lipids) can reduce the risk of a heart attack. Judaism requires communities to not only provide for the medical and social needs of their citizens but also to alert people about drug recalls, epidemics, and the dangers of substance abuse. Judaism thus responds to modern technology by harnessing it for the benefit of mankind.

Electronic mail between physicians and patients offers substantial promise as a way to improve access to healthcare, let physicians reach out to patients, and increase the involvement of patients in their own care. Elderly patients can consult their physicians by "electronic house call" to record their vital signs and discuss their condition. Prescription refills, lab results, appointment scheduling and reminders, insurance questions, routine follow-up inquiries, and reporting of home health measurements such as blood pressure and glucose are well suited to e-mail. Highly confidential information or medically urgent or emergent situations should not be communicated by e-mail.

Jewish concerns about the potential dangers of the indiscriminate use of the Internet must be addressed. Pornographic and other prurient and/or defamatory material must be blocked out to avoid violating the biblical and rabbinic laws concerning immorality. The placing of misleading or potentially harmful information, medical or otherwise, violates the prohibitions against deception (Chullin 94a) and against placing a stumbling block before the blind (Leviticus 19:4). *Cursed is he who leads the blind astray* (Deuteronomy 27:18). The addictive qualities of the Internet result in sleep deprivation for many people who spend more time online than they intended. Such addiction may take its toll on one's health, school grades, employment, marriage, and Torah study.

The Internet is a wonderful scientific and technological advance with enormous beneficial potential for mankind. Its use must certainly be sanctioned in Jewish law. However, good often is not pure good, but may contain potentially dangerous elements.

Confidentiality and the Internet

Patients have the right and perhaps the obligation to use the Internet to prevent and to treat illnesses. For some patients the Internet may be an absolute necessity. Patients with very rare conditions or diseases can "talk" to physicians and experts all over the world about their cases. Lay people who need sources of help such as support groups, medical care, and specialists can obtain such assistance and information on the Internet. For physicians, the Internet is an indispensable tool for continuing medical education, for patient care and patient education, and for information exchange with colleagues. For the general Jewish public, accurate medical information is crucial for healthy living and disease prevention. Confidentiality of medical information is one of the major concerns relating to the Internet. There are no major ethical difficulties if physicians provide generic medical information on the Internet. However, patients' private medical information transmitted by e-mail from patient to physician, and vice-versa, is accessible to many people with computer expertise, and therefore requires special and careful consideration. Patients must be told that the Internet is not a secure means of communication, because Internet messages can be intercepted, viewed, and altered by unauthorized individuals. Material that is "deleted" may still be recoverable. Therefore, sensitive information should not be sent over the Internet. Furthermore, the Internet should not be used for urgent or emergency medical conditions. Direct communication with the physician or ambulance service should then be used.

Other than clerical or administrative communications such as billing, appointments and insurance matters, all e-mail communications related to patient care should be considered sensitive and confidential. Patients must also consider the security of their own home or office computers in regard to the confidentiality of their medical information. The challenge to preserve confidentiality must be pursued and met by the adoption of technologically secure means of data transmission.

The obligation to maintain confidentiality is one of the cornerstones of medical ethical practice and is clearly stated in the Oath of Hippocrates and many subsequent deontological oaths and declarations. This obligation is based on the general ethical principles of doing good for others (beneficence), not to harm others (non-maleficence), patient autonomy, and the right to privacy. This obligation is also based on the trusting relationship between patient and physician and the need to protect and preserve that relationship by not disclosing private and personal information about the patient.

Maintaining professional confidentiality is a subject which Jewish thought and literature have dealt with extensively over the centuries [11]. In Judaism, the rights of privacy of an individual are balanced against the rights of others and of society as a whole [12]. Jewish law regards as inviolate the privacy of personal information that a person does not wish to disclose to others. Jewish law demands that confidences be respected not only by professionals with whom one has entered into a fiduciary relationship but also by friends and acquaintances and even strangers to whom such information has been imparted [13]. The obligation of confidentiality is far broader in Judaism than in any other legal, religious, or moral system [14].

There is no specific term in Jewish law for professional confidentiality because this topic is subsumed under the general obligation or prohibition against talebearing and evil gossip (Leviticus 19:16, Proverbs 25:9, Psalms 34:14).

According to these laws, a physician may not share privileged information with his colleagues, his family, or anyone else if no benefit to the patient would result therefrom [15]. However, if the maintenance of confidence might cause harm to another person, the latter may be informed. If the individual's right to privacy conflicts with the need of society to prevent harm to others, the prohibitions against talebearing and evil gossip are waived and the information must be disclosed to protect other people. The disclosure must be factual, accurate, and not exaggerated.

Specific medical situations where disclosure is required include the possible transmission of illness to another person, the presence of a serious medical condition in a potential spouse, and the reporting of certain infectious diseases to public health authorities. The overriding obligation to protect the lives of others requires that confidential information be disclosed if the withholding of that information might lead to serious harm to someone else. Judaism thus balances the obligation and duty to maintain confidentiality with the obligation and duty to protect others.

The Future of Jewish Medical Ethics

According to Lord Jakobovits, Jewish medical ethics is built on rulings given by leading experts on Jewish law. When collected and published, these rulings are known as responsa. By definition, such rulings are reactive rather than proactive and meet a demand for guidance by patients, physicians, scholars, or others who seek to practice Judaism according to traditional teachings. The rulings become normative and assume the force of law by virtue of the universal recognition accorded to their authors. These conditions show every sign of remaining a permanent feature of Jewish medical ethics [16].

A second crucial factor determining the future course of medical ethics will be the development of medicine itself. Most important from a Jewish point of view will be where to draw the line between the "blind march to mechanical perfection and the capacity to control the forces science and technology can now generate at our bidding for the exploitation of nature's infinite energies" [16].

In some areas, halachic issues raised by modern medical technology are still unresolved and subject to heated controversy. One such example is the definition of death. Within the next few years, one hopes that this dispute will be resolved—if only by the preponderance of halachic verdicts one way or the other. The decision depends on facts, and facts are bound to emerge convincingly in the end. When heart transplants began, the procedure was condemned by most halachic authorities. The increasing success rate (80 percent survival for five years) has been accompanied by increasing permissive rulings, which now seem to predominate.

Areas of Jewish medical ethics that require additional study and research are professional ethics, such as secrecy, confidentiality, truth telling, and the public good; genetics, including genetic screening, gene therapy, gene surgery, and cloning; and mental health issues, such as sex therapy, homosexuality, drug addiction, and alcoholism.

A large area that has, to date, been inadequately discussed, and is bound to engage ever increasing attention, is the distribution of scarce resources and the allocation of limited funds. Among the limited resources is the Jewish source material. This need, too, will eventually be met by intensified search for precedents in earlier statements of principles and decisions.

Finally, the significant growth of Jewish medical ethics, both for practical guidance and as an academic discipline of ever-greater sophistication, will call for the more intensive training of experts proficient in both Jewish law and medicine. Such professional specialists are beginning to emerge, both practicing rabbis and practicing physicians. Some are both rabbis and doctors in the spirit of the famous talmudic and medieval physician-rabbis. All these modern Jewish bioethicists are indebted to, and many were stimulated by, the pioneering work in this field of the late Rabbi Lord Immanuel Jakobovits. That is why he is more correctly identified today not as the father of Jewish medical ethics but the grandfather of Jewish medical ethics "through the disciples who now themselves have raised generations of scholars devoted to this field" [17].

Summary and Conclusion

The attitude toward healing in Judaism has always been a positive one. A physician is obligated to heal and is given divine license to do so. A physician must be well trained and licensed in his discipline. A physician must apply his skills for the benefit of the patient and be careful not to do harm. Thus, the ethical principles of beneficence and non-maleficence are deeply rooted in Judaism. A patient is also obligated to seek healing, because one must be healthy in order to serve the Lord by doing His will in the service of mankind.

A second cardinal principle of Judaism is the infinite value of human life. The preservation of life takes precedence over all biblical and rabbinic commandments except three: murder, idolatry, and forbidden sexual relations such as incest or adultery. The Talmud states that all lives are equal because one person's blood is not redder than that of another person (Pesachim 25b).

Preventive medicine is the centerpiece of the Jewish system. The Jewish view toward the practice of medicine emphasizes prevention over treatment. Prevention of danger and thereby the preservation of life and health are biblical mandates. One must observe rules of personal hygiene, such as hand washing before eating. Diet, exercise, sexual and bodily functions must all be properly tended to. Preventive medical services and patient responsibilities are fully consonant with Judaism. Thus, emphasis on prevention of illness and personal responsibility are deeply rooted in Judaic teaching and tradition.

With regard to the Internet, Judaism views any new technology or scientific advance with favor if it is used for the betterment of mankind, such as the prevention and treatment of illness. Such harnessing of the natural sciences is not considered an encroachment upon divine prerogatives. On the contrary, God gave us dominion over the world to use nature to subdue the earth (Genesis 1:28) by transforming its secrets into products and technology to benefit mankind. The Internet is a wonderful tool to accomplish this purpose, with some caveats as discussed above.

These principles of Judaism guide the Jewish physician in the practice of medicine. As new Jewish bioethical questions arise, rabbinic decisors will provide answers based on the expert medical and technical information provided by physicians and scientists. Such answers must be consonant with the physician's ability to practice medicine, using the most up-to-date advances in medical science and biomedical technology. However, such answers must also remain true to traditional Judaic teachings as transmitted by God to Moses and the children of Israel.

PART I
The Beginning of Life

1

Genetic Screening and Genetic Therapy

Genetic screening, gene therapy, and other applications of genetic engineering are permissible in Judaism when used for the treatment, cure, or prevention of disease. Such genetic manipulation is not considered to be a violation of God's natural law, but a legitimate implementation of the biblical mandate to heal. If Tay-Sachs disease, diabetes, hemophilia, cystic fibrosis, Huntington's disease, or other genetic diseases can be cured or prevented by "gene surgery," then it is certainly permitted in Jewish law.

Genetic premarital screening is encouraged in Judaism for the purpose of discouraging at-risk marriages for a fatal illness such as Tay-Sachs disease. Neonatal screening for treatable conditions such as phenylketonuria is certainly desirable and perhaps required in Jewish law. Preimplantation screening and the implantation of only "healthy" zygotes into the mother's womb to prevent the birth of an affected child are probably sanctioned in Jewish law. Whether or not these assisted-reproduction techniques may be used to choose the sex of one's offspring, thereby preventing the birth of a child with a sex-linked disease such as hemophilia, has not yet been ruled on by modern rabbinic decisions. Prenatal screening with the specific intent of aborting an affected fetus is not allowed according to most rabbinic authorities, although a minority view permits it "for great need." Not to have children if both parents are carriers of a genetic disease such as Tay-Sachs is not a Jewish option. Preimplantation screening is preferable. All screening test

3

results must remain confidential. Judaism does not permit the alteration or manipulation of physical traits and characteristics, such as height, eye and hair color, and facial features, when such change provides no useful benefit to mankind. On the other hand, it is permissible to clone organisms and microorganisms to facilitate the production of insulin, growth hormones, and other agents intended to benefit mankind and to cure and treat diseases.

Genetic information about a person's health and health prospects can be inferred from family history or by direct genetic testing. Such testing can involve sophisticated molecular analysis for the mutant gene (e.g., cystic fibrosis) or simple biochemical (e.g., hypercholesterolemia), enzymatic (e.g., Tay-Sachs disease), hematological (e.g., Sickle cell diseases), or chromosomal (e.g., Down's syndrome) analysis of blood or body fluids or tissues.

Points to consider before embarking on carrier-screening programs include the nature and frequency of the disorder and the availability and effectiveness of treatment, community perception of the disorder and attitudes to screening, motivation for screening, how the test is done and what the results mean, obtaining informed consent and maintaining confidentiality of results, when to screen, education before screening, possible stigmatization and discrimination, and the organization of the screening program [1]. The Council on Ethical and Judicial Affairs of the American Medical Association has addressed ethical issues related to prenatal genetic testing [2], genetic testing by employers [3] and insurers [4], and carrier screening for cystic fibrosis and other disorders [5].

How does society control the way genetic information is obtained and used? How does society monitor and review genetic screening programs? What criteria should be set to make maximum use of the potential good that the Human Genome Project offers, without infringing on the ethical and legal principles of privacy, autonomy, beneficence, confidentiality, and nondiscrimination? Who owns genetic information? How should genetic information be used? Who decides which people should be screened? Are there or should there be limits to preimplantation, prenatal screening, and neonatal screening? How should employers and insurers receive and use genetic information? Do we have sufficient data to judge the pros and cons of genetic testing and screening? The Orthodox Jewish community relies on the traditional use of biblical and talmudic law and rabbinic responsa to answer such questions. This approach is described in this essay on traditional Jewish views on genetic issues.

The genetic testing and counseling of children and adolescents is associated with special ethical, legal, and psychological implications [6]. The risks and benefits of testing have to be assessed to determine whether it is in the child's best interests to be tested [7].

Breast Cancer

About 5–10 percent of all breast cancer cases are hereditary. The breast cancer genes known as *BRCA1* and *BRCA2* are responsible for most inherited breast cancer, especially in women who develop the disease before the age of 40 years. The *BRCA1* mutation known as 185delAG is found in approximately 1 percent of the Ashkenazi Jewish population [8] and in 20 percent of Ashkenazi Jewish women who develop breast cancer before 40 [9] or 42 [10] years of age. This gene is also associated with an increased risk of ovarian cancer. These findings and observations are cause for concern [11]. Early interventions may be appropriate in high-risk women who test positive (e.g., more frequent breast examination and mammography, prophylactic mastectomy, hormone prophylaxis). There are many other issues of concern, including confidentiality, access, autonomy, and informing the patient about the implications of a positive or negative test, including its technical accuracy and cost.

The availability of a test does not require that it be offered universally. The American Society of Clinical Oncology recommends that cancer predisposition testing be offered only when the person has a strong family history of cancer or very early age of onset of disease, when the test can be interpreted adequately, and when the results will influence the medical management of the patient or family member [12]. However, many other prestigious organizations emphasize that *BRCA1* testing remains a research activity for the time being [13]. The pitfalls of genetic testing [14] and the psychological issues in testing for breast cancer susceptibility [15] should not be minimized. People at risk must fully understand the risks, benefits, and limitations of genetic testing, the risk of psychological harm, and the possibility of insurance discrimination and subsequent loss of healthcare coverage, before they undergo testing [16].

Tay-Sachs Disease

Debate continues about the screening of large populations of Jewish people for the carrier state of Tay-Sachs disease to prevent the "inappropriate" marriage of two carriers. Also controversial is the performance of amniocentesis for the prenatal detection of the fatal disease, with the subsequent possible abortion of an affected fetus. Selected termination of affected fetuses may not be acceptable in Judaism, although some rabbis might sanction it. Mass screening programs may produce a psychological burden on young people who screen positive. Should a carrier of the Tay-Sachs gene refuse to marry an individual who has not been tested? Should a couple break up their engagement if they learn that both are carriers? Should a young person inquire about the Tay-Sachs status of a member of the opposite sex prior to meeting that individual on a social level? Must a person who knows he or she is a carrier divulge this fact to an intended spouse?

The stigma of being a carrier of the Tay-Sachs gene may not be fully appreciated. Misinformed or uninformed people may shun and ostracize carriers. Job and insurance discrimination is also possible if confidentiality of testing results is not assured. If the purpose of Tay-Sachs screening is to provide information and genetic counseling about mating and reproductive options, few will oppose screening. If the purpose, however, is to suggest prenatal diagnosis with the specific intent of recommending abortion of affected fetuses, religious and moral objections might be raised. Preimplantation diagnosis of *in vitro* fertilized eggs, with the discarding of affected zygotes, if any, avoids the issue of pregnancy termination, since pregnancy in Judaism does not begin until zygote implantation into the wall of the uterus.

Genetics and Eugenics in Classic Jewish Sources

Ancient Jewish writings, including the Bible and Talmud, are not devoid of material relating to genetics. One writer describes in some detail how the laws of Mendelian genetics were applied by Jacob in the biblical narrative of the speckled and spotted sheep (Genesis 30:32 ff.) [17]. Hemophilia and its precise genetic transmission is described in the Talmud (Yebamot 64b). The sages in the Talmud and subsequent rabbinic authorities had a remarkable knowledge of the genetics of this sex-linked disorder [18]. All rabbis recognized that females transmit the disease but do not suffer from it. A few rabbis also considered the possibility of its transmission through males.

Elsewhere (Ketubot 10b), the Talmud portrays a family whose women had hereditary absence of menstruation and no blood of virginity, and were obviously childless. The exact nature of the anatomical or physiological abnormality is not described.

It is prohibited in Jewish law to marry a woman from a family of epileptics or lepers lest the illness be genetically transmitted to future generations (Yebamot 64b; Maimonides' *Mishneh Torah*, Issurei Biyah 21:30; Karo's *Shulchan Aruch*, Even Haezer 2:7). According to Rashi (Yebamot 64b), any hereditary disease is included in this category. This talmudic ruling "may well represent the first eugenic enactment, and the only legislative bar to the procreation of a diseased progeny, in ancient and even medieval times" [19]. On the basis of the higher frequency of defective births resulting from unions among blood relatives, Rabbi Judah the Pious, in his ethical will, prohibited marriages between first cousins and between uncles and nieces. Yet such marriages are sanctioned in the Bible and expressly encouraged in the Talmud (Yebamot 62b, Sanhedrin 76b). Since consanguineous marriage increases the probability of birth defects, some rabbis ban such marriages [20, 21], while others strongly caution against them [22–24].

Genetic disease was recognized by Maimonides, who prescribes a regimen of health for all Jews that will enable them to remain healthy, since one cannot serve the Lord when one is ill (*Mishneh Torah*, Deot 4:1). He guarantees that anyone who follows his regimen will be healthy all his life, except for those who were born with hereditary or genetic defects (ibid. 4:20).

The Genome Project

Is the genome project an encroachment on the divine plan for this world that interferes with nature as God created it? Would genetic engineering tamper with the divine arrangement of Creation? Although one rabbi answers in the affirmative [25], most rabbis consider the acquisition of knowledge for the sake of finding cures for human illnesses to be divinely sanctioned, if not in fact mandated. God blessed mankind with the phrase *replenish the earth and subdue it* (Genesis 1:28). This phrase is interpreted by Nachmanides (Ramban) to mean that God gave man dominion over the world to use animals and insects and all creeping things for the benefit of mankind (Ramban, Genesis 1:28). To subdue the earth, according to Samson Raphael Hirsch (on Genesis 1:28), is to master, appropriate, and transform the earth and its products for human purposes. To have *dominion over the fish and over the birds and over every living thing on earth* (Genesis 1:28) means to use them for the benefit of mankind. The pursuit of scientific knowledge does not constitute prohibited eating from the tree of knowledge (Genesis 2:17). Whatever is good for mankind must be permissible and praiseworthy. However, good often is not pure good, but may contain dangerous elements. Although the genome project is intended to cure diseases, it has raised many concerns.

In the general introduction to his *Commentary on the Mishnah* [26], Moses Maimonides discusses the existence and purpose of all living and inanimate things in the world. He clearly enunciates the thesis that the purpose of everything that God put on this earth is to serve mankind. Thus, scientific experiments on laboratory animals, during the course of medical research that might find cures for human illnesses, are sanctioned in Jewish law as legitimate utilization of animals for the benefit of mankind [27]. However, whenever possible, pain or discomfort should be avoided or minimized in order not to transgress the prohibition in Jewish law against cruelty to animals.

King David said, "The heavens are the Lord's heavens, but the earth He has given to mankind" (Psalms 115:16), further supporting the concept that knowledge and its pursuit are legitimate activities for human beings and not considered an encroachment upon divine prerogatives. Thus, therapeutic genetic engineering and gene therapy that may result from the knowledge derived from the genome project do not undermine God's creation of the world by manipulating nature (Ramban, Leviticus 19:19). On the contrary, it is a legitimate modification of the natural order. The use of scientific knowledge to benefit mankind is biblically mandated (Ramban, Genesis 1:28). The use of such knowledge to heal illness and cure disease is also allowed biblically, based on the talmudic interpretation (Baba Kamma 85a) of the phrase *and heal he shall heal* (Exodus 21:19), or even biblically mandated, based on Maimonides' interpretation (*Mishnah Commentary*, Nedarim 4:4) of the biblical obligation to restore a lost object (Deuteronomy 22:2) to include the restoration of one's lost health. The healing of illness includes the use of genetically engineered medications such as insulin and various antibiotics. The cure of disease by gene therapy, if possible, is also sanctioned in Jewish law.

Genetic Screening

Many years ago, Rabbi Moshe Feinstein [28] was asked whether it is advisable for a boy or girl to be screened for Tay-Sachs disease and, if it is proper, at what age the test should be performed. His answer was:

> . . . it is advisable for one preparing to be married to have himself tested. It is also proper to publicize the fact, via newspapers and other media, that such a test is available. It is clear and certain that absolute secrecy must be maintained to prevent anyone from learning the result of such a test performed on another. The physician must not reveal these to anyone . . . these tests must be performed in private, and, consequently, it is not proper to schedule these tests in large groups as, for example, in yeshivas, schools, or other similar situations.

Rabbi Feinstein [29] also points out that most young people are quite susceptible to nervous tension or psychological stress, and therefore, young men (below age 20) and women (below age 18) not yet contemplating marriage should not be screened for Tay-Sachs disease. Finally, Rabbi Feinstein strongly condemned abortion for Tay-Sachs disease and even questioned the permissibility of the amniocentesis that proves the presence of a Tay-Sachs fetus, since amniocentesis is not without risk, albeit small.

Rabbi J. David Bleich [30] indicates that the elimination of Tay-Sachs disease is, of course, a goal to which all concerned individuals subscribe. He points out, however, that the obligation with regard to procreation is not suspended simply because of the statistical probability that some children of the union may be deformed or abnormal. While the couple may quite properly be counseled with regard to the risks of having a Tay-Sachs child, according to Jewish law (Halachah) the failure to bear natural children is not a viable alternative. He further voices concern that if the fetus is found to have Tay-Sachs disease by prenatal testing, abortion may not be sanctioned in Jewish law. Rabbi Bleich concludes that screening programs for the detection of carriers of Tay-Sachs disease "are certainly to be encouraged." He suggests that the most propitious time for such screening is childhood or early adolescence, since early awareness of a carrier state, particularly as part of a mass screening program, is advantageous. He is critical of Rabbi Waldenberg, pointing out that the latter's permissive ruling on abortion for Tay-Sachs disease is contrary to the decisions of other contemporary rabbinic scholars, including Rabbi Feinstein.

Two methods now exist for totally eliminating the need for prenatal screening for Tay-Sachs disease and thus averting the serious halachic objections to abortion if the fetus should be found to be affected. The first method is to perform confidential premarital screening and strongly discourage the marriage of two carriers. This approach, widely utilized in many Orthodox Jewish communities, is sponsored by the Dor Yeshorim organization (429 Wythe Avenue, Brooklyn, NY 11211-5933, 718-384-6060), which claims to have tested more than 70,000 people and identified more than 100 at-risk couples, who were advised not to marry. In the United States, the program has significantly reduced the number of Jewish babies born with the disease. In Israel, a similar screening program has resulted in no Tay-Sachs children being born to newlywed couples in the ultra-Orthodox Ashkenazi Jewish community in more than ten years [31].

The second method of preventing the birth of a baby with Tay-Sachs disease, hemophilia, or Huntington's disease is to perform preimplantation screening of *in vitro* fertilized zygotes if both husband and wife are known carriers and to use only the unaffected ones for implantation. Whether one may screen these *in vitro* fertilized zygotes for genetic diseases has yet to be ruled on decisively by modern rabbinic authorities. However, *in vitro* fertilization is sanctioned by many rabbis for couples who cannot conceive in the normal way [32]. Moreover, the discarding of the affected zygotes would not be considered abortion, because Jewish law considers life to begin only when the living embryo has been implanted in the mother's womb and continues to grow.

It is not clear whether Judaism sanctions genetic screening for diseases for which no effective treatment yet exists. The rabbis are greatly concerned about the emotional burden (*tiruf hadaat*) that such knowledge may place upon a person found to have the gene for Huntington's disease in the presymptomatic stage. Judaism would not sanction amniocentesis or chorionic villi sampling to rule out Huntington's disease if the only purpose is to abort the fetus if it is found to be affected. However, preimplantation screening of Huntington's disease and choosing only unaffected zygotes for implantation may be permissible to prevent the birth of an affected child, as described above for the prevention of Tay-Sachs disease. The same permissive view might apply to the prevention of hemophilia births by preimplantation screening.

Newborn screening for treatable diseases, such as phenylketonuria and congenital hypothyroidism, should certainly be done. Judaism subsumes such testing under the biblical and rabbinic mandates to seek healing from the medical profession.

Judaism requires that confidentiality of test results for all types of genetic screening be maintained. The prohibitions in Judaism against talebearing (Leviticus 19:16) and evil gossip (Psalms 34:14) are discussed at length in the Talmud (Yoma 4b, Sanhedrin 31a) and in the codes of Jewish law, such as Maimonides' *Mishneh Torah* (Deot 7:2). An entire book was written on this subject by Rabbi Israel Meir Hakohen of Radin, popularly known as Chafetz Chayim [33]. Whenever the physician obtains confidential medical information, genetic or otherwise, he is forbidden to disclose that information or share it with anyone, including the patient's family and even professional colleagues, if no benefit to the patient would result. However, if keeping confidence might impact adversely on the health of another person, the latter may be informed. In Jewish law, a person who is the carrier of a serious and potentially lethal genetic disorder is obligated to divulge that information to a prospective spouse.

More difficult to resolve is the question of whether an Ashkenazi Jewish woman with the *BRCA1* or *BRCA2* gene for breast cancer is obligated to tell a prospective spouse or her husband if she is already married. Modern rabbinic authorities have not yet ruled on whether it is even appropriate to test for that gene in all Jewish women. It may be reasonable to do so in women with very strong family histories of breast cancer. But to what end? Even if they are found not to have the gene, the risk of developing breast cancer is still high. But women found to be positive for the gene may wish to take action, such as more frequent mammography, prophylactic hormonal treatment, or even prophylactic mastectomies. Current rabbinic authorities need to address how such matters might impact on therapeutic choices within the context of Judaism.

Gene Therapy and Genetic Engineering

The literature in Jewish law on gene therapy and genetic engineering is very sparse. Two rabbinic articles with "genetic engineering" in their titles [34, 35] deal primarily with artificial insemination, *in vitro* fertilization, and surrogate motherhood, and only briefly mention cloning. The production of hormones such as insulin and erythropoietin, and antibiotics and other therapeutic substances, by genetic engineering through recombinant DNA technology is certainly permissible in Jewish law, because nature is being used properly by man to his benefit in the treatment and cure of illnesses. Gene therapy, such as the replacement of the missing enzyme in Tay-Sachs disease and the missing hormone in diabetes, and the repair of the defective gene in hemophilia or Huntington's disease, if and when these procedures become scientifically feasible, is also probably sanctioned in Jewish law, because it is done with the intention of restoring health, and preserving and prolonging life. The technical medical problems of modifying the defective gene or genes in an individual sperm, ovum, or zygote by gene surgery and implanting the replaced or repaired genes into the mother in order to produce a healthy child have not yet been surmounted. However, assuming such surgery can be performed successfully, gene surgery will probably be sanctioned by rabbinic authorities as a legitimate implementation of the mandate on physicians to heal the sick.

Another argument favoring the permissibility of gene surgery or genetic manipulation is the fact that neither the sperm nor the ovum nor even the fertilized zygote is a person. Thus, gene manipulation is not considered to be tampering with an existing or even a potential human being, because in Jewish law that status is only bestowed upon a fetus implanted in the mother's womb. One can also argue that any surgery performed on a live human being must certainly be permitted on a sperm, ovum, or fertilized zygote. For example, if a surgical cure for hemophilia, Tay-Sachs disease, or Huntington's disease were possible, it would surely be permissible. Hence, it should certainly be permissible to cure or prevent these diseases by gene surgery.

Rabbi Moshe Hershler [25] warns against blinding ourselves to the potential of genetic engineering and gene therapy, which are no longer a dream or a fantasy but are becoming medical and scientific realities. Hershler raises the question of the permissibility (or lack thereof) of experimenting with gene therapy to try to save the life of a child with thalassemia or Tay-Sachs disease if the unsuccessful outcome of the experimentation would be a shortening of the child's life. Hershler is of the opinion that gene therapy and genetic engineering may be prohibited because "he who changes the [divine] arrangement of creation lacks faith [in the Creator]," and he cites as support for this view the prohibition against mating diverse kinds of animals, sowing together diverse kinds of seeds, and wearing garments made of wool and linen (Leviticus 19:19). This line of reasoning is rejected by Rabbis Shlomo Zalman Auerbach and Yehoshua J. Neuwirth [36], on the grounds that genetic engineering does not seem to be comparable to the grafting of diverse types of animals or seed. The main purposes of gene therapy are to cure disease, restore health, and prolong life, all goals within the physician's divine license to heal. Gene grafting is no different from an "organ graft," such as a kidney or corneal transplant, which nearly all rabbis consider permissible.

The ethical and halachic problems associated with genetic engineering include "speciation." Does a certain species lose its identity if other genes are introduced into it? Would the citron or *etrog* (*Citrus medica* Linn) used on the Tabernacles holiday (Sukkot) for religious purposes lose its identity if lemon genes were introduced into it? How many transplanted lemon genes are needed for the *etrog* to be considered a lemon? Can the rabbinic concept of nullification (*bitul*), whereby one part of a prohibited substance becomes nullified if mixed with sixty parts of a permitted substance, be applied to this situation? Another example is the need for fins and scales for fish to be kosher for consumption. If genes introduced in a scaleless catfish induce scalation, does the catfish then become a kosher fish? Yet another example is the conversion by genetic engineering of annual plants into perennials. The latter are not subject to some of the laws of the Sabbatical year. Thus, perennial wheat, corn, or tomatoes would be permitted in Jewish law even if grown during the Sabbatical year. These problems and issues have not yet been decisively discussed and resolved by current halachic authorities.

It seems clear that genetic engineering and gene therapy can and should be used to promote the human condition and treat, cure, and prevent disease. But should these techniques be allowed to alter human traits, such as eye color, height, personality, intelligence, and facial features? The Talmud relates (Pesachim 54a) that God inspired Adam with a type of divine knowledge, and he took two heterogeneous animals and crossed them and created a mule. Elsewhere, the Talmud asks (Chullin 7b) why they are called mules (*yemim*) and answers, "Because they cast fear [*emah*] upon men." This inappropriate use of nature by Adam is what Ramban condemns in his biblical commentary (Leviticus 19:19) as "changing and denying the divine creation of the world."

There is no specific halachic prohibition against attempting to clone a human being. An example of the creation of an artificial human being, or *golem*, is cited in the Talmud (Sanhedrin 65b). The *golem*, however, was not formed in and born from a woman's womb. It was therefore not considered to be human and was destroyed without it considered an act of murder. A cloned human being, on the other hand, has the full status of a human being. Although

Jewish law does not prohibit cloning a human being, one should be very cautious and not do so indiscriminately. Many scientific and Jewish legal problems would first need to be dealt with. The risks of producing serious birth defects through human cloning are not known. In Judaism, paternity is determined by the sperm [37]. But in human cloning, no sperm is used; so who is the father?

The possibly deleterious effects of genetic engineering and gene therapy are not yet fully known. And in addition to the medical and scientific aspects of genetic engineering, DNA recombinant research, and human cloning, the spiritual and theological aspects also require exploration. Rabbis must examine these issues from the Jewish viewpoint and offer halachic guidance to the medical and lay communities.

Conclusion

Genetic screening, gene therapy, and other applications of genetic engineering are permissible in Judaism when used for the treatment, cure, and prevention of disease. Such genetic manipulation is not considered to be a violation of God's natural law but a legitimate implementation of the biblical mandate to heal. According to Jewish law, if Tay-Sachs disease, diabetes, hemophilia, cystic fibrosis, Huntington's disease, or other genetic diseases can be cured or prevented by "gene surgery," it is certainly permitted.

Genetic premarital screening is encouraged in Judaism for the purpose of discouraging at-risk marriages for a fatal illness, such as Tay-Sachs disease. Neonatal screening for treatable conditions, such as phenylketonuria, is certainly desirable and even required under Jewish law. Preimplantation screening and the use of only unaffected zygotes for implantation into the mother's womb to prevent the birth of an affected child is probably sanctioned in Jewish law. Whether these assisted-reproduction techniques can be used to choose the sex of one's offspring to prevent the birth of a child with a sex-linked disease, such as hemophilia, has not yet been ruled on by modern rabbinic authorities [38]. Prenatal screening with the specific intent of aborting an affected fetus is not allowed according to most rabbinic authorities, although a minority view permits it "for great need." Not to have children if both parents are carriers of a genetic disease, such as Tay-Sachs, is not a Jewish option. Preimplantation screening is preferable. All screening test results must remain confidential. To improve physical traits and characteristics, such as height, eye and hair color, and facial features, is frowned upon in Judaism if it serves no useful medical or psychological purpose. The cloning of man is not prohibited as a violation of the divine arrangement of the world and the creation of man in the image of God. However, Lord Rabbi Immanuel Jakobovits [19] expressed sentiments that we should all take to heart:

> It is indefensible to initiate uncontrolled experiments with incalculable effects on the balance of nature and the preservation of man's incomparable spirituality without the most careful evaluation of the likely consequences beforehand. . . . "Sparepart" surgery and "genetic engineering" may open a wonderful chapter in the history of healing. But without prior agreement on restraints and the strictest limitations, such mechanization of human life may also herald irretrievable disaster resulting from man's encroachment upon nature's preserves, from assessing human beings by their potential value as tool-parts, sperm donors, or living incubators, and from replacing the matchless destiny of the human personality by test-tubes, syringes, and the soulless artificiality of computerized numbers. Man, as the delicately balanced fusion of body, mind, and soul, can never be the mere product of laboratory conditions and scientific ingenuity.

2

The Ethical Use of Stem Cells

Background

A stem cell is so named because it resembles the stem of a planted seed that then grows to a mature plant. So, too, a stem cell is the earliest stage of a human cell that is designated to mature into a specific cell and then grows into a complete organ. A cardiac stem cell, if properly treated and cared for, will mature into cardiac tissue. Hence its name. Cardiac stem cells originated in the bone marrow, where all blood cells, which are at first multipotential blood stem cells, develop and grow into either red blood cells, white blood cells, platelets lymphocytes, or fibroblasts depending upon which hormone stimulates the bone marrow stem cell to develop into its designated adult blood cell. These hormones include erythropoietin, leukopoeitin, and thrombopotien, which respectively stimulate bone marrow stem cells to mature into red blood cells, white blood cells, or platelets. The new stem cell technology attempts to stimulate human embryonic stem cells to develop into totipotential cells, which could mature to become any kind of adult cell, such as a kidney cell, cardiac cell, muscle cell, or central nervous system cell. Once that becomes possible, repair of damaged cardiac muscle from a heart attack may become feasible. Similarly, a brain damaged by Alzheimer's disease or Parkinson's disease may be repairable by the use of stem cells programmed to become healthy neurons. The possible application of this new technology when perfected seems limitless. The ethical issues involved are of paramount importance and are discussed later in this essay. Just because medicine is capable of doing something does not necessarily mean that we should do it. What is feasible and legal is not necessarily ethical. Religious considerations must also be dealt with, and these are discussed at length later in this essay.

Stem cells can be retrieved from human bone marrow and human circulating blood. These bone marrow stem cells are called multipotential because they can develop into white blood cells, red blood cells, platelets, lymphocytes, or fibroblasts. Stem cells can also be retrieved from other body organs, such as the kidney and the heart, and if processed in a certain way, may be programmed to make new kidney or heart cells to repair a damaged kidney or a heart that has suffered damage following a heart attack.

These are called unipotential stem cells because they are limited, if programmed properly, to produce only one type of mature cell. The most ideal stem cell is called a totipotential stem cell, which has the capacity to differentiate into any type of cell desired, including neurons or nerve cells, to possibly ameliorate or eventually cure degenerative diseases of the nervous system, such as Alzheimer's or Parkinson's disease. Such totipotential stem cells can be obtained from human embryos, and that is where the controversy begins about the use of human embryonic stem cells for medical research and who should fund such research, which may eventually lead to the cure of neurological diseases and others, such as diabetes and multiple sclerosis, because the human embryos are discarded or destroyed after use.

Does this act constitute the killing of a human being? If so, it would be a sin in the eyes of all religions, or is an early human embryo not yet a human being or potential human until it is implanted into a woman's womb and becomes a full human being when it is born? This question is controversial and has generated much debate, as discussed later in this essay.

Perhaps one solution to avoid any religious objection to harvesting stem cells from human embryos would be to limit the retrieval of stem cells to spontaneous miscarriages in which no killing of a human being would be involved (assuming that an embryo is a human being) because a spontaneous miscarriage is an act of God.

Introduction

When the President's Council on Bioethics began to discuss embryonic stem cells in the 1980s, it focused on new therapeutic approaches to chronic, debilitating, and incurable diseases such as

Parkinson's disease and diabetes mellitus [1]. For many years, the U.S. government would not fund research on stem cells that had been derived from human embryos. On August 9, 2001, President George W. Bush proposed a compromise in which he would permit federal funding for stem cell research using stem lines derived from human embryos that had been killed before that date. The National Institutes of Health made available 15 to 20 human stem cell lines for federally supported research. Privately funded research on stem cells was not restricted and is in fact proceeding with some urgency in several countries, such as Australia, Britain, Korea, and other European and Asian countries.

Discussion

Kaji and Leiden point out that the isolation of stem cells from organs previously thought to have no regenerative potential, plasticity, and the creation of human embryonic stem cells clearly demonstrate the feasibility of human stem cell therapy [2]. They also insist that the ethical issues surrounding cell-based therapies must be confronted. Hard questions arise regarding the respect that the human embryo deserves, which must be balanced against the needs of living patients. In a commentary in the prestigious British publication *The Lancet*, Neil Scolding points out that in the United Kingdom, the House of Commons and the House of Lords both voted to legalize research involving stem cells derived from cloned human embryos [2]. The public health minister, articulating government support, said that it "could prove the Holy Grail in finding treatments for cancer, Parkinson's disease, diabetes, osteoporosis, spinal cord injuries, Alzheimer's Disease, leukemia and multiple sclerosis . . . transforming the lives of hundreds of thousands of people" [1].

Summary and Conclusions

The subject of embryonic stem cell research has evoked passionate and sometimes heated debate on a global scale. Stem cells are potentially immortal cells, capable of self-renewal, and under enormous scrutiny by the research community, both private and governmental, because of the potential to treat and even cure certain degenerative diseases, such as Parkinson's disease, Alzheimer's disease, multiple sclerosis, spinal cord injury, and even diabetes and other chronic illnesses. No area of research since gene therapy, genetic engineering, and cloning has evoked so much enthusiasm and debate [3]. Many countries in Europe and elsewhere have enacted legislation dealing with stem cell research. In the United States, the federal government will not fund such research, but private companies are using their own resources to further the research. The opposition to the creation of human embryos for the sole purpose of extracting stem cells is motivated by a deeply held belief in the personhood of the human embryo from the moment of conception, whether *in vivo* or *in vitro*, and the intrinsic value of every human being. This is the Catholic religious viewpoint. The Jewish view on embryonic stem cell research differs [4]. The overwhelming majority of rabbinic authorities do not accord a fertilized egg or pre-embryo the same legal status as the fetus *in utero*. Personhood is defined in Judaism as the birth of a human being from its mother's womb. Prior to birth, the fetus is considered a potential person who may not be harmed except to save its mothers life. As a result, Judaism has no objection to the donation of surplus embryos to infertile couples who might benefit by thus being able to have a child of their own. Judaism, following the same logic of the nonpersonhood of an embryo in a petri dish, would allow the discarding of surplus embryos and, by logical extension, the use of embryos for stem cell research, since this would be use for a potentially life-saving purpose [4].

3

Medical Research in Children

In 1966, Henry Beecher published a now classic article about unethical or questionable ethical procedures in clinical research, citing 22 instances where informed consent was not obtained in potentially hazardous human experimentation [1]. One of the 22 instances was a series of experiments conducted at Willowbrook Hospital on Staten Island, New York, involving handicapped or disabled children in a study of hepatitis. An editorial in *The Lancet* stated that the research was unjustifiable [2]. Some ethicists, such as Norman Fost, have argued that Krugman's hepatitis experiments at Willowbrook met the ethical standards of the day and did not impose undue burdens on the subjects. The Nuremberg Code (1946), the first international code of research ethics, required that informed consent be obtained from any individual asked to participate in research. Children were thus excluded because they were not considered capable of giving consent [3]. The Declaration of Helsinki (1964) allowed proxy consent for children and others not capable of giving their own consent. In 1977, the National Commission for the Protection of Human Subjects of Biomedical and Behavioral Research issued its Report and Recommendations about research involving children [4]. The additional historical record of research in children is detailed by Burns [5], Ross [6], and Ross, Newburger, and Sanders [3]. The current code of federal regulations concerning research in children, first adopted in 1983 [7], states that children can participate in federally funded research that poses greater than minimal risks to the subject if a local review committee, such as an institutional review board (IRB), finds that

21

the potential risk is justified by the anticipated benefit if the anticipated benefit is at least as favorable as that of standard or alternative approaches, and adequate provisions are made for soliciting the assent of the children and the permission of the parents or guardian [5]. Research is classified in the federal regulations in four categories:

1. Research involving greater than minimal risk.
2. Research involving greater than minimal risk but has the prospect of direct benefit to the study child subject. The research must have relevance to a condition that the subjects have (e.g., a particular disease).
3. Research involving greater than minimal risk with no prospect of direct benefit to the study subject.
4. Research not otherwise allowed but presents an opportunity to understand, prevent, or alleviate a serious problem affecting the health or welfare of children. Such research requires approval of a special panel convened by the secretary of health and human services if a local IRB forwards the protocol to the federal government. IRBs may not themselves approve research in category 4. Additional recommendations for the protection of children in medical or other research have been proposed by numerous authors [3, 5, 6, 7, 8].

Discussion

Research in children is a complicated and sensitive subject with ethical, legal, and philosophical components. Many articles and even several books [9–11] have been written on the subject. Ross, a philosopher and pediatrician, discusses whether healthy children deserve greater protection in medical research than sick or handicapped children [6]. She describes minimal-risk research and a minor increase over minimal risk. She cites Steinbrook [12], who argues that research involving healthy people requires a higher standard for minimizing risk. Ross asserts that this position is entrenched in the federal regulations and is the prevailing norm regarding children in research [6]. She concludes, "We need to be wary of exposing any child to risks when there is no direct therapeutic benefit." If children are to participate in such research and there are strong utilitarian reasons to permit it, then the federal regulations must be revised and she makes specific suggestions for such revisions.

Burns [5] reminds us of the importance of medical research to the diagnosis and treatment of human diseases. He points out that children represent an especially vulnerable population needing special protection against violation of individual rights and exposure to undue risk. He reviews the guidelines and policies developed to protect children as research subjects. He shows that special focus is given to the present federal regulations that are intended to provide an ethical context for the performance of pediatric research, including the distinction between therapeutic and nontherapeutic research. He concludes by stating that federal and professional initiatives are bringing renewed focus on the need for rigorous study of childhood development and disease.

One group of authors [3] summarizes additional ethical concerns about research in children, including issues of confidentiality and privacy, compensation for children harmed by medical research, and the use of stored specimens after children who were study subjects reach maturity. Furthermore, do the federal regulations allow placebo-controlled trials in children? [3]

The Catholic position on health care and research issues is discussed in some detail by Loretta M. Kopelman [10]. The Jewish view on human experimentation including children was first enunciated in a pioneering article by the late chief rabbi of the British Commonwealth of Nations, Lord Immanuel Jakobovits in 1966 [14]. In summary, human experimentation may involve healthy volunteers and/or sick patients. In Judaism, healthy people, including mature children, may altruistically volunteer for a research study that involves little or no risk (e.g., blood drawing). A seriously ill patient is required to accept standard medical therapy that is known to be efficacious even if side-effects may occur. If standard therapy has failed or is not available, a patient is allowed but not obligated to accept experimental therapy even if the risks are significant. Experimental medications or surgical procedures may not be undertaken solely to determine toxicity or possible benefit to others. They must at least have the potential to benefit the patient at hand. The decision to assume the risk of high mortality or severe morbidity with hope of benefit from the experimental treatment must, if possible, be made by the patient.

The most recent discussion of the position in Jewish law of human experimentation including children is that of Abraham Steinberg in his monumental three-volume *Encyclopedia of Jewish Medical Ethics* [15]. Steinberg provides a historical background, the immoral hypothermia experiments performed by the Nazis to preserve the Aryan race, and the immoral experiments of mass sterilization. He then discusses specific laws in Judaism concerning studies involving healthy volunteers with no anticipated side-effects, studies involving healthy volunteers but with anticipated side-effects, and studies on dangerously ill patients. He provides the ethical background for such experiments, research study design, the duties and professional obligations and requirements of the experimental scientists, and the rights of research subjects. He finally provides an extensive bibliography for further reading.

Conclusions

Human experimentation on children is associated with numerous ethical, legal, moral, social, and philosophical questions, many of which are addressed in this article. With adequate protective measures in place, such research can be ethically and philosophically justified in Western secular societies and also religiously allowed in both Catholicism and Judaism. In Judaism, four requirements must be satisfied before human experimentation of new therapies in adults and children can be justified. First, standard therapy, if available and successful, must be used before experimental medical or surgical experimental therapy may be tried. Second, the new therapy must be tested and show success in animals and tissue culture systems or other subhuman systems. Third, only the most expert and knowledgeable physicians and/or scientists may perform the experiment. Last, there must be at least the remote possibility that the ill patient may be benefited by the experimental therapy. All these considerations are based on the assumption in Judaism that human life is sacrosanct and of supreme value. Any chance to save a life, however remote, must be pursued. Thus, the issue raised by Burns et al. and by Ross can be resolved in both Judaism and Catholicism. Every life is equally valuable and inviolable, including minority groups and susceptible groups, such as children, prisoners, and the mentally ill. Measures involving risks to life may be taken in an attempt to prevent certain death. There is no restriction on animal experimentation for medical purposes to find the cure for disease or remission of illness. The animal must be spared all pain and suffering, however [17]. This paper was prompted by a discussion with pediatric residents about ethical issues pertaining to children.

4

Human Cloning

The ethics of human cloning has been an intensely and widely discussed topic ever since Dr. Ian Wilmut in 1996 announced the
cloning of Dolly the sheep. Whether human cloning should be
banned is a difficult question because it involves ethical, legal,
social, religious, and political considerations over and above the
scientific issues. This essay presents some elements of the debate
by reviewing the recent literature on human cloning with an analysis of the positions taken by different authors.

Literature Review

The debate about whether human cloning should be allowed was
recently reinvigorated by the announcement that Korean scientists
had cloned 30 human embryos [1] and the very recent bankrolling
of stem cell research in California with state funds in order to cir-
cumvent the U.S. ban on federal funding for such research except
for a limited number of already existing cell lines [2]. The February
12, 2004 announcement by the Korean scientists made global
headlines. At least one writer is greatly concerned that the demon-
stration by these scientists of the practical ability to manufacture
stem cell lines from scratch will lead to a global market or business
in stem cells [3]. The author points out that only 10 private firms
in the United States were actively involved in embryonic stem cell
research in 2003. Although the Korean accomplishment turned out
to be fabricated, it is surely only a matter of time before real results
are achieved.

Human cloning or reproductive cloning is the asexual production of a human being whose genetic makeup is nearly identical to that of a currently or previously existing individual. Research cloning involves the creation of a cloned human embryo for the purpose of scientific research about early human development or research aimed at developing treatments for chronic and debilitating diseases, such as Parkinson's disease, Alzheimer's disease, diabetes, and others, by the use of pluripotential and totipotential stem cell research and research cloning. One prominent group of bioethicists has concluded that human cloning, for whatever purpose, represents an abuse of scientific freedom, not its realization [4]. "These authors state that this new technology should adhere to the standard that science should always serve humanity, never that a segment of humanity would be created to serve science." They remind the reader that history has conspicuously recorded that no program sacrificing those at the margins of humanity to science has ever stood the test of time. The authors continue by positing that ethical reflection always reaches, in due course, the conclusion that the least of human beings deserve the care and concern that the medical profession presumes is due all other human beings. "Whether the ethical cinder of human cloning will lodge in the eye of society's conscience is an issue still within reach of sensible preventive intervention" [4]. For the sake of their patients, as well as the future of humanity, these bioethicists urge healthcare professionals to oppose all forms of human cloning. In keeping with the Hippocratic ethic, they recommend that biomedical research on nonembryonic stem cells should be pursued and funded aggressively. They also recommend legislation and policies at all levels that will protect people from the unfavorable outcomes of human cloning, both now and for generations to come. Only a ban prohibiting both research and reproductive cloning will offer such protection [4].

Fully in support of banning reproductive cloning is the article by Landry and Zucker [5]. They claim that the creation of human embryonic stem cells through the destruction of a human embryo puts the value of a potential therapeutic tool against that of an early human life. This contest of values, claim the authors, has resulted in a polarized debate that neglects areas of common interest and perspective. They suggest that common ground be found for pursuing research on human embryonic stem cells by reconsidering the death of the human embryo and by applying to this research the ethical norms of essential organ donation [5]. Only a ban prohibiting both research and reproductive cloning will offer protection to prevent research cloning from evolving into reproductive cloning.

On the other hand, Hochedlinger and Jaenisch state that therapeutic cloning, in combination with the differentiation potential of embryonic stem cells, offers a valuable means of obtaining autologous cells for the treatment of a variety of diseases [8]. The abnormalities associated with reproductive cloning are not expected to impede the use of this technique for therapy, they continue, since the process seems to select for functional cells. However, before these principles can be applied clinically, it will be essential to improve differentiation protocols for human embryonic stem cells and to evaluate the effect of the oocyte-derived mitochondrial proteins in somatic cells obtained by nuclear transfer. In the future, state the authors, it might be possible to generate embryonic stem cells directly from somatic cells. They conclude that it is, therefore, important to continue research aimed at improving our understanding of the molecular events that take place during nuclear reprogramming in order to develop these potential new therapies [5].

McHugh discusses the ethical use of embryonic stem cells by inventing the term "clonote" [6]. As a member of the President's Council on Bioethics, he speaks with authority and prestige. Continuing the ethical and moral debate, Fischbach and Fischbach [7] point out that human embryonic stem cells offer the promise of a new regenerative medicine in which damaged adult cells can be replaced with new cells. The council's seminal publication *Human Cloning and Human Dignity: An Ethical Inquiry* provides insights into the moral reasoning behind both sets of arguments. Opposing arguments were articulated by several other members of the council, such as George, Meilaender, Hurlbut, and Gomez-Lobo. The authors continue by stating that research is needed to determine the most viable stem cell lines and reliable ways to promote the differentiation of pluripotent stem cells into specific cell types (neurons, muscle cells, etc.). To create new cell lines, it is necessary to destroy pre-implantation blastocysts, which has led to an intense debate that threatens to limit embryonic stem cell research. The authors conclude that the profound ethical issues raised call for informed, dispassionate debate [7].

Jaenisch provides his own perspective of the science and ethics of nuclear transplantation in human cloning [8]. He points out that whereas reproductive cloning is rejected almost unanimously, the use of embryos generated either by *in vitro* fertilization or by nuclear cloning for the purpose of generating embryonic stem cells remains controversial. He contends that there is a difference between the two methods of obtaining embryonic stem cells that makes biologic sense, is consistent with available evidence, and may contribute to a more rational discussion of nuclear transfer technology. Vastag postulates that embryos cloned for stem cells do not represent a leap toward reproductive cloning [9].

On the political scene the United Kingdom has banned implantation of human blastocysts or embryos for reproductive cloning but allows therapeutic cloning [10]. The South Korean scientists whose work is described above called for a worldwide ban on reproductive cloning [10]. In Canada, the Assisted Human Reproduction Act prohibits research on therapeutic cloning, although some authors question whether such a ban can be justified on the basis of scientific freedom [11]. France has banned both reproductive and therapeutic cloning [12]. In late 2003 the United Nations General Assembly failed to pass a treaty on reproductive cloning, and the European Union failed to agree on conditions for funding stem cell research [13]. But in March 2005 the UN General Assembly adopted a Declaration on Human Cloning, which solemnly declares, "Member states are called upon to prohibit all forms of human cloning inasmuch as they are incompatible with human dignity and the protection of life." In 2002 Australia prohibited human cloning for reproduction or research.

Most countries, including the United States, distinguish between reproductive cloning, which most prohibit, and research cloning or stem cell research, which most permit but usually with restrictions. After Professor Panos Zabos claimed in early 2004 that he had implanted a fertilized egg obtained by reproductive cloning into a woman's uterus, outcries from numerous sources called for an international ban on human reproductive cloning [14]. In the United States, on August 9, 2001, President Bush addressed the issue of stem cell research and cloning. A series of congressional bills were proposed to limit or ban therapeutic and/or reproductive cloning but none of the bills reached the president's desk for his signature. Individual states also passed a gamut of laws ranging from the prohibition of all forms of human cloning (in Arkansas, Iowa, Michigan, and North Dakota) to bans on reproductive cloning alone (in Louisiana, Missouri, and Rhode Island) to a bill passed in California in 2002, which expressly promotes stem cell research, including nuclear transfer studies. The California statute has since become a model for several other states (Massachusetts, Illinois,

Maryland, New Jersey, New York, Pennsylvania, Texas, Vermont, and Washington) [15].

In 2003, the American Medical Association approved physicians' participation in cloning stem cells for research and treatment but not for making babies [16]. The AMA noted that this position does not conflict with President Bush's opposition to all cloning on ethical grounds and has restricted funding and research to existing cell lines [16]. An author who is a member of the President's Council on Bioethics decries the political distortion of biomedical science by the ethical debate surrounding reproductive and therapeutic cloning and stem cell research [17]. In 2006, President Bush vetoed a bill that would have relaxed federal funding restrictions on embryonic stem cell research, but supported so-called fetal farming legislation.

In Britain, the Human Fertilization and Embryology Authority granted Britain's first cloning license to the Newcastle Center for Life for the purpose of harvesting insulin-producing cells for transplantation into diabetic patients [18]. Even more recently, a request from Professor Ian Wilmut and his group, who created Dolly the sheep, for a license to clone human embryos for the purpose of research into motor neuron disease was approved [19]. Professor Wilmut himself states that current methods of cloning are repeatable but inefficient [20].

In the United States, a writer has accused Congress of legislative myopia in the areas of cloning and stem cell research [21]. Phimister and Drazen point out that embryonic stem cell lines are required to clear the hurdles between concept and practice [22]. They decry the fact that federal regulations limit their use because of the concern cited by President Bush in 2001 that blastocysts "have at least the potential for life" and that destroying them would cross "a fundamental moral line" [22].

Summary and Conclusions

Rapid advances in research into the pluripotent nature of stem cells derived from human embryos, including their potential use in treating degenerative diseases such as Parkinson's disease, Alzheimer's disease, heart failure [23], and diabetes, have collided with opposing views regarding the morality of using human embryos for these purposes [24]. Physicians need to become educated about the science and ethics of cloning [25], to understand the difference between therapeutic or research cloning and reproductive cloning or the cloning of babies, and to become familiar with the moral and ethical arguments for or against the use of unenabled embryos [26]. If procreative cloning someday becomes as safe as natural conception, moral objections will still be articulated by those who believe that human life begins at the time an egg is fertilized either *in vivo* or *in vitro*, and that the destruction of a human fertilized egg or zygote or blastocyst is the equivalent of killing a living human being, which is prohibited even to save the life of another human being because of the axiom "Thou shalt not destroy one human life to save another human life or even several other human lives."

The use of terms like blastocyst and zygote and fertilized egg is not meant to evade the fundamental biological nature of the embryonic human being. Therapeutic cloning, which is the use of somatic cell nuclear transfer to produce embryonic stem cells, has its strong proponents [27]. Wilson [28] cites Vogelstein, who said, "Although animal stem-cell work is important to pursue, they can't supplant work on human embryonic stem cells. The only way to learn how to use these cells is to do experiments with them." Wilson also quotes Bloom, who said, "For the moment, it's a battle of ideologies and abstractions, and I don't expect the debate to change until the science has something to offer in a practical way." Thus, Vogelstein and Bloom seem to sum up the present status of cloning, which could change medicine in dramatic ways.

In this age of advanced information technology, MedGene is a freely available interactive database that summarizes and organizes the vast biomedical literature with respect to diseases and genes [29]. More research is needed on human embryos because of a deficiency of literature about human epigenetic programming and the propensity for epigenetic errors with embryo technologies and how to minimize or eliminate them [30].

5

Separating Siamese Twins

In recent years, attempted separations of Siamese twins in the United States and Britain have received much prominence in the mass media. In fact, the detailed description of one famous case written by Donald C. Drake in the *Philadelphia Inquirer* on Sunday, October 16, 1977, entitled "One Must Die So the Other Might Live" earned Drake a Pulitzer Prize.

The term "Siamese twins" is derived from the case of the twins Eng and Cheng, who were born as conjoined twins in 1811. They were widely exhibited by P.T. Barnum. Eng and Cheng each had a full complement of normal limbs and organs but were joined at the sternum by a flexible band of cartilage several inches thick. A British merchant discovered them in 1824. After tours of the United States and Europe, they adopted the surname Bunker and settled as farmers in North Carolina. At the age of 44 they married two British sisters, ages 26 and 28. The twins maintained their wives in separate households and alternated weekly in visiting each wife. Cheng fathered six children, and Eng had five. All the children were normal and healthy. The brothers lived until 1874 and died within hours of each other.

Brief Literature Review of Recent Cases

Conjoined twins are a rare occurrence, with an incidence of about 1 in 250,000 live births. Approximately 60 percent are stillborn. Although they can be joined at the hip, abdomen, chest, or head, the majority are joined at the chest and share a heart. Although

31

conjoined twins are fascinating to the public, they present complex and challenging ethical, medical, and legal issues to everyone involved in their care. Among the issues discussed by one author [2] are: right to life, presumed consent, physician duty, quality of life, allocation of resources, and futile care. The author also discusses the pros and cons of separation and offers alternative solutions, such as transplant surgery, and experimental therapies made on a limited basis, perhaps by the creation of experimental therapy centers of excellence [2].

The Lakewood Case

In 1977, dicephalous twins who shared a single heart were born to a couple in Lakewood, New Jersey—devout Jewish parents who were members of a family of rabbinic scholars. The parents sought the sanction of the late Rabbi Moshe Feinstein before consenting to the procedure. The story of the separation of these twins and the tragic outcome of both twins dying is recounted in detail by Drake in his Pulitzer Prize–winning article [3] as well as by other authors [1, 4]. The chief of pediatric surgery at Philadelphia's Children's Hospital where the surgery was performed was Dr. C. Everett Koop, later to become surgeon general of the United States. Since separation of the twins necessitated sacrificing one to preserve the life of the other, who unfortunately died 47 days later of unrelated causes, several Catholic nurses asked to be excused from assisting at the surgery even though reassurance by a Catholic moralist was forthcoming. The opinion rendered by Rabbi Feinstein allowing the surgery is discussed and criticized by a renowned Jewish medical ethicist [1].

Several cases of conjoined twins from foreign countries (e.g., Honduras, Guatemala) who came to the United States for attempted separation received much attention by the mass media, but there was very little discussion of the ethical issues involved, including the allocation of enormous resources (both financial and otherwise) to the care of these foreign patients and their families.

The Case of Mary and Jodie

Conjoined twins named Mary and Jodie were born in Malta and brought to England by their parents to seek out the competent specialized medical assistance not available in their native land. The twins' parents, who are Catholic, did not want the twins surgically separated, whereas the physicians and the hospital believed that they had an obligation to save one girl, even with the certain fore-knowledge that the other girl would die as a result of the separation. The matter was brought to the High Court, which decided in favor of the physicians and the hospital. The family sought relief from the Court of Appeals. All three justices on the Court of Appeals unanimously voted to dismiss the appeal after a careful review of the medical facts. The justices interviewed the involved surgeons and the parents, pondering the relevant medical laws, family laws, and criminal laws.

The surgical separation was accomplished. Jodie survived, while, as expected, Mary quickly died.

The Catholic View

In light of the Catholic Church's moral tradition, one might ask whether the parents' decision should have been honored and the children allowed to live, even if for only about six months, since they would eventually both die naturally of their pathological condition. One Catholic theologian gives a detailed moral analysis of this case [5]. He discusses the principle of double effect, where one good effect (the survival of Jodie) and one bad effect (the death of Mary) are opposing moral forces. For the single surgical act to be morally good, four conditions have to be met.

1. The act itself must be good, or at least neutral.
2. The intention of the acting person must be good.
3. The good effect must not flow from the evil effect.
4. The evil effect (the good lost) must not be greater than the good obtained (i.e., the good effect.)

The author argues that since not all four conditions of the principle of double effect were met, the surgical separation of Mary and Jodie must be judged as objectively immoral, notwithstanding the good intentions of the surgeon and hospital. It is prohibited to kill one person to save another. The author concludes that whether the firm decision of the parents to allows the twins to die naturally should have been overridden by the courts is another issue, which he does not discuss in the present article [5].

Another writer addresses the ethics of separating Siamese twins and cites a British poll, which found that respondents seemed to agree that parents should not always have the final say. A full 78 percent of the respondents said it is ethical to separate dying con-joined twins to save the life of one [6]. Another Catholic theologian concludes that because of what he terms circumstantial necessity, it is not possible to justify the separation of Jodie and Mary by appealing to the principle of double effect [7]. The doctors did intend Mary's death as an end in a secondary sense and did not choose to kill Mary as a means to achieving their primary end, which was to save Jodie. Certainly, the decision that confronted the parents, judges, and doctors who were designated by Providence to choose the fate of the twins was about as difficult a moral dilemma as we can imagine. Unfortunately, the decision by the courts to grant legal permission for the doctors to separate the twins was gravely imprudent because it legally sanctioned the killing of an innocent human being [7]. The author concludes that good would have truly been done if all involved had simply allowed the twins to die a natural death [7].

Latbovic and Nelson [8], in a lengthy article on the Catholic moral perspective on the separation of the conjoined twins Jodie and Mary, provide the general medical facts and legal background, and then survey and critique the various moral analyses of the case by Cardinal O'Connor, Albert Morazewski, Helen Watt, Michel Terrien, Benedict Guevin, William E. May, Christopher Kaizor, Therese Lysaught, and Daniel Sulmasy. The paper by Latbovic and Nelson is entirely devoted to analysis and critique of the responses by the aforementioned Catholics to the question of whether it was morally upright to separate Mary and Jodie, rather than to the legal decision of the court. They argue that they do not view the separation of Mary and Jodie as intentional killing or as intentional mutilation. They sympathize with those who think that it would have been best for the final decision concerning separation to have been made by the parents.

However, Latkovic and Nelson [8] also think that the decision of the physicians to intervene and the decision of the courts to allow them to intervene was morally justified, given the unique circumstances of the case, even though the moral reasoning underlying the opinions of the courts was not always satisfactory.

The Jewish View

The writers who discuss the famous Lakewood case described previously [1, 3, 9] provide Jewish insight into the problem of separating Siamese twins and other related Jewish laws. Historical backgrounds are provided, and numerous cases cited in early Jewish writings are quoted, going all the way back to the Talmud and early post-talmudic Hebrew writings up to the rabbinic responsa literature of the last 300 years [1].

Discussion

The famous Jodie and Mary case and its outcome, as described earlier, generated a torrent of discussion and writing in medical, legal, ethical, religious, and philosophical circles. A few samples follow. Helen Watt [10] considers the separation of Siamese twins as mutilation. To avoid deliberate killing, argues Watt, doctors should respect the lives and bodies of those on whom they intervene. It is unacceptable to invade the body of a patient if this will do the patient no good, but serious and permanent harm. Cutting into Mary, which did her serious and permanent harm, was a bad means of the good end of saving her twin sister's life. Another author [11] questions the assumption that conjoined twins are necessarily two people or persons. The article concludes with a critical evaluation of the tendency in bioethics to regard ethical challenges as rivalry between individuals competing for scarce resources. Yet another writer [12] attacks the British court's decision to allow the separation of Jodie and Mary on the basis of various inconsistencies. Most fundamentally, the leading judgment appears to involve a relative devaluation of Mary's life in consequentialist terms. One life is better than no life appears to be the message, an evaluation apparently reached by reference to quality-of-life considerations. Yet this approach was explicitly rejected in an oral presentation by the judge.

Christopher Crowley [13] considers the relationship between the court's legal decision and the moral reasons adduced in its support, which gain their force against the framework of mainstream normative ethical theory. He argues that in a few dilemmatic situations, such a legalistic theoretical approach cannot plausibly accommodate certain irreducible and uneliminable features of the ethical experience of any concrete individual implicated in the situation, and that this failure partly undermines the self-appointed role of guiding such an individual's conduct. He does not reject law or moral theory but challenges their explicit claim to comprehensiveness and their "fixation with an idealized and protectively universal rationality modeled on converging scientific inquiry."

McCullough [14] describes personal identity, individuals, and substances in clinical ethics. He states that contrarian ways of thinking are generally good for the intellectual life and clinical ethics. He applies his proposal to discussions of cloning, separation of conjoined twins, and the coming into existence of human beings.

Appel [15] points out that the Jodie and Mary case drew international attention when their parents sued to prevent physicians at St. Mary's Hospital from sacrificing the weaker twin. The case also proved highly divisive within the medical community. He quotes a similar American case of conjoined sisters in 1993. At Philadelphia's Children's Hospital, physicians separated Amy and Angela Lakeberg, attempting to sacrifice one twin to save the other, but both ultimately died. He discusses the question of parental autonomy and the denunciation of the appeals court for trying to force the parents to violate their fundamental beliefs [15].

Rosalie O. Maimous brings a nursing perspective to the issue of separating conjoined twins [16]. She asks and discusses answers to a series of ethical questions, including: Is there an ethical right to separation? Is it morally permissible to let both infants die? Does distributive justice play a role in the separation of conjoined twins with multiple anomalies? Where are we today? Her thesis is to argue for separation, and she gives several reasons to bolster her argument.

Dickens and Cook [17] discuss the management of severely malformed newborn infants with specific reference to conjoined twins. They recapitulate the story of Jodie and Mary. Parental duties to the viable twin were formed consistent with allowing but not intending the natural death of the nonviable twin. The right to human dignity of both twins supported the justification of separation surgery. The decision did not elevate physicians' choices over parents', but subjected both to the law.

A lengthy editorial about the court-imposed separation of Mary and Jodie [18] states, "Undoubtedly, many people," the writer included, "would agree with the English Courts that 'the least worst option was to separate the twins and save one at the cost of killing the other.'" The editorial writer then provides a lengthy discussion of the various ethical questions and views on this subject.

Another editorial in the prestigious journal *The Lancet* [19] discusses the moral, ethical, and legal arguments in the Jodie and Mary case. The editorial writer states that under the circumstances of this case, British legal opinion has to prevail, separation is deemed lawful, and there is only one sensible decision. The only choices are between two certain deaths and one death accelerated with one child surviving, albeit with an uncertain future.

"The latter would be the correct decision in this appallingly difficult case." [19].

Another perspective on the Maltese conjoined twins presents two views of their separation, one in favor of separation and one opposed [20]. The opposing view states that it is difficult to see how Mary's right to life could encompass a right to the organs and life of her sister as well, especially in light of her very grim prospects even with that support.

Paris and Elias Jonas [21] also are opposed to the court-imposed separation of Jodie and Mary. They discuss at length the complex medical, moral, and legal issues raised by this case. They conclude with a suggestion that we heed Justice Cardozo's counsel of restraint and reconcile ourselves to the idea that there are myriads of problems and troubles that judges are powerless to solve; and this is as it should be.

Thomasma and colleagues describe in detail the case of the Lakeberg twins and discuss the ethics of caring for conjoined twins [22]. In 1993,the conjoined twins Amy and Angela Lakeberg became the focus of national attention. They shared a complex six-chambered heart and one liver. Only one could survive separation surgery, and even her chances were slim. The medical challenge was great, and the ethical challenges were even greater. The authors describe the preoperative discussions, the surgery, and the difficulty of applying ethical standards to the complex issues relating to deciding what is best for children who cannot speak for themselves. The twins would both die if nothing were done. One had to be sacrificed, in other words killed, to save the other. The authors bemoan the fact that past moral experience contributing to the ethos of an institution does not guarantee that current behavior is ethical. They also assert that there is an American propensity to rescue identified lives—those that we see on television and magazine covers—at the expense of acting to benefit the unidentified masses, an arguable premise. The authors conclude that "what we learned most of all was that the duty to life must, in high technology environments like U.S. Healthcare, be reinterpreted as a duty to preserve, as far as possible normal human life."

Conclusion

George Annas [23] provides us with an analysis of the Jodie and Mary court-ordered separation of the Maltese Siamese twins in Britain and provides what may serve as an appropriate conclusion

for this difficult dilemma in the last section of his paper, entitled
"Lessons." Annas first describes the circumstances of the case,
then discusses and criticizes the opinions of the three lord justices
of the British court that ordered the separation in defiance of the
parents' wishes: Lord Justice Alan Ward, Lord Justice Robert
Brooke, and Lord Justice Robert Walker. He also describes the
aftermath of the surgery, the problems with the legal analysis, the
failure to identify with the parents, the problems with analogies to
other cases and precedents, and problems with conjoined twins
themselves. In the final section of his paper Annas states that perhaps the most important lesson of the case of Jodie and Mary is
that there are severe limits to the law in making unprecedented,
complex life-and-death decisions. The most important shortcoming
of the decision of the judges, argues Annas, is that it did not rest
on any legal principle. That is why, if a similar case were to present
itself, the physicians involved could, on the basis of the reasoning
in this case (and contrary to its conclusion), decide to follow the
wishes of the parents and let both twins die. What is the court's role
in similar cases? asks Annas. Is it to determine whether a particular course of action, chosen by both parent and physician, is legally
permissible, or is it to determine whether a particular medical
intervention is required by law? The first role seems reasonable, the
second seems justified only in cases in which the failure to act (on
the part of either parent or physician) is child neglect. I agree with
Annas, who says that in this case, it would have been better had
the physicians not sought court intervention. It would have been
preferable to convince the parents to agree to the separation (since
giving Jodie a chance to live at the cost of cutting Mary's life short
seems to have been the lesser of two evils). I further agree with
Annas that the case for separation is not so strong that it demands
that the authority to make the decision on the medical care of their
children be taken away from the parents.

6

The Treatment of Newborns with Ambiguous or Traumatized Genitalia

Under current medical practice, when a child is born with ambiguous genitalia, sex is assigned and medical/surgical intervention is undertaken even though it is now possible to promptly determine the true sex of the newborn by chromosomal analysis. Such analysis is not always accurate, because there is the phenomenon of transsexualism in which a person's sense of his or her "true" sex goes completely counter to the chromosomal. In addition, there are instances of confused chromosomal sexuality (xxy, xxo, etc.). Early assignment of sex is considered ideal, and its goal is to enable a satisfactory adjustment to the sex of rearing. This process is fraught with many ethical decisions and dilemmas, which have gone largely unnoticed in the medical ethical literature [1]. This practice is criticized by the Intersex Society of North America and by feminist scholars, who together are creating a "politics of difference approach in which differences are not seen as defects to be corrected" [1]. The reasons offered to support current medical practice are analyzed, and arguments are put forth for a move toward the politics of difference [1].

Since the treatment of newborns with ambiguous genitalia is fraught with medical, surgical, personal, psychological, ethical, legal, social, religious, and political considerations, it seems reasonable to briefly review some of the recent medical literature on the subject and to present recommendations for the future.

A Landmark Case

One of the most widely cited cases of a patient with surgical sex change is known as "John/Joan" [2–5].

John's penis was accidentally severed during a circumcision accident. Most specialists consulted thought John should be left alone and not reassigned. Other specialists decided that life as a boy or man without a penis would be impossible, and that John would be better off as a girl. Surgeons removed his testes and performed plastic surgery to make his damaged male genitals look somewhat more feminine. The parents were advised to raise John as Joan. Years later, sex researcher Milton Diamond and his associate, Sigmondson, published the details of John/Joan's life, which revealed that he had never developed a female identity and considered his medical treatment to have been abusive [6]. These authors give specific recommendations as to how to deal with intersex infants [7]. John had reasserted himself [6] as a male [7] during his adolescence, against the resistance of his doctors [8]. Today, John lives as a man, is married to a woman, and has adopted her children. He takes testosterone to replace what would have been produced by his testicles. He had a mastectomy to remove the breasts produced by the estrogen he was given. He also had a phalloplasty to make his genitals look more masculine [2, 6–8]. This landmark case has "proved wrong" [1]. The remarkable case of John/Joan is described in greater detail by Beh and Diamond [9], who discuss some of the ethical and medical dilemmas associated with the case.

Brief Literature Review

The landmark case of John/Joan has already been discussed above. Beh and Dian [9] discuss the development of the surgical approach to treat intersex infants and others with congenital anomalies that began in the late 1960s and became standard in the 1970s. Sex-reassignment surgery for intersex babies became routine, and parents were persuaded to consent to radical surgeries on their infants. The authors discuss in detail the remarkable case of John/Joan, how medical standards develop, and how a poorly grounded standard of care became entrenched with anecdotal reporting but without scientific validation. The next part of the lengthy article by Beh and Dian explores the role of the informed-consent doctrine, particularly in regard to parental decision-making responsibility in cases of ambiguous or traumatized genitalia. Beh and Dian are very critical of the way formidable informed-consent obstacles are handled or ignored.

The last part of their paper offers the recommendations for change endorsed by critics of such surgery, including both medical ethicists and the Intersex Society of North America. They assert that although surgical intervention became the "standard of care" for intersex rather than considering a proven protocol, it would have been appropriate to characterize it as innovative therapy all along because treatments for intersex have not been adequately grounded in long-term studies. They also state that newborns with genitalia outside our normal expectations can achieve a satisfying psychosexual adjustment without surgical intervention. Other criticisms of the "standard of care" are also discussed by Beh and Diamond [9]. The American Academy of Pediatrics standard operating procedure published in 2000 fairly well retains the idea of sex reassignment and surgery as acceptable. The British, however, have accepted the more conservative approach of not doing infant cosmetic surgery. The final section of their paper deals with parental consent to genital surgery sex reassignment on behalf of children whose chromosomal or genetic sex can be easily established. There are many problems of informed consent and infant surgery, including the aura of urgency, imparting incomplete information by the physicians, perpetuating secrecy from the child as to his/her real sex, and failure to disclose the uncertainty of long-term outcome. The authors conclude that a fuller airing of the ethical dimensions of treatment and informed consent may prompt a more cautious approach to surgical intervention. Importantly, recognizing the child's right to an open future as part of the calculation may yield a more measured approach in the difficult cases of newborns with ambiguous genitalia, who should have the final say in how they want to live. The article concludes with the adage "The most important sex organs are between the ears rather than between the legs" [9].

Minto, Liaro Woodhouse, Ramsley, and Greighton performed a cross-sectional study of the effect of clitoral surgery on sexual outcome in individuals who have intersex conditions with ambiguous genitalia [10]. Of the 39 individuals enrolled, 28 had been sexually active and all had sexual difficulties—the 18 women of nonsensuality (78%) and of inability to achieve orgasm (39%) were compared to the 10 women who had not had surgery. The authors conclude that sexual function may be compromised by clitoral surgery. Debate on the ethics of the use of such surgery on children should be promoted, and further multicenter research is needed to ensure representative samples and comprehensive outcome assessment. Meanwhile, parents and patients who consent to clitoral surgery should be fully informed of the potential risks to sexual function [10].

Dreger discusses the ethical issues in the treatment of intersexuality [11]. She describes the frequency of intersexuality as approximately 1 in 500 births. She then provides a historical background, discusses dominant treatment protocols, the problem of normality and psychological health, and the problem of deception. She argues that today, typically after the identification of an "ambiguous or intersex baby, teams of specialists are immediately assembled and these teams of doctors decide to which sex/gender a given child will be assigned." Dreger is surprised that feminists and intersexuals have objected to presumptions that there is a "right" way to be a male and a "right way to be a female and that children who challenge these categories should be constructed to fit into them." She continues that it is not at all clear whether all or even most of the intersex surgeries done today involve what would legally and ethically constitute informed consent. She is pleased, however, with the fact that new guidelines have been proposed for dealing with persons with ambiguous genitalia [7].

Daaboul and Frader [12] review the controversies surrounding the management of patients born with ambiguous genitalia to determine the strengths and weaknesses of recommendations for clinical practice. Traditional practice involves paternalistic decision-making by medical practitioners, including the use of deception and/or incomplete communication of facts about the infant's condition and early surgical intervention, to make a "definitive" sex and gender assignment. However, the authors point out that modern scientific evidence about sex-role determination refutes earlier theories supporting the need and appropriateness for early decisions. "Some intersex individuals have begun to speak out against their treatment, denouncing the secretive approaches and cosmetic surgery without the specific consent of the (mature) affected individuals. They argue for complete disclosure of information regarding the condition and deferral of all surgery until at least adolescence" [12]. The authors assert that the traditionalist practices no longer conform to modern legal or ethical standards of care. They point out that the position of some intersex activists ignores the potential for psychosocial harm to intersex children and our society's general and strong deference to parental discretion in decisions for and about their children. The authors argue for a middle way, involving shared decision-making with intersex patients and the honoring of parental preferences for or against surgery [12]. However this approach does not take into account the substantial harm that may be done to some patients because of secrecy and deception.

The theory of gender neutrality espoused by Money [4, 5] is no longer tenable. Adults who have had intersex surgery may grow up with tendencies of the opposite sex or gender in which they were raised. There seem to be no perfect solutions, although rules for handling and treatment of babies born with ambiguous genitalia are being promulgated. [1, 2, 6, 7, 10, 11, 12]

Concluding Note

More and more ethicists are taking note of the traditional practice of performing immediate sex- and gender-assignment surgery shortly after birth. The many ethical questions raised by this traditional practice make it obsolete and require rethinking the treatment for ambiguous genitalia [2]. The famous landmark John/Joan case described earlier illustrates many of these ethical concerns. A new, enlightened model for the treatment of newborns with ambiguous genitalia would provide an interdisciplinary clinic that could provide counseling, peer referrals, sex therapy, and surgery if decided upon after "appropriate informed consent." One proposal is that newborn intersexual children would be diagnosed and labeled boy or girl. Emotional distress of the parents would be addressed by counseling and information sharing, including the best available evidence about gender-identity outcomes. Parents should be told that their child may end up with an atypical gender identity or sexual orientation and may change sex role. Well-informed parents and their intersex children would be allowed to choose cosmetic surgery or change of sex role if they so wish [2].

A recently published book entitled *Lessons from the Intersexed* [13] describes a small political group which has evolved "to lift the shame and secrecy" from congenital intersex conditions. They want to halt nonconsensual infant surgeries and allow intersex to be considered an identity, not an abnormality, unless there is a threat to life. They seek to eliminate the term "ambiguous" and replace it with "variant." The author emphasizes the need for long-term follow-up of intersex babies. How soon and how ardently will untreated intersexuals seek change so that they can disappear into the two-sex culture? Being different, states the author, is difficult and lonely for each child and family. The uneasy, provocative questions raised in this book deserve consideration. If one reads this book and other related books, one becomes aware of the tremendous complexity of human sexuality and gender identity beyond genitals, hormones, enzymes, and even chromosomes and genes. Behavior, feelings, and values blend with intellect and how each individual behaves sexually. Recent literature on the subject [14, 15] concludes that a moratorium on sex-reassignment cosmetic surgery should be imposed. Also recommended are follow-up studies on past cases, with honesty and counseling as the core of initial and subsequent treatment [15].

PART II

Patients' Rights, Informed Consent, Confidentiality, and Related Topics

7

Physicians' Fees in Jewish Law

In Jewish tradition, the physician is given specific divine license to practice medicine. The biblical verse *and heal he shall heal* (Exodus 21:19) is interpreted by the talmudic sages as teaching us that God grants authorization to the physician to heal (Bava Kamma 85a). In Jewish law, a physician is not merely allowed to practice medicine but is in fact commanded to do so if he has chosen to become a physician. This biblical mandate is based upon two scriptural precepts. *And thou shalt restore it to him* (Deuteronomy 22:2) refers to the restoration of lost property. Moses Maimonides, in his Commentary on the Mishnah (Nedarim 4:4), states that "it is obligatory from the Torah for the physician to heal the sick, and this is included in the explanation of the scriptural phrase and *thou shalt restore it to him,* meaning to heal his body." Thus, Maimonides and the Talmud (Nedarim 38b) both state that the law of restoration also includes the restoration of the health of one's fellow man. If a person has "lost his health" and the physician is able to restore it, he is obligated to do so.

The second scriptural mandate for the physician to heal is based on the phrase *neither shalt thou stand idly by the blood of thy neighbor* (Leviticus 19:16). The passage refers to the duties of human beings to their fellow men and the moral principles that the sages expound and apply to every phase of civil and criminal law. If one stands idly by and allows one's fellow man to die without offering help, one is guilty of transgressing this precept. A physician who refuses to heal, thereby resulting in suffering and/or death of the patient, is also guilty of transgressing this commandment.

Thus, permission for the physician to heal is granted in the Bible from the phrase *and heal he shall heal* (Exodus 21:19). Some scholars, notably Maimonides, claim that healing the sick is not only allowed but is actually obligatory. Rabbi Joseph Karo, in his code of Jewish law (*Shulchan Aruch*, Yoreh Deah 336), combines both thoughts:

> *The Torah gave permission to the physician to heal; moreover, this is a religious precept and it is included in the category of saving life; and if he withholds his services, it is considered as shedding blood.*

If one asks why God granted physicians license and even mandate to heal the sick, one can offer the following explanation: A cardinal principle of Judaism is that human life is of infinite value. The preservation of human life takes precedence over all commandments in the Bible except three: idolatry, murder, and forbidden sexual relations. Life's value is absolute and supreme. In order to preserve a human life, the Sabbath and even the Day of Atonement may be desecrated, and all other rules and laws save the aforementioned three are suspended for the overriding consideration of saving a human life. He who saves one life is as if he saved a whole world (Sanhedrin 37a). Even a few moments of life are worthwhile. Judaism is a "right-to-life" religion. The obligation to save lives is an individual as well as a communal obligation. Certainly a physician, who has knowledge and expertise far beyond that of a layperson, is obligated to use his medical skills to heal the sick and thereby prolong and preserve life.

Physicians' Compensation and Fees

The biblical verse *and heal he shall heal* relates to compensation for personal injuries and is usually translated "he shall cause him to be thoroughly healed." This is an obvious reference to the payment of medical expenses by one who inflicts an injury on his neighbor. In fact, the three most ancient translations, the Septuagint (Greek), the Targum (Aramaic), and the Vulgate (Latin) all render the phrase "he shall pay the doctor's fee." Healing expenses are one of five items of compensation due by law to an injured party (Baba Kamma 8:1).

Numerous references in classical Jewish sources speak of physician's fees and compensation. Heirs who are obligated to provide medical care for their chronically ill mother can contract with a physician for an all-inclusive fee (Ketubot 52b). A person who has pain in his eyes should pay the physician in advance (Ketubot 105a). A sectarian once threatened to kick a hunchback and strip him of his hump, to which the hunchback retorted, "If you could do that, you would be called a great physician and command large fees" (Sanhedrin 91a). A similar statement was made by another hunchback in reply to the same threat (Genesis Rabbah 61:7). When the Roman emperor Vespasian had physicians feed Rabbi Tsadok to restore the latter's health, his son said to him, "Father, give the physicians their reward in this world" (Lamentations Rabbah 1:5:31). A physician who heals for nothing is worth nothing (Baba Kamma 85a).

Lord Immanuel Jakobovits points out that the Talmud and the codes of Jewish law legislate at considerable length on legal claims in respect of sickness benefits and medical expenses, including the liability to the payment of doctors' bills [1]. He adds:

> The law determines the husband's responsibility for medical expenses incurred by his wife on account of sickness (Shulchan Aruch, Even Haezer 69:2 and 79:1-3) or injuries (ibid. 83:1), even if she turned insane (ibid. 70:4); the obligation of heirs to defray the cost of medical attendance on the deceased (ibid., Chosen Mishpat 108:1, gloss) and his widow (ibid., Even Haezer 79:2); the division of medical costs among business partners if one of them fell ill (ibid. Chosen Mishpat 177:2-3); and, above all, the compensation due to victims of violence and the basis on which the doctor's and other healing charges are to be assessed (ibid. 420:3-23).

Limitation on Physicians' Fees

The Talmud states that if one takes payment to act as a judge, his judgments are void (Bechorot 29a). The Talmud then offers the reason why it is forbidden to take payment for giving decisions on Jewish law and teaching the Torah:

> Scripture says, Behold, I [God] have taught you (Deuteronomy 4:5); just as I teach gratuitously, so you should teach gratuitously. It has also been taught to the same effect that Scripture says, Even as the lord my God commanded me (ibid.), [intimating], just as I

teach gratuitously, so you should teach gratuitously. And whence do we derive that if he cannot find someone to teach him gratuitously he must pay for learning? The text states, Buy the truth (Proverbs 23:23). And whence do we infer that one should not say "As I learned the Torah by paying, so I shall teach it for payment"? The text states, And sell it not (ibid.).

The codes of Jewish law authored by Jacob ben Asher (1269–1343), known as the *Tur*, and Joseph Karo (1488–1575), known as the *Shulchan Aruch*, rule that a physician is prohibited from accepting compensation for his medical expertise and knowledge, but is allowed to receive payment for his trouble and his loss of time (*Tur,* Yoreh Deah 336; *Shulchan Aruch*, Yoreh Deah 336:2). The limitation on physicians' fees is already found in the thirteenth-century *Sefer Hasidim* (no. 810) by Rabbi Judah the Pious and the fourteenth-century *Kaftor Vaferakh* (chap. 44) by Eshtori Haparhi.

One of the earliest Jewish writers to deal with the issue of physicians' remuneration was Moses Nachmanides (1194–1268), known as Ramban, himself a physician. In his famous work entitled *Torat Ha'dam*, Nachmanides writes as follows:

Concerning physician compensation, it appears to me that he is allowed to accept payment for his loss of time and for his trouble but may not receive payment for teaching [and instructing the patient about the illness], since it is a matter of the loss of the patient's body [i.e., health] concerning which the Torah states, Thou shalt restore it to him (Deuteronomy 22:2). And in regard to the fulfillment of precepts, we apply the principle that "just as I [God] act gratuitously, so you should act gratuitously" (Bechorot 29a). Therefore, it is forbidden to receive payment for one's medical knowledge or instruction [2].

Nachmanides supports his position with a quotation from the Talmud, which states that if someone helps an old man onto a horse, he is entitled to payment "like a workman idle from his particular occupation" (Bechorot 29a–b). Nachmanides also rules that if a person possesses medications or drugs that his sick neighbor requires, he is forbidden to charge more than the standard price. Furthermore, even if they agreed to pay him an excessive price due to the need of the hour because only he possessed the drugs, he is entitled only to the price of their actual value. This ruling was later codified by Karo (Yoreh Deah 336:3). Nachmanides proves his point from the talmudic discussion of a widow who falls to the lot of a levir who is unworthy of her (Yebamot 106a). The sages advised her to promise him a great sum of money in return for performance of the ceremony of *chalitsah*, which would exempt her from marrying the levir. After the ceremony the sages told her that she need not pay the sum that she promised, since she could claim, "I was merely fooling you." This advice by the sages was based on another talmudic passage which discusses the case of an escapee who promises a ferryman a large sum of money to take him across the river (Baba Kamma 116a). The sages ruled that the ferryman was only entitled to the standard fare because the escapee could claim, "I was only fooling you." Similarly, the widow could make the same claim.

Nachmanides also subscribes to the principle that one is not obligated to pay an excessive fee if the promised fee was made under severe pressure or duress. This principle also applies to someone who overcharges a patient for medication. However, Nachmanides qualifies the principle with respect to physicians' fees by stating that if the patient stipulates an excessive sum of money as payment to the physician, he is obligated to give it to the physician, because the latter sold him his expert medical knowledge, which is invaluable. A similar statement was later codified by Karo (Yoreh Deah 336.:3). Thus there is an apparent contradiction in Nachmanides' position. On the one hand, he states that a physician may not accept compensation for his expert medical knowledge. On the other hand, he asserts that this knowledge is invaluable (i.e., priceless), and the patient must pay even an excessive fee. Hayyim David Halevi explains that Nachmanides' intent is to indicate that although it is against the law for a physician to charge an excessive fee, if he nevertheless does so, the patient is obligated to pay the fee [3].

Nachmanides points out that some rabbis disagree with his view and state that a physician is only entitled to payment for lost time and may not collect any more. This contrary opinion, expressed by Yom Tob ben Abraham Al-Ashbili (1270–1344), known as Ritva, in his *Novellae* (Nedarim 38b), takes issue with Nachmanides' principle that one cannot be held to a promise to pay an excessive fee if the promise was made under duress. Ritva opines that the reason the escapee is not obligated to pay the ferryman is not because he can claim "I was merely fooling you," but rather because the ferryman is obligated to take him across the river anyway and can therefore only collect the fare equivalent to his lost time. This obligation, states Ritva, is based on the biblical verse *And thou shalt restore it to him* (Deuteronomy 22:2). The physician is similarly obligated to restore the patient's lost health and is, therefore, only entitled to payment for his lost time. However, concludes Ritva, even if the patient does not pay for the lost time, the physician is nevertheless obligated to treat him and save his life.

Nachmanides rejects Ritva's opinion because the Talmud compares the case of the ferryman to that of the widow. In the latter case, the levir is under no obligation to agree to the ceremony of *chalitsah* because he can marry the widow instead. The ferryman is also not specifically obligated to take the escapee across the river, perhaps because there are other ferrymen available. Similarly, asserts Nachmanides, the physician is not specifically obligated to heal the patient and is perhaps, therefore, entitled to whatever fee is agreed upon. Nachmanides explains that the verse *And thou shalt restore it to him* does not convey a specific obligation on the physician to heal but a commandment to any and every person who is able to help. Nachmanides concludes by saying that if a person only agrees to fulfill a positive precept if he is paid a fee, he does not have to return the fee if it is paid.

In addition to Ritva, Rabbi Judah the Pious in *Sefer Hasidim* (no. 810) and Shlomo Kluger (*Chochmat Shlomoh*, Yoreh Deah 336:3) also disagree with Nachmanides. The former states that a physician should not heal for a fee but may accept payment for his expenses. Kluger cites Meir ben Gedaliah (1558–1616), known as Maharam, who rules that marriage brokers are only entitled to payment for their efforts despite the widespread custom of paying them large fees. Maharam does not suggest that marriage brokers are entitled to large fees "because they sell their expert matchmaking knowledge." This is the rationale behind Nachmanides' allowing a physician to charge a large fee. Maharam thus only allows a physician to collect payment for lost time and effort.

On the other hand, most codifiers of Jewish law agree with Nachmanides and quote him almost verbatim. Karo rules that a physician is forbidden to accept payment for his expert medical knowledge but may receive payment for his trouble and lost time (*Shulchan Aruch*, Yoreh Deah 336:1–2). The *Tur* (Yoreh Deah 336) makes a similar statement, and quotes Nachmanides' principle that if a person only agrees to fulfill a positive precept if he is paid a fee, he does not have to return it if it is paid. In his gloss on Karo's *Shulchan Aruch* (Yoreh Deah 336:2), Isserles (Rema) also notes Nachmanides' principle.

Physicians' Compensation in Modern Times

Some of the talmudic commentaries explain the concept of lost time. Rashi (1040–1105) opines that one examines the type of work a person ordinarily performs and his income and pays him for the lost time required to fulfill the precept (Bechorot 29b, s.v. *kepo'el batal*). For example, if he deals in precious stones and has a very large income, his lost time may be quite expensive. The sages collectively known as Tosafot (twelfth and thirteenth centuries) object to this method of assessing lost time, because one would be paying the person to fulfill a commandment, and this is forbidden (Bechorot 29b, s.v. *kepo'el batal*). Instead, Tosafot suggest, one should estimate how much a person with that trade or profession would be willing to accept to abstain from work altogether, and that is the sum one should pay.

In modern times, however, the concept of lost time needs to be reexamined. Physicians no longer derive their income from other endeavors, as they did in ancient times. Tosafot comment on the judges in Jerusalem who derived their total income from the holy treasury because they did nothing else but serve as judges (Bechorot 29a, s.v. *ma ani bechinam*). Tosafot and Asher ben Yehiel (1250–1327), known as Rosh, point out that the same reasoning applies to teachers who are fully engaged in their occupation and therefore derive their income solely from a salary for their teaching duties (Bechorot 29a).

In talmudic times, physicians, teachers, judges, and rabbis were all categorized together as professionals who should not receive or accept compensation for their professional services (Karo, Yoreh Deah 246:5 and Chosen Mishpat 9:5, Rema's gloss to Yoreh Deah 246:21). At that time they could only receive payment for the interruption or time lost from their ordinary occupations to engage in their communal activities. Nowadays, however, physicians, teachers, judges, and rabbis have no other occupations and are therefore fully occupied with their professions and thus are entitled to receive full compensation for their services. The talmudic commentary of Yom Tob Lippman Heller, known as *Divre Hamudot*, states that the Jewish community is obliged to provide an income for its teachers and judges (Bechorot 29a). The same reasoning can be applied to physicians.

Abraham Steinberg suggests that the basis for the physician's fee nowadays can be derived from the law concerning paid witnesses to a divorce. If their actions or improper signatures result in the invalidation of the bill of divorce, they can be made to pay damages by the courts (Rema's gloss on Even Haezer 130). For that reason they can charge a fee for their services. Similarly, states Steinberg, a physician who undertakes the risk and liability for malpractice suits is entitled to charge a fee for his services [3]. Shaul Yisraeli offers another justification for physicians' compensation [4]. The phrase *Just as I* [God] *teach gratuitously* was only applicable in the days when the Jews were in the desert and all their needs were provided for. Nowadays, however, since everyone must earn a livelihood, the rule does not apply, and physicians are entitled and allowed to be paid for their services.

Other Rabbinic Rulings

Earlier we pointed out that Nachmanides rules that an individual physician is not necessarily obligated to care for a specific patient. Rather, all physicians are obligated to heal the sick. Everyone who can help the patient and restore his lost health, even someone who is not a physician, is obligated to do so. Therefore, an individual physician is allowed to charge a fee. Nowadays, however, since a license is required to practice medicine, it is difficult to say that healing is a commandment which "all can perform." Therefore, why is a physician allowed to charge a fee? Yisraeli suggests that since other physicians are available, the individual physician is not obligated to heal a given patient without receiving payment [4]. However, if he is the only qualified physician available, he is only entitled to charge for his expenses and lost time.

Yehiel Michel Epstein, author of *Aruch Hashulchan*, writes that a physician may charge for writing a prescription but not for giving verbal instructions (*Aruch Hashulchan*, Yoreh Deah 336:3–4). Eliezer Yehuda Waldenberg, however, citing several earlier rabbinic writings, prohibits both (*Responsa Tsits Eliezer* 5:24). Epstein reiterates the rulings of Nachmanides, Tur, and Karo that if the patient agreed in advance to pay a large fee to the physician, he is obligated to pay because he is paying for the physician's expert medical knowledge, which is priceless. Epstein concludes by saying that if the physician has to travel a great distance to the patient, he is entitled to whatever fee is stipulated.

If a physician charges a large fee after he has treated the patient, Joel Sirkes (1561–1640), known as Bah, and Shabtai ben Meir Hakohen (1621–1662), known as Shah, both rule that he can claim the payment in court (Yoreh Deah 336:3). Kluger, however, disagrees, claiming that the courts cannot force the patient to pay after the fact (Yoreh Deah 336:3). Abraham ibn Tova, in his commentary on Simon ben Zemah Duran's *Sefer Hatashbats*, states that there must be clear agreement between the physician and patient before treatment to allow the physician to claim a large fee [6]. Thus, the patient must be made fully aware of the charges before treatment.

David Ibn Zimra, known as Radbaz, reiterates the principle that a physician should only charge an appropriate and not an excessive fee (Responsa Radvaz 3:986). However, if the patient agrees in advance to pay a large fee, it is considered like a gift to the physician.

Waldenberg [6], Halevi (*Novellae Ritva*, Nedarim 38b), Jakobovits [7, p. 224], and others clearly point out that a physician is obligated to treat the poor free of charge. The courts can, if necessary, force a physician to heal an indigent patient gratuitously [8] Jakobovits cites a talmudic passage (Taanit 21b) that commends the ideal of free treatment for the poor. He further quotes several Jewish medical authors, including Asaf Judaeus, Isaac Israeli, Amatus Lusitanus, and Jacob Zahalon, all of whom reiterate the ideal of not taking a fee from the poor.

Other twentieth-century rabbis who discuss the issue of physician fees and compensation include Yitshak Zilberstein [10] Abraham Steinberg [3], and Abraham S. Abraham (*Nishmat Avraham*, Yoreh Deah 336:2–3). One author even writes about fees for a veterinary physician [10].

Conclusion

In Judaism, a physician is given divine license and biblical mandate to heal. The physician is entitled to reasonable fees and compensation for his services. In talmudic times, when physicians, rabbis, teachers, and judges served the community on a part-time basis only and had other occupations and trades, their compensation was limited to lost time and effort. Nowadays, however, when physicians have no other occupation, they can charge for their expert medical knowledge and receive full compensation.

Excessive fees are discouraged but are not prohibited if the patient agrees to the fee in advance. Indigent patients should be treated for reduced or no fees at all. These principles are applicable both to salaried physicians and to physicians in private practice who charge fee-for-service.

8

Medical Confidentiality and Patient Privacy

Confidentiality has its roots in the human practice of sharing and keeping secrets [1]. The responsibilities of health professionals, as articulated in codes of professional ethics, reinforce the value of confidentiality [14]. For example, the Hippocratic oath says, "I will keep to myself that which I may see or hear in the course of treatment." The Principles of Ethics of the American Medical Association instruct physicians to "safeguard patient confidences within the constraints of the law." The American Bar Association, in its handbook *AIDS/HIV and Confidentiality*, Model Policy and Procedures, addresses the value of confidentiality [10]. The American Psychiatric Association has issued detailed guidelines on confidentiality [7]. Confidentiality between physicians and patients is clearly central to the physician-patient relationship; hence confidentiality of patient information must be guaranteed [11]. The National Health Service in Britain is currently debating and will shortly issue rules about what can and cannot be done with a patient's personal data. Major changes in practice throughout the United Kingdom will insure patient privacy and confidentiality [4].

In one of his final acts as president, Bill Clinton unveiled the first federal rules governing medical privacy and patient confidentiality [9]. The new rules set national standards for protecting the privacy and distribution of Americans' personal health records. In addition they established fines and penalties for violating those standards. The Bush administration has also released rules governing federal protection for the medical privacy of patients in the United States [9].

Several key concepts relate to confidentiality [5]. First, the concept of privacy reflects the desire of patients to limit the disclosure of personal information. Second, confidentiality is a condition in which information is shared or released in a controlled manner. Third, security involves measures to protect the integrity, confidentiality, and availability of information. By April 14, 2003, physicians in the United States were required to fully comply with legislation known as the Health Insurance Portability and Accountability Act (HIPAA) privacy rule [8]. The HIPAA privacy rule creates national standards to protect individuals' medical records and other health information. The rule gives patients more control over their health information, sets boundaries on the use and release of health records, and establishes appropriate safeguards that healthcare providers must achieve to protect the privacy of health information. Civil and criminal penalties can be imposed for violation of the rules and standards, although some forms of patient data may be disclosed to protect the public health [8].

Confidentiality for the General Public

For physicians, the Internet is an indispensable tool for continuing medical education, patient care and education, and information exchange with colleagues. For the general and Jewish public, accurate medical information is one of the major concerns relating to the Internet. There are no major ethical difficulties if physicians provide generic medical information on the Internet. However, patients' private medical information transmitted by e-mail from patient to physician, and vice-versa, is accessible to many people with computer expertise, and therefore requires special and careful consideration. Patients must be told that the Internet is not a secure means of communication because Internet messages can potentially be intercepted, viewed, and altered by unauthorized individuals. "Deleted" messages may still be recoverable. Therefore, sensitive information should not be sent over the Internet. Furthermore, the Internet should not be used for urgent or emergency medical conditions. In such cases, direct communication with the physician or ambulance service (#911) should be used.

Other than clerical or administrative communications such as billing, appointments, and insurance matters, all e-mail communications related to patient care should be considered sensitive and confidential. Patients must also consider the security of their own home or office computers in regard to the confidentiality of their medical information, because external sources can access and obtain information. The challenge to preserve confidentiality must be pursued and met by the adoption of technologically secure means of data transmission.

The obligation to maintain confidentiality is one of the cornerstones of medical ethical practice and is clearly stated in the Oath of Hippocrates and many subsequent deontological oaths and declarations. This obligation is based on the general ethical principles of doing well for others (beneficence), not harming others (nonmaleficence), patient autonomy, and the right to privacy. This obligation is also based on the trusting relationship between patient and physicians as shown by not disclosing private and personal information about the patient to others.

Confidentiality from the Jewish Perspective

Maintaining professional confidentiality is a subject which Jewish thought and literature have dealt with extensively over the centuries [6]. In Judaism, the rights of privacy of an individual are balanced against the rights of others and of society as a whole [13]. Jewish law regards as inviolate the privacy of personal information that a person does not wish to disclose to others. Jewish law demands that confidences be respected not only by professionals with whom one has entered into a fiduciary relationship, but also by friends, acquaintances, and even strangers to whom such information has been imparted [3]. The obligation of confidentiality is far broader in Judaism than in any other legal, religious, or moral system, but it "is neither all-encompassing in scope nor, when it does exist, is it absolute in nature" [2].

There is no specific term in Jewish law for professional confidentiality because this topic is subsumed under the general obligation or prohibition against talebearing and evil gossip (Leviticus 19:16, Proverbs 25:9, Psalm 34:14). The prohibition against divulging confidential information is discussed in the Talmud (Yoma 4b), which states that if a man says something to his neighbor, the latter is not allowed to repeat it without the man's specific consent; this conclusion is based on a biblical verse (Leviticus 1:1). Another talmudic discussion of confidentiality (Sanhedrin 31a) states that judges may not reveal confidential discussions that take place behind closed doors. The prohibition against talebearing (Leviticus 19:16, Proverbs 25:9) is in reference to harm. The Talmud indicates that this prohibition has no statute of limitations. In fact, a scholar was rebuked for having revealed a secret after 22 years (Sanhedrin 31a). The biblical prohibitions against talebearing and gossip are codified by Maimonides in his *Mishneh Torah* (Deot 7:2).

According to these laws, a physician may not share privileged information with his colleagues, his family, or anyone else if no benefit to the patient would result thereby. However, if the maintenance of confidence might cause harm to another person, the latter may be informed. If the individual's right to privacy conflicts with the need of society to prevent harm to others, the prohibitions against talebearing and evil gossip are waived and the information must be disclosed to protect other people. The disclosure must be factual, accurate, and not exaggerated.

Specific medical situations where disclosure is required include the possible transmission of illness to another person, the presence of a serious medical condition in a potential spouse, and the reporting of certain infectious diseases to public health authorities. The overriding obligation to protect the lives of others requires that confidential information be disclosed if the withholding of that information might lead to serious harm to someone else. Judaism thus balances the obligation and duty to maintain confidentiality with the obligation and duty to protect others. Lengthy and detailed discussion of this topic is available [3, 12].

The most extensive discussion of confidentiality in Jewish law is that by Avraham Steinberg [12] in his massive and now classic multivolume reference work entitled *Encyclopedia of Jewish Medical Ethics*, where he expounds on general Jewish principles and specific laws relating to medical confidentiality and patient privacy, specific and special medical situations, as well as the general secular ethical views on this subject.

Conclusion

This essay presents the approach of Jewish law to the major issue of medical confidentiality and patient privacy. For an extensive discussion of Jewish medical ethics and an in-depth presentation of the Jewish view of 39 major issues in medical ethics, the reader is referred elsewhere [15]. Briefly, the Jewish view toward medical ethical subjects is predicated on the general principle of the supreme value of human life. In Judaism, all biblical and rabbinic laws except the cardinal three of idolatry, murder, and forbidden sexual relations such as incest are temporarily waived in order to save a human life. Physicians are obligated to heal patients from their illness, to induce remission and cure disease whenever possible. Similarly, patients are obligated to lead healthy lifestyles, to consult physicians when they are sick, and to comply with the physician's therapeutic recommendations. The Jewish view on medical confidentiality and patient privacy as presented in this essay flows from these general principles of Jewish medical ethics.

9

Court-Ordered Medical and Surgical Interventions

Over the past several decades, the medical, nursing, and legal literatures have been replete with articles discussing court-ordered medical interventions, especially cesarean sections to save the baby late in pregnancy, often over the protestations of the mother, who tries to assert her autonomous right of refusal [1–17]. These articles have generated considerable discussion about the ethics of court-ordered medical interventions [1–18]. The present article provides a brief review of the literature on court-ordered cesarean sections, briefly describes other court-ordered medical interventions, such as abortions and fetal surgeries, the separation of Siamese twins with the full advance knowledge that one must die to save the other, and the court-ordered nontreatment of a 56-year-old retarded man with acute myelocytic leukemia although his chances of achieving a complete remission with modern chemotherapy was about 70 percent.

Cesarian Sections and Other Obstetric Interventions

In a very lengthy article on the constitutionality of court-ordered cesarean surgery, Eric Levine [1] examines the numerous precedents of court-ordered cesarean sections, discusses their constitutional implications, and reviews abortion precedents, privacy interests, and due process. He points out that no trade-off is permitted for privacy rights under the Constitution and questions whether the state interest applicable in abortion cases pertains to the cesarean context. Of enormous importance in this age of autonomous decision-making by the patient, the author discusses the constitutional right to refuse treatment and the countervailing state interests in cesarean refusal cases. Also discussed in his paper are the prevention of suicide, the preservation of the ethical integrity of the medical profession, the preservation of life, the protection of third parties, preserving potential life, and the pregnant woman who lacks decision-making capacity and has failed to make her wishes clear. Other constitutional issues described in this review include equal protection as a Fourteenth Amendment safeguard, Fourth Amendment protections, and First Amendment issues.

Levine concludes that fortunately, the cases in which pregnant women refuse to undergo cesarean surgery necessary to preserve fetal health are few and far between. In those rare instances, a physician and the hospital in which the refusal is given can be expected to petition a court to order the cesarean section. Seeking a court order should be second nature given what is at stake: a potential malpractice suit, state licensure board discipline, moral and ethical dilemmas, and, more important, the bodily integrity of a human being, potential life, and in some instances, the woman's life or health. Given these high stakes, a court may be tempted to grant the petition. Undoubtedly, judges often have results in mind when they make decisions, especially those involving life-and-death matters. Judges are human and have moral, ethical, and personal views that may taint their legal analysis and ultimate decision in these cases. The author further concludes that although physicians mean well, they fail to consider the constitutional implications of forcing a woman to undergo major medical treatment against her will. While judges are presumably knowledgeable in constitutional law, he continues, it is quite infrequent that a trial judge is called on to order major surgery against the patient's wishes. Nor are the judges likely to receive an excellent brief on the constitutional issues arising in such cases when counsel is appointed only hours before the scheduled bedside or telephone hearing. Moreover, the author correctly points out, the emergency nature of these cases leaves a judge little time to reflect on the constitutional and other legal issues posed by the compelled cesarean surgery. In his well-documented and well-argued lengthy review of this subject [1], Levine attempts to resolve these complex issues "with the advantage of having had several months of research and reflect on the law relevant to those decisions" [1]. His final conclusions, based on available precedent and constitutional doctrine relevant to the issue, hold that "compelled cesarean surgery is unconstitutional in those cases which involve competent refusal in which the cesarean is indicated merely for fetal health or survival and provides no additional benefit for the woman herself." Levine states that he came to this conclusion only after carefully weighing the state's interests and those of the mother. In doing so he admits that his intention was not to encourage courts to balance these interests on an *ad hoc* basis, because such an approach might lead to unpredictable results and would impose additional obligations on physicians to seek a court order every time a woman refuses a cesarean section against their advice. Rather, he would like the constitutional analysis set forth in his article to determine the outcome in all cesarean refusal cases, but admits that courts are reluctant to adopt *per se* rules, especially when high stakes are involved.

Levine confides to the reader that were he writing on the moral and ethical issues rather than the constitutional issues, he might have concluded otherwise to some extent. He supposes that once a woman chooses to carry a fetus to term, she has a moral duty to act in the best interests of the fetus. However, the discussion in the article is limited to the threshold question of whether a court can, consistent with the dictates of the United States Constitution, require a woman to uphold that supposed moral duty and compel her to undergo a cesarean section, notwithstanding her refusal. As long as the Constitution remains the law of the land, Levine argues, and as long as the Supreme Court does not radically depart from current precedent, compelled cesarean section is unconstitutional when a woman gives her competent refusal or where the cesarean is indicated merely for the fetus. He admits that this conclusion may very occasionally result in undesired injury or death to the fetus; such a rare sacrifice is "vital in preserving the Constitution's high regard for personal autonomy and self determination that society holds so dearly." In an epilogue to his paper, Levine details another case that was decided before the paper went to print, in which the appellate court refused to order a cesarean section against a woman's competent refusal. The court's decision, based on constitutional grounds similar to those he presents in his lengthy analysis of the constitutionality of court-ordered caesarean surgery, seemingly supports his analysis and conclusions.

Michael Flannery [3] takes a totally different approach to this issue of court-ordered prenatal intervention. In his view such intervention is a final means to end the gestational substance abuse by the mother, where applicable. Flannery discusses fetal rights and the legal status of the fetus. He also describes abortion law, the abuse and neglect law, tort law, maternal rights, including the right to privacy, the right to refuse medical treatment, and the right to withhold treatment. Flannery then discusses state interests, drug prohibition, and how to balance the interests of all parties involved. He proposes various standards of care that may determine when to intervene. These include the *Roe v. Wade* standard, the neglected-child standard, the reasonable-mother standard, and the independent strict-liability standard. Next Flannery presents the options for the courts in terms of the type of intervention to be implemented in any given case. These include mandatory toxicological screening, criminalization, and civil commitment. An effective means must be found to protect the fetus. Such means may include medical intervention or surgical intervention, such as cesarean section, sterilization, or fetal surgery. Flannery concludes that courts are beginning to take advantage of the opportunity to become a means of intervention on behalf of the child, recognizing the fact that the state necessarily violates the woman's right to privacy but this intrusion is "legally tolerable." The decisions whether to intervene and what type of intervention is appropriate, he argues, are not solely legal determinates. A series of rare medical, social, financial, and even psychological factors need to be considered. Flannery omits to mention moral, ethical, cultural, and religious considerations which may also play a role in the decision-making process. In balancing maternal and fetal rights, developments in the status of the fetus, and advances in neonatal medicine give added force to the interest of the fetus in a healthy drug-free gestation.

Flannery quotes another source, which states, "To get off drugs, one must be motivated by love or dedication to something greater than personal pleasure or pain." If this statement is true, he concludes, perhaps in the end the only effective means of (drug abuse) prevention is a mother's love for her child [3].

Charity Scott [2] argues against the views of Flannery. She urges physicians and courts to resist the temptation to turn medical recommendations into judicial orders and advocates a reconsideration of court-ordered surgery for pregnant women. In a lengthy discourse, she discusses judicial precedent, reproductive rights and the right to refuse medical treatment, cases authorizing judicial intervention in a woman's pregnancy, and cases not authorizing judicial intervention in a woman's pregnancy. Scott continues with legal considerations, including support protecting the fetus, the abortion law, state tort and criminal law, child-neglect laws and the state's interest in the ethical integrity of the medical profession, maternal rights waiver and autonomy, and pregnancy conclusions in advance medical directives. Scott proceeds with descriptions of the opposition to judicial intervention, the medical profession, maternal rights, including autonomy, pregnancy exclusions in advance medical directives, the state's interest in protecting the fetus, the abortion law, state tort and criminal law, child-neglect laws, and the state's interest in the ethical integrity of the medical profession. She then presents an analysis of all the above by providing the abortion analogy, the child analogy, the technological imperative, the possibility of mistakes, the medicalization of childbirth, and major surgery. The last major section of the discussion, entitled "The Ends Justify the Means," describes the effect of court-ordered pregnancy interventions in other women, the effect on the medical profession, including increased liability by the use of force, and the effect on the legal system, including the poor forum for decision-making and the weak jurisdictional basis for such court-ordered decisions. Scott states in conclusion that her lengthy review article attempts to explore the underlying assumptions and intentions of doctors and judges who seek to compel pregnant women to undergo cesarean surgery. Accepting arguments that their intentions are understandable and motivated out of genuine concern for maternal and fetal health, she states that her article also attempts to explain why acting on these medical and legal intuitions is unwise. The legal intentions, she concludes, find little to support them. The judicial sense that *Roe v. Wade* provides authority for court intervention is misguided. The judicial reliance on child-neglect laws to support intervention reflects a view, in her opinion, that the fetus is tantamount to a child and should be protected as such. This analogy of a fetus to a child is not yet accepted in American law or as public policy. The trend toward judicial intervention could threaten a general deterioration in relations between doctors and patients. Scott admits that there are cases concerning that right of pregnant women to express competent refusal of recommended surgery to deliver the child which have come to opposite conclusions. She points out the American Medical Association and the American College of Obstetrics and Gynecology have adopted policies that oppose seeking court orders to override a pregnant woman's medical decision except in rare and truly exceptional circumstances. She advances a number of policy considerations to support judicial nonintervention in all such cases.

Ouellette [5] is strongly opposed to court-ordered surgical intervention during pregnancy and describes several cases discussed in detail in various law reviews. She strongly advocates a rethinking of court-ordered interventions, and states that the advent of new medical technology, including fetal surgery *in utero*, enables physicians to save formerly doomed fetuses and provide a medical miracle to some pregnant women and their families. Unfortunately, she continues, if courts blindly apply the flawed precedent set in the forced cesarean sections, women will be confined, drugged, anesthetized twice, and twice subjected to major abdominal surgery on behalf of their fetuses, albeit without full constitutional rights. The slippery slope will become the reality, and the women "could logically be forced to become virtual slaves to their fetuses." Courts should not blindly expand the precedent but should rethink the analysis used in those hastily made decisions. Under no circumstances, concludes the author, should women be compelled to undergo surgery on behalf of the fetus. This is particularly clear with fetal surgery, where there is no health benefit to the pregnant woman but substantial risk and violation of her constitutional right to competently refuse. Courts presented with such cases should analyze them without reference to fetal rights and instead focus on maternal rights and informed consent. These are much more established and fundamental concepts than the new and controversial concern for fetal rights. Appellate courts should overturn the forced cesarean cases. Ouellette's strong opposition to court-ordered medical or surgical interventions during gestation is evident throughout her manuscript.

Further opposition to judicial involvement in medical decision-making is provided by Brent T. Stanyer [9]. His opening statement, without documentation, reads: "Recent evidence suggests that physicians are becoming more willing to seek judicial intervention into the treatment of pregnant women and the courts are willing to accommodate these requests." He further states that previous discussions of court-ordered cesareans have focused primarily on the conflict between mother and fetus created by the refusal of treatment by the competent mother expressing her autonomous, constitutionally guaranteed wishes and desires. This conflict raises substantial legal, social, and ethical issues. Stamyer discusses in detail several of the precedent case law cases, including *Jefferson v. Griffen*, *Spalding County Hospital Authority*. and *in re A.C.* (Angela Carder). He then discusses the problem of judicial intervention in the cases of Jesse Mae Jefferson and Angela Carder. He suggests other approaches to court-ordered treatment, including the George Washington University Medical Center's approach and the American Medical Association's approach and offers a critique of these alternative approaches. Stamyer concludes that there are sound procedural reasons why decisions about medical and surgical treatment of pregnant women who refuse treatment should not be made in court. The good of all parties involved in these cases should be to ensure that treatment decisions are made by those with full information on the risks and benefits of treatment, the greatest sensitivity to the interests of the mother and the fetus, responsiveness to the values and preferences of the patient, and the professional standards of the caregivers. Thus, the best plan for making these decisions is in the patient-physician relationship, even though this may result in a few cases where a pregnant patient's decision to refuse treatment results in harm to the fetus [9].

Brenner and Burnet [10] present a case where the courts authorized an obstetric intervention deemed necessary for the well-being of both mother and child. Although the case is one of maternal psychosis, the authors state that there are legal and ethical concerns whenever court-ordered intervention is deemed necessary. Approaches to this difficult maternal decision-making problem in the form of utilitarian "burden versus benefit" ratio analysis or the recognized additional ethical principles beneficence, nonmaleficence, justice, and acting in the patient's best interest are considered. They question the guidelines of the Royal College of Obstetrics and Gynecologists suggesting that it is inappropriate to invoke judicial intervention to overrule an informed and competent woman's refusal of a proposed medical treatment, even though her refusal might place her life and that of the fetus at risk.

Sheila Kitzinger [14] describes a case in the United Kingdom where a judge ruled that a woman can be compelled to have a cesarean section. The cesarean was performed; the patient offered no physical resistance but said she was submitting to surgery against her will. A three-judge panel in this case ruled that both detention of the patient and the cesarean operation were unlawful, even though a high court judge had sanctioned it. The woman had a right to damages against the National Health Service for false imprisonment (hospital detention) and trespass to her person. They also ruled that a declaration made in a court hearing when someone is not represented does not protect doctors and hospitals from being sued for trespass. The three-judge court reaffirmed the right of any competent adult, male or female, to refuse medical or surgical intervention, even if the result is certain death for the individual or for a fetus. Kitzinger points out that British law is unequivocal. Comprehensive surgical or invasive treatment of a male or female patient is illegal. It is as illegal to force a woman to submit to a cesarean section as it would be to force anyone to give bone marrow or a kidney, even to someone who desperately needs a transplant, and even if that person is the donor's own child. The author of the article, Sheila Kitzinger, and a consultant gynecologist both support the legal decision of the three-judge court. The British Medical Association welcomed the ruling. A spokeswoman said, "The fact that a woman has moral obligations to her baby does not mean the health professionals or the courts can compel her to be fulfill them" [19].

Heather Cahill [17] also objects to court-ordered cesarean sections as a violation of women's autonomy. She uses several actual cases as contextual illustrations for the article, which focuses on the complex interplay of process that has brought the medical profession, in her opinion, to a position in which physicians' own self-conviction and determination to do what they believe is best for their patients has resulted in gross denial of woman's autonomy and the use of the law to override pregnant women's refusal of consent. Cahill argues that all professionals in maternity care should be working together toward the goal of healthier mothers and babies, but this cannot be achieved by coercing and deceiving women, overriding their competent refusal to consent. Although fetuses clearly have interests that should be protected, this must not be at the expense of competent women's autonomy and self-determination. To do otherwise is to treat women as less than persons. Not to do so is to create a slippery slope toward further erosion of women's rights, forced compliance with a medically defined "healthy" antenatal lifestyle, and possible incarceration of those who default—"Such an Orwellian scenario can have no place in contemporary healthcare"[17].

Kristina Stern [11] asks whose interests are served by court-ordered cesarean sections. In a specific case, she discusses the following questions: Did the court have jurisdiction to make a declaration? Could the operation be justified solely in the interests of Mrs. S? Could the operation be justified solely in the interests of the unborn child? Was it lawful to carry out the cesarean section after the death of the unborn child? Stern concludes that the implications of the decision may promote a growing acceptance of a broad public interest defense to liability in assault and battery. She further concludes that this would be a welcome development in the law and would require explicit consideration of the demands of public policy in each case. Such a pragmatic approach is a positive development in the law. However, judicial caution is necessary when applying such a battery defense. In each case it is essential, she concludes, to identify which public interest is to be furthered by the intervention and to take into account the implications and ramifications of the decision. Stern finally points out that in the United States, the courts consider the maternal-fetal conflict, and there is a growing acceptance that the public interest of protecting unborn life will override the public interest in protecting patient autonomy only in truly exceptional circumstances (if at all).

Cathy Rowan [12] rediscusses the case cited by Kitzinger described previously. Rowan discusses the role of the midwife and concludes that it is very clear from that British case and others elsewhere in the world that court-ordered cesarean sections are not legally or morally acceptable when a competent woman makes her own autonomous decision to refuse the surgery. In the United States, Rowan points out, court-ordered cesarean sections have been performed since 1973. American obstetricians carried out a cesarean section on a patient suffering from terminal cancer. She had refused consent, so the doctors obtained a court order. Both the mother and the baby died soon after surgery. The parents obtained substantial damages. The court of appeals upheld the woman's right to refuse treatment [12].

Kelly Lindgren [16] points out that advances in prenatal care have related areas of conflict between the pregnant woman and her fetus. Court orders mandating cesarean section deny the pregnant woman the rights accorded to all other competent adults in the United States. The caregiver-patient relationship can be adversarial in such situations. Nurses participating in the decision-making process when judicial involvement is being considered must be informed of the issues. Lindgren emphasizes that court-ordered treatment pits the pregnant woman against caregiver and fetus. Furthermore, court-ordered cesarean section invades a woman's privacy, limits her autonomy, and takes away her rights to informed consent.

Priya S. Morgan-Stern [13] describes a case from the District of Columbia in 1990 where a trial court ordered a cesarean section to be performed. This ruling was vacated by the court of appeals of the District of Columbia. Morgan-Stern also discusses the case of Angela Carder (in re A.C., already mentioned above).

The court-ordered cesarean section was performed and a baby girl was delivered. Tragically, the baby died within a few hours, and the mother died two days later of terminal breast cancer. Morgan-Stern also discusses common law and constitutional principles, describes the opinion of the dissenting judge, and the impact of the decision in the Carder case. She concludes that the issue of fetal rights, especially as the rights are perceived to conflict with maternal rights, is not limited to the practice of medicine. It surfaces in the workplace when employers enact fetal-protection policies, and in the criminal and social services arenas when pregnant women who use drugs or alcohol are "preventively detained" for minor crimes, charged with child abuse, or separated from the newborns because they are "unfit." These are agonizing issues for the legal system and for society in general. In relation to medical treatment, at least, we have a clear and long-standing body of law that establishes the right of competent individuals to make informed treatment decisions, and to refuse to indulge medical treatment for the sake of the mother. *In re A.C.* takes an important step in establishing that these principles hold true for pregnant women as well. This should be our guide, concludes Morgan-Stern [13].

In a lengthy review of court-ordered cesareans in pregnant women, Barbara Leavine [8] summarizes a collected series of cases of court-ordered cesareans and abortion cases and discusses the impact of abortion cases on court-ordered cesareans in some detail. Leavine also discusses the right to refuse medical treatment and the duty of care. She draws numerous conclusions from her lengthy discussion. First, the court *in re A.C.* properly ruled in favor of respecting the right of pregnant women to refuse medical treatment. This case turns back a growing body of precedent that encroaches on the rights of pregnant women by balancing their interests with the state's interests in protecting potential life. The *A.C.* court reasoned that there is little if any room for the interest-balancing test in the case of a pregnant woman refusing medical treatment. Instead the court held that, as in cases involving any other competent adult, the pregnant patient's wishes must be respected. If a pregnant woman is incompetent or does not have decision-making capacity, the court should then apply the substitute-judgment test to determine what her wishes would be were she competent. Leavine further concludes that if other appellate courts persist in following the balancing analysis, greater and more frequent intrusions into women's rights are likely to result. The *Webster* decision, she admits, may justify intrusions based on a state interest in the fetus that is compelling throughout the pregnancy and not just after the stage of viability has been reached. She is concerned that the balancing analysis, which historically subordinated the state's rights to those of women, will become a mere pretense, and that pregnant women will effectively lose their right to refuse treatment. Morgan-Stern also concluded that the medical community will face the consequences, and Leavine describes those consequences. Finally, she concludes that *in re A.C.* "takes a crucial step towards restoring the rights of pregnant women to refuse medical treatment. Its holding should and must be followed." Finally, she expresses the hope that pregnant women will not be subject to intrusions on their privacy and bodily integrity, and that the medical profession and not the courts will play an increasing role in defining the rights of pregnant women [8].

A correspondent who wrote a letter to the prestigious *British Medical Journal* [15] states that "court ordered cesarean sections are discouraging women from seeking obstetric care" [15]. In the prestigious *New England Journal of Medicine*, William J. Curran [6] describes in detail the case of A.C., including the ruling of the court of appeals in the District of Colombia. Curran concludes that the debate over women's rights in pregnancy is far from over. The decision in the matter of A.C, however, provides strong support for the privacy of women's rights when the woman's own welfare is endangered by any procedure designed to safeguard the fetus and its potential for life. In Curran's judgment, "the decision in this case turns the law in the proper direction" [6]. Several correspondents commented on Curran's report [7], and he replied to their comments [7]. Thomas E. Elkins and his colleagues conducted a study of physician concerns in court-ordered cesarean sections [4]. They conclude from their study that most obstetric physicians concur with the 1987 statement of the American College of Obstetricians and Gynecologists that court-ordered intervention should "almost never" be considered. However, the respondents indicated that when faced in clinical settings with rare cases involving grave fetal risks at term, gestation without similar maternal risk, they will often give higher priority to respect for fetal life, medical tradition, and beneficence than to maternal autonomy, bodily integrity, and privacy. The authors state that this approach to decision-making should be strongly criticized but need not be prejudged as unreasonable [4].

Separation of Siamese Twins

Intervention by the courts is not limited to pregnant women. A recent case of Siamese twins, born in Malta and brought to England for the expert and specialized medical assistance not available in their native land, caused a tremendous outcry in the mass media and in the medical literature [20]. The twins' parents, who are Catholic, did not want the twins surgically separated, because one of them would die while the other might live. The twins were attached at the chest but shared a heart that could not be divided to give them each a chance for life. The choice was between two deaths or the killing of one twin in an attempt to let the other live. The case was brought to the High Court, which ruled in favor of the physicians and the hospital, stating that they had an obligation to save the one girl with the certain fair knowledge that the other girl would die as a result of the separation. The parents appealed the decision. All three appeals justices dismissed the appeal and upheld the High Court's order to separate the twins. The surgical separation of Jodie and Mary was accomplished. Jodie survived, while, as expected, Mary quickly died. I have discussed the ethics of this case in detail elsewhere [20], including the Catholic and Jewish views on the subject.

George Annas provides a legal analysis of the court-ordered separation of the Maltese Siamese twins [18]. He criticizes the opinions of all three justices of the British appeals court and their decision, which was contrary to the parents' wishes. Annas concludes that in this case it would have been better had the physicians not sought the court's intervention. It would have been preferable to convince the parents to agree to the separation, since giving Jodie a chance to live at the cost of cutting Mary's life short was the lesser of the two evils. Annas further concludes that the case for separation was not so strong that it required legal authority to take the decision about the medical care of their children away from the parents. I agree.

Nontreatment of a Retarded Man with Acute Myelocytic Leukemia

I now present an example where a court ordered the nontreatment of a patient who had a 70 percent chance of achieving a complete remission from his disease and a 20 percent chance of cure from his disease.

Mr. Caikowicz was a 56-year-old man, retarded since birth, who had lived all his life at the Belchertown Residential Facility for the retarded. At age 56 he developed acute myelocytic leukemia. The case was brought to a Massachusetts court for adjudication. Physicians testified that with modern chemotherapy, the man had a 70 percent chance of achieving complete remission of his disease, and if that occurred, he had a 20 percent chance of being completely cured from that life-threatening illness. The court ruled that since the patient could not give informed consent and would not understand what was happening if he were to develop side-effects from the chemotherapy, he should not be treated at all. The physicians protested but had to comply with the court order and did not treat the patient, who died shortly thereafter of his leukemia. The Massachusetts Medical Society was understandably upset and strongly criticized the court-ordered nontreatment of the patient.

Appropriate Court-Ordered Interventions

A court-ordered medical or surgical intervention is not always subject to criticism. Some court orders may be totally appropriate and reasonable. For example, consider the case of a woman who brings her 4-year-old daughter who is bleeding to death to the emergency room, but clearly refuses blood transfusions to save her daughter's life because that is contrary to her religious beliefs, since Jehovah's witnesses interpret the Bible to prohibit the acceptance of blood or blood products even as a life-saving procedure. In most such cases, the physicians and the hospital will ask a judge or court to order the blood transfusions to be given despite the protestations of the mother because the child, when he or she grows up, may not subscribe to that religion or its tenets in prohibiting blood transfusion. The child can make its own competent autonomous choice when it grows up as to what religious faith it wishes to follow and adhere to. In such cases, judges will always support the physician's petition and grant authorization or order blood transfusions to save the life of a child. Such judicial orders of intervention for children are totally appropriate and are rarely if ever considered a violation of the parental right to decide on behalf of the child.

Another example of appropriate court-ordered intervention is the case of a psychotic patient who, according to the testimony of a psychiatrist, is an imminent danger to himself and possibly others. Physicians will petition the court to involuntarily commit this patient to a psychiatric facility to prevent possible harm to the patient or to others. A court-ordered commitment in such a case is totally appropriate and reasonable, and is not a violation of the patient's constitutional right of refusal or autonomous decision-making which must be followed in order not to invade the patient's privacy and body integrity. The decision is made by the court and implemented for the safety of the patient and of others. The state's interest in protecting the health and welfare of its citizens would then override the patient's refusal.

Other examples of appropriate court-ordered medical or surgical interventions could be cited. Objections only arise if the court order violates the competent patient's constitutional right to privacy and refusal of an invasion of his or her bodily integrity.

Summary and Conclusions

Since the first court-ordered cesarean section in the United States in 1973, many additional cases have been described in the medical, legal, and nursing literatures. The actual number of such cases may be greater than thought, because many cases may go unreported. The trend in recent years is for fewer such court orders to be issued. Some writers consider court-ordered medical or surgical interventions in pregnancy, overriding the mother's competent refusal, to be illegal on the grounds that they violate the constitutional right of a competent woman to refuse an invasion of her privacy and body integrity. Fewer physicians will request such court orders, and fewer will be issued as the illegality thereof is disseminated in the medical and legal literatures.

Court-ordered medical or surgical interventions are not limited to pregnant women, as shown by the example discussed above of a court-ordered surgical separation of Siamese twins. The Massachusetts court's order of nontreatment of a man with acute leukemia is an example of the flip side of our topic.

The advent of medical technology that allows physicians to surgically repair fetal defects *in utero* is another aspect of our topic. The preferable approach to many of these issues is extensive communication between the medical caregivers and their patients, pregnant or not, and negotiations between the parties to attempt to reach agreement on the proper course of action, following the standards of the medical profession to use their talents in the best interests of their patients. A fetus is not legally considered a person but a potential life or person. Hence, the mother's wishes and autonomous constitutionally protected decision-making must be given precedence.

10

Informed Consent

The concept of informed consent is not as recent as most people think. In 1914, Judge Benjamin Cardozo issued a ruling: "Every human being of adult years and sound mind has a right to determine what shall be done with his own body and a surgeon who performs an operation without his patient's consent commits an assault for which he is liable in damages." The clear implication of the judge's ruling is that a person who lays a hand on or does anything to a fellow human being without the latter's consent can be sued for assault and battery, and the latter can collect damages in court.

Consent need not always be expressed by direct words, either spoken or written. Implied consent arises from reasonable inference or from the conduct of the patient. For example, if a patient answers all the physician's questions during a history-taking session, the patient obviously consents to the doctor's taking his medical history. If the patient undresses and allows the physician to examine him and, if necessary, perform a complete physical examination, including pelvic and rectal, the patient is obviously consenting to the performance of the physical examination. If the patient rolls up his sleeve and allows the physician to take a sample of blood from his arm, the patient is obviously consenting to the venipuncture.

The legal doctrine of informed consent and the standards of disclosure in obtaining it changed around 1970. Prior to that time, professional standards were the rule, which means that the physician had to disclose to the patient whatever another reasonable physician would disclose under similar circumstances. Since 1970, patient-oriented standards must be used. This means that a physician must disclose to the patient whatever another reasonable patient would want to know from the physician under similar circumstances.

The elements of disclosure are: the diagnosis and prognosis of the illness; the nature and purpose of the diagnostic procedure or therapeutic intervention the physician is recommending; the probability of success of the procedure or treatment; the nature, magnitude, probability, and imminence of possible risks or side-effects; alternatives or other options; and the prognosis if the patient refuses the diagnostic test or therapeutic intervention.

Exceptions to the legal requirements for obtaining the patient's informed consent include the following. In an emergency life-threatening situation, the physician may act in the patient's best interests and do what is necessary to save the patient's life without first obtaining consent. Another exception occurs if the patient waives the right to be informed and/or to consent. A third exception to the requirements of informed consent is called the therapeutic privilege, whereby disclosure to the patient might cause harm to the patient. In cases of incompetent patients or incapacitated patients, informed consent must be obtained from surrogates, such as close family members or a designated health-care proxy or even a court of law. If all else fails, the physician must act without consent in the best interests of the patient.

The ethical foundations for the concept and doctrine and now legal requirement of informed consent are the maximization of good to the patient (i.e., beneficence), the minimization of harm to the patient (i.e. nonmaleficence), the patient's right to self-determination (i.e., autonomy), and the maximization of good to society (i.e., utilitarianism).

Sometimes fully informed consent is impractical or impossible to obtain. For example, if a physician prescribing an aspirin tablet told his patient that death may occur if the patient is one of the very rare people who may have a fatal anaphylactic or allergic reaction to aspirin, no patient would ever consent to taking the aspirin. Opponents to fully informed consent therefore characterize it as a fairy tale (*University of Pittsburgh Law Review*, 1977), fiction (*Journal of the American Medical Association*, 1976)), myth (ibid., 1966), uneducated (*New England Journal of Medicine*, 1972), bad medicine (*Western Journal of Medicine*, 1977), an illusion (*Emery Law Journal*, 1974), a farce (*Informed Consent*, Oxford University

Press, 1987), hazardous to your health (*Science*, 1979], and unbearable (*Journal of Medical Ethics*, 1979). Yet the law in the United States and in most civilized countries is that informed consent must be obtained from a patient before any procedure or treatment is undertaken, and the law must be obeyed by all medical practitioners.

The incision and drainage of an abscess constitutes an invasion of the integrity of the patient and, when unauthorized, constitutes an act of assault and battery. A patient who voluntarily consults a physician and voluntarily submits to treatment relies entirely on the physician's skill and care, thus giving general consent by implication; the patient may at any time withdraw or limit such consent [1].

Several writers have proposed a new approach to informed consent involving two processes but one goal [2]. They claim that because informed consent and shared decision-making can serve the same purpose of enhancing the patient's control over his or her medical care, it is natural to ask whether they are, or should be, the same process, as some commentators have asserted. Two means, one developed for the most part in ethics (shared decision-making) and the other developed primarily in law (informed consent), would both operate to create the same collaborative environment and serve the same goal [2]. They conclude that this normative account of shared decision-making, informed consent, and simple consent accommodates physicians' values while recognizing the continued central importance of patients' right and responsibility to make their own choices. Informed consent enhances patient control in situations of significant risk, and shared decision-making applies when there are two or more reasonable medical options. We thus modify the current account of informed consent in the following way: consent is always required; informed consent is not.

Although the concept of informed consent has evolved over the past century, as recently as the 1970s most physicians and patients believed that medical decisions should be made by the physician without participation from the patient. Prior to the 1970s, society accepted that physicians not only possessed the technical knowledge required to make the best decisions possible on behalf of the patient, but were also guided by the overriding principle of beneficence. The former made consent by the patient difficult; the latter perhaps made it unnecessary. This approach spared the patient and family from the burdens associated with difficult choices. The paternalism of the approach emphasized beneficence to the exclusion of other important principles, particularly autonomy. This former system of paternalism over autonomy has been criticized in that physicians are not always able to determine what is in their patients' best interests [3], and biases are unavoidable. [4]

By the mid-1980s, the concept of paternalistic beneficence was replaced by an emphasis on patient autonomy and patient decision-making. This was the era of cost containment, where physicians became providers, and patients became clients. In recent years the pendulum has begun to swing back from absolute patient autonomy to a more balanced approach sometimes called enhanced autonomy [5]. These new models recognize that a model based solely on one principle such as autonomy is no better than one based solely on another such as beneficence.

Incompetent or incapacitated patients who are unable to participate in the decision-making process do not lose their autonomy. The medical team and persons who are well acquainted with the patient attempt to reconstruct the patient and incorporate the patient's overall values and beliefs into a substituted judgment and make the decision. In the absence of reliable information about the patient's wishes, the decision is made in the patient's best interests. The renewed emphasis on informed consent may lead to physicians shifting the decision-making process entirely to the patient or the family. This approach is incorrect, because informed consent is a process that requires the involvement and input of both the patient and the healthcare team.

An extensive literature is now discussing whether consent should be necessary for using leftover body material for scientific purposes [6–7] or for research involving the nearly dead and/or training on the newly dead [8–10], or for research such as resuscitation research [11]. This relatively unexplored field in medical ethics is now receiving considerable attention. A related question asks whether informed consent should be required for laboratory testing of drugs or abuse in medical settings [12]. Consent is also an issue in pediatric critical care [13] as well as in research in critically ill adult patients [14–15].

Many years ago I wrote about informed consent as one of the ethical issues in randomized clinical trials [16]. The implications and limitations of the moral justifications for surrogate decision-making in the intensive care unit are discussed by Arnold and Kellum [17]. Roberts concludes that improved understanding of voluntarism will help in our efforts to fulfill autonomy in clinical care and research [18]. Yet some authors question whether or not the concept of informed consent is applicable to clinical research involving critically ill patients [15]. Even in this era of evidence-based medicine, careful consideration must be given regarding patients as both recipients and decision-makers about their own proven and unproven forms of medical care. Informed consent should not be overlooked during this trend toward evidence-based medicine [19], although consent should be patient-centered by tailoring disclosure of information to individual patients' needs and by not neglecting the patient's objectives [20]. How do the rules of confidentiality and consent apply to adolescent substance abusers? [21].

Obtaining informed consent is a particularly difficult problem prior to anesthesia [22]. Since British law rejects the need for specific written consent for anesthesia, a position also adopted in other Western jurisdictions. Some authors propose that the Association of Anesthetists of Great Britain and Ireland should change its guidelines and advise anesthetists to obtain separate, written affirmation from patients that certain risks and consequences of anesthesia have been explained to them [23]. They further suggest that a standardized consent form for anesthesia be developed and may prove invaluable in retrospectively defending a claim of negligence founded around information disclosure by recording exactly the risks and consequences of interventions discussed by the patient and the anesthetist [23].

Lessons about informed consent that the American medical community can learn from Australia is that courts in both England and Australia have begun applying a tougher standard to the information doctors should give their patients: namely, the standard of what a reasonable patient might expect (i.e., the patient standard) rather than of what a reasonable body of doctors might think (i.e., the professional standard). Some writers argue that many doctors have not yet caught up with this change in judges' thinking and are thus laying themselves open to negligence claims [24].

Catholic and Jewish Views

The Catholic view on informed consent is quite similar to that of the secular ethical system as described above [25]. The history of informed consent is detailed by Tom Beauchamp and Ruth Faden [26]. The meaning and elements of informed consent are also described by Beauchamp and Faden [27]. Consent issues in human research are discussed by Robert J. Levine [28]. Clinical aspects of consent and healthcare are written by Robert M. Arnold and

Charles W. Lidz [29]. Legal and ethical issues of consent in health-care are described by Jay Katz [30]. Finally, issues of consent in mental healthcare are discussed by Alan P. Brown and Troyen A. Brennan [31].

The Jewish approach to informed consent is described in great detail by Avraham Steinberg [32]. Steinberg first defines the term, and then writes a historical background of the term in secular and general ethics. He discusses the fundamental basis for the need for informed consent, the terms and conditions of informed consent and their practical application, how much to tell and what to tell the patient, the patient's level of understanding and capacity to participate in the decision-making process, additional issues, and refusal of medical treatment.

Steinberg then presents the halachic (Jewish legal) view on informed consent. This term is not found in halachic literature. The fundamental values upon which the concepts and parameters of informed consent are formulated nowadays are not always conso-nant with Jewish law. The principle of autonomy has only limited validity and application in Jewish law, because Judaism requires the physician to heal but also requires the patient to seek healing. Informed consent is also predicated on the ownership rights over one's body. The principle of full ownership rights over one's body is not consonant with Jewish thinking and literature, wherein God is the owner of all bodies and gives us ours to care for like a bailee entrusted with a valuable object. A variety of recent rabbinic rul-ings and statements by rabbinic decisors are cited by Steinberg. If a specific treatment is indicated and is medically necessary in a Jewish patient, one need not obtain the patient's consent, since the patient is obligated to accept the treatment in order to be healed. However, concludes Steinberg, in medical matters that are not con-trary to Jewish law and where two equally effective options are available, one should the take patient's viewpoint and desires into account. If a patient is comatose or otherwise incapacitated and cannot make decisions for himself, a guardian or relative can par-ticipate with the physician in the decision about treatment.

11

Informing the Patient about a Fatal Disease: From Paternalism to Autonomy

In 1974, I published a paper about informing the patient that he has a fatal disease [1]. I subtitled the paper "To Tell or Not to Tell." That paper could never get published today, because there is now no question about telling the patient. One is legally and morally obligated to tell the patient. The patient has the right to know his diagnosis and prognosis. At the time the paper was written, the concept of paternalism reigned supreme. I remember my training as a hematology fellow in the early 1960s. We told patients very little, especially if it was bad news. For a patient with acute leukemia we would say, "You have too many white blood cells" or "You have abnormal, sick-looking white blood cells." "However, we'll take good care of you." "We'll do some tests, including a bone narrow aspiration, and we will give you treatment to try and rid your body of the abnormal white blood cells." The same inadequate explanation or noninforming of the patient with a solid tumor such as Hodgkin's disease or other cancer was routine practice in those days. After all, the doctrine of paternalism meant that the doctor knew best and the patient was to follow all the doctor's instructions and recommendations concerning diagnostic workup and therapeutic interventions.

Those days are gone forever. We now live in the era of patient autonomy and patient rights. The patient has a right to know what is wrong with him. He has a right to know his diagnosis and his prognosis. The patient has a right to read his chart. The patient has a right to refuse any diagnostic test or therapeutic suggestion. The patient has a right to question everything. The patient has a right to appoint a healthcare proxy to make decisions if and when the patient has no capacity to do so. The patient has a right not to be resuscitated. In the state of Oregon, the patient has a legal right to physician-assisted suicide. These rights are all over and above the patient's constitutional rights of life, liberty, and the pursuit of happiness and the right to privacy and confidentiality, among others. The ethical principle of autonomy means that a patient has the autonomous right to make all healthcare decisions after being truthfully informed about the diagnosis and prognosis, the nature and purpose of the diagnostic test or recommended treatment, the probability of success, the nature, magnitude, and probability of risks and side-effects, other options or alternatives, and the prognosis without the test or treatment. These are the elements of disclosure to a patient when obtaining informed consent for a procedure or treatment.

In addition to all the aforementioned rights, there are additional rights to be considered. Does every person in this country have the right to be treated? By law, the only people who have an absolute right to medical care are prisoners in federal penitentiaries. This essay will not discuss the problem of millions of uninsured or underinsured Americans. Everyone has access to medical care. As a last resort, the municipal hospitals around the country serve as a safety net to ensure that everyone receives proper medical care. With the number of patients' rights entitlements constantly increasing, one may ask a series of questions to clarify the extent of these rights: Does a critically ill patient have the right to costly, uncertain, or experimental treatments opposed by the physicians or family? Does a competent patient have a right to receive palliative care if he has rejected standard potentially curative therapy? Most people would answer yes to such questions. However, the patient's right to know the truth and be fully informed about his illness in order to make autonomous decisions about his healthcare only works one way. If the family asks the medical staff not to disclose any information to the patient about his diagnosis and prognosis, the physicians may not follow that request and must tell the patient everything because he has a right to know. However, if the patient asks his doctor not to disclose the diagnosis and prognosis to the family, the doctor must honor that request as part of the patient's right to privacy and confidentiality—the physician may use his best persuasive powers to convince the patient otherwise, but the patient has the final word.

The art of telling the patient and disclosure of negative information is an art in itself and is associated with a series of practical questions: Who should do the telling? Where should the patient be told? When should the patient be told? What should the patient be told? Not always is the physician the best person to disclose the information to the patient. For a sick child, the parents will probably be the ones to disclose the diagnosis and prognosis, perhaps in the presence of the doctor. For some patients, a clergyman with or without the physician present may be the one to tell the patient, either at the patient or family's request or at the physician's request. In a municipal hospital where third- and fourth-year medical students spend a lot of time with the patient and obtain the patient's trust, a medical student may be the preferred discloser of information. Again, in the municipal hospital situation, it is not appropriate that the information be disclosed on an open ward of patients. Privacy must be assured by pulling the curtains around the bed or moving the patient into a private room or lounge. It is also not advisable to tell such a patient his diagnosis and prognosis and other information at the first patient-doctor encounter. Patients in municipal hospitals have often never seen their doctors before, and it would seem advisable for the house staff or students or even attending physicians to wait until some rapport and trust have developed between the patient and the medical team after several visits to the patient's bedside.

The single most important question remaining is how to disclose the truth to the patient. It must be done with compassion and sensitivity, attempting at all costs to avoid the patient's becoming despondent. Hope must never be abandoned. The doctor must paint the rosiest picture possible under the circumstances of the individual case but without lying to the patient. The glass should be described as half full and not half empty. The doctor must assure the patient that he will be cared for until the very end and that any pain he may suffer will be relieved with potent analgesics if necessary.

The patient's right to know and the patient's right to make autonomous decisions about his medical care, now that we are no longer in the era of paternalism but the era of patient autonomy, can create some absurd situations in medical practice. For example, if a woman's aspirated breast lump turns out to be cancer, the physician must not only disclose the diagnosis, prognosis, and other pertinent information but must offer the patient a menu of therapeutic options from which to choose. The physician may say: Do you want a lumpectomy? Do you want a simple mastectomy? Do you want a radical mastectomy or a modified radical mastectomy? Do you want adjuvant chemotherapy? Do you want preoperative or postoperative radiation therapy? How is the patient to make her decision? She is not a physician, nor a breast surgeon or medical oncologist, nor a radiotherapist. It all seems absurd. But we live in an era of autonomous patient decision-making, so she is entitled to make the decision even without the expertise and/or experience to make the correct decision. Often the problem is solved by the patient following the doctor's recommendations—but not always. The patient may seek additional expert opinions before she decides, and has every right to do so. She may discuss her problem with neighbors and friends, some of whom may have had breast cancer. She may seek out alternative therapists and reject traditional medical care. Such therapies are becoming more and more popular among the general lay public worldwide, with visits to alternative therapists in the United States exceeding those to traditional physicians practicing modern medicine.

The Jewish View

Judaism has serious reservations about disclosing the diagnosis of a terminal or fatal illness because that might lead to serious emotional trauma (*tiruf hadaat*) in which the patient may give up on life and become despondent to the point that his life is shortened by the divulgence of the diagnosis [2]. This reservation is especially cogent when informing patients on their deathbed [3]. The preponderance of rabbinic opinion is heavily weighed in opposition to full truthful disclosure despite biblical commandments to tell the truth and to keep far away from falsehood (Exodus 23:7). This opposition is based on the reasoning that survivability and longevity are dependent upon hope and high morale, which may be undermined, but the knowledge of the full truth of a serious or fatal illness may harm the patient by causing him to die earlier if he becomes emotionally distraught from the information. In Judaism, the duty and obligation to save and preserve life overrides the duty to be truthful. Lying or withholding some of the "bad news" from the patient is thus permissible and even obligatory under such circumstances. The Jewish legal concern about *tiruf hadaat*, or emotional trauma, following the disclosure of bad news has been scientifically confirmed by Wixon, who reported that abrupt disclosure of very bad news can trigger panic or severe depression and can set into motion a psychological response described by Gisela Bok as the "dying response" and may even lead to suicide [5].

Even if disclosure is the chosen option in a given case, it should be done with the utmost care and sensitivity to the mental anguish of the patient. Any poor diagnosis should be couched in the context of optimism. All writers, both secular and religious, emphasize the importance of not depriving the patient of any hope for recovery. The recently published *Encyclopedia of Jewish Medical Ethics* gives a detailed exposition of the Jewish view on the subject of disclosure of illness to the patient, including scientific background, survey studies, and general ethical and legal principles of truth-telling in both secular ethics and Jewish medical ethics [6].

The arguments for full disclosure include a simple denial of the phenomenon of emotional distress as a life-shortening factor. A second argument is that full disclosure is actually beneficial to a terminally ill patient in a variety of ways [2], including the reduction of fear and anxiety, improvement in the patient's cooperation with treatment, pain is better tolerated, and isolation from family and caregivers is relieved [5]. A third argument in favor of full disclosure is that the patient has the right to know the truth, and no one can abrogate that right except the patient himself if he specifically asks not to be told. A fourth reason in favor of full disclosure of the truth is that lying is a sin and absolutely unmoral. The patient's right to know obviously flows from the concept of personal autonomy, which is nearly universally accepted in Western society. In Judaism, the right of full autonomy does not exist because our bodies are given to us by God on loan, and we are commanded to care for them until God decides to take the body and soul back. Jews have no right to intentionally injure themselves or to commit suicide.

Yet there are cogent reasons in Judaism why full disclosure may benefit the patient in spite of the risk of producing mental anguish. The patient may wish to recite his final confession (*Viduy*) before God and repent. He is given the opportunity to set his affairs in order and to make provisions for his family [2].

In all cases, however, the physician must not tell the patient that nothing more can be done for him. The nature and severity of the illness should be spelled out in a manner that is supportive, hopeful, reassuring, and conveys the message that everything that can be done on behalf of the patient, including pain relief and emotional support and other supportive care, will be done [3].

Another writer has summarized the Jewish view on telling terminally ill patients their diagnosis and prognosis as follows: Many people afflicted with terminal illness desire information about the illness and about the nature and purpose of procedures and treatments. These patients benefit from such information, honestly and sensitively presented, in the following ways: amelioration of anxiety and fear, hopefulness for the potential benefits of treatment as described by the physician, better toleration of pain and discomfort, enhanced cooperation in and response to treatment, alleviation of much-feared alienation. All of these benefits make for a psychological climate conducive to a positive will to live [4].

One must always remember, however, that Jewish law is particularly sensitive to the debilitating effects that mental stress may have on an enfeebled or moribund patient. Since Judaism views every moment of life as sacred, care must be taken not to foreshorten life even by a short time. Therefore, it is common practice in Judaism not to disclose the full truth to a terminally ill patient and even to lie if necessary to prevent mental anguish, which may foreshorten the patient's life [7].

Catholic and Secular Views

The revised edition of the fifth volume of Georgetown University's *Encyclopedia of Bioethics* discusses the topic of information disclosure under the following headings: attitudes toward truth-Telling, to tell or not to tell, why tell a lie, the patient's perspective, and HIV/AIDS disclosure [8]. The author concludes that research about attitudes toward information disclosure reveals a diversity of opinion on the subject. Numerous factor enter into considerations of whether and what to tell patients and research subjects about their condition, treatment, or the risks of experimentation. Variations in the cultural expectations of patients and caregiver's influence what information will be told, to whom, and in what manner. Personal and social characteristics of providers and patients, such as age, social class, and orientation to death, also shape the content and process of communication in clinical encounters. The specific clinical, environmental, and economic circumstances of such encounters can further define preferences for what is told and how it is told. Given this contextual complexity, ethical concerns regarding information disclosure are likely to continue to demand sensitivity, thoughtfulness, and skillful communication from clinicians, patients, and ethicists in the future. [8]

Summary and Conclusions

Until the late twentieth century, withholding a fatal diagnosis functioned as a paradigm for sharing other medical information with patients. The obligation of confidentiality was emphasized, and disclosure was ignored. Ethicists perceived the doctor-patient relationship as oriented to therapy, reassurance, and avoiding harm. Physicians were to provide lies and truth instrumentally only insofar as they aided therapy [9]. This was the era of paternalism. Since the 1960s, opinion on the role of disclosure has changed rapidly in the United States, stimulated by the patients'-rights movement and the rise of bioethics. The current climate supports honest and complete disclosure of medical information. In 1972, the board of trustees of the American Hospital Association affirmed a Patient's Bill of Rights, which states that the patient has the right to obtain from the physician complete current information concerning his diagnosis, treatment, and prognosis in terms the patient can be reasonably expected to understand [10]. Bioethicists now favor full disclosure as a means of respecting patient autonomy [11]. The American College of Physicians' ethics manual states that disclosure to patients is a fundamental ethical requirement [12]. The era of patient autonomy ended the traditional pattern of withholding information that was characteristic of the previous era of paternalism.

The Jewish view toward full disclosure of a fatal illness to a patient, and especially a patient who is terminally ill, is in general a negative one because of the fear that the patient may give up hope, suffer severe mental anguish (*tiruf hadaat*), become despondent, and die sooner than otherwise. Shortening a patient's life is strictly forbidden because Judaism espouses the concept that God-given life is sacred, even only a short period thereof. Disclosure should be couched in the context of optimism. The most positive outlook should be imparted to the patient. Disclosure must be imparted with compassion, sensitivity, and hope, thus giving the patient an opportunity to "set his house in order" and recite the confessional penitent prayer known as *Viduy*.

12

Medical Malpractice, Negligence, and Liability in Jewish Law

In the Bible (Exodus 15:26) God clearly states that He is the healer of the sick. Nevertheless, the rabbis in the Talmud (Baba Kamma 85a) interpret another biblical passage (Exodus 21:19) to mean that God grants human physicians a divine license to heal the sick as His agents or messengers. Moses Maimonides considered the healing of the sick to be a positive biblical commandment. He states that the precept of returning a lost object to its rightful owner (Deuteronomy 22:2) includes the healing of the sick (i.e., if a doctor is able to restore a patient's "lost" health, he is obligated to do so). Failure or refusal to heal the sick is a violation of the negative biblical commandment of not "standing idly by the blood of one's fellow human being" (Leviticus 19:16).

Patients have the responsibility and obligation to seek healing when they are sick, based on several biblical commandments (Deuteronomy 4:15 and 22:8). Man does not have full title over his body and life. He must eat and drink and live a healthy lifestyle in order to sustain himself, and must seek healing when ill.

Another cardinal principle in Jewish law is the sanctity and infinite value of human life. In order to save a human life that is in imminent danger, all biblical and rabbinic laws except the cardinal three (idolatry, murder, and forbidden sexual relations, such as incest or adultery) are suspended for the overriding consideration of saving a human life. Since the value of human life is nearly absolute and supreme, even the Sabbath or the Day of Atonement (Yom Kippur) may be desecrated, and all other rules and regulations are waived temporarily in order to save a human life. The Talmud states that he who saves one life is as if he saved a whole world (Sanhedrin 37a).

While much of the secular ethical system is based on rights (e.g., the right to die, the right to refuse therapy, the right to abortion), Judaism is an ethical system based on duties and responsibilities. The late Chief Rabbi of Great Britain, Lord Immanuel Jakobovits, eloquently articulated the Jewish view as follows [1]:

> *Now in Judaism we know of no intrinsic rights. Indeed, there is no word for rights in the very language of the Hebrew Bible and in the classic sources of Jewish Law. In Judaism, we speak of human duties, not human rights, of obligations, not entitlement. The Decalogue is a list of Ten Commandments, not a Bill of Human Rights.*

Statement of the Problem

In Jewish law, in order for a physician to practice medicine, he must be properly trained (i.e., graduate of an approved medical school) with postgraduate training in the area of medicine in which he practices. In addition, a physician must be licensed by the government authorities to practice medicine. For example, in New York, the State Education Department licenses physicians to practice medicine and/or surgery. In Jewish law, a physician is liable if he is obviously negligent by not exerting his full effort or by not consulting with colleagues when appropriate or by practicing medicine outside his area of competence. However, is a Jewish physician responsible for the inadvertent or unintentional death of his patient from surgery or chemotherapy or other potentially lethal therapy if the patient was previously fully informed about the benefits and risks of the procedure? Is a Jewish physician liable for an honest mistake or error in judgment that results in an adverse effect, even including death? Is a Jewish physician liable for a mal-outcome in the patient's therapy even if the physician made no mistake or error in judgment and is well trained and fully licensed and practicing only in his area of specialization?

Another Jewish legal principle holds that one is forewarned that one is strictly liable for all harm caused by his actions (adam muad l'olan). It is not totally clear whether this law is based on a no-fault system where liability attaches for all acts of negligence (peshiyah) or only those committed under circumstances approaching or approximating negligence (ones k'ein aveirah). Jewish law totally exempts a person who causes damage by pure accident (ones gamur) or damage resulting from circumstances approximating an accident (ones k'ein aveidah) [2]. Where does a physician fit into this tort system? Is a physician considered as adam muad l'olan claims, so that he is automatically forewarned and is liable for all acts of medical practice that result in damage or harm to the patient even if the harm was accidental and/or unintentional? Are there exemptions for physicians in Jewish law if they inflict damage or harm to a patient during their usual medical care of the patient?

Classic Jewish Sources

Although the Talmud makes no direct reference to physician negligence or liability, several key quotations are found in the post-talmudic rabbinic writings known as Tosefta (literally: "additional," or outside the Talmud discussions).

The Tosefta (Baba Kamma 6:5–6) reads as follows: "A skilled physician who treated a patient with the permission of the court [i.e., a fully licensed physician] and caused damage in the process is not liable by human law, but his judgment is given to Heaven." The rabbinic commentaries explain that the damage was unintentional. The code of Jewish law authored by Rabbi Joseph Karo rules that if the licensed physician erred and harmed the patient, the physician is exempt from human law but liable by heavenly law. However, if the physician was not licensed, and he erred and harmed the patient, he is liable in a court of law even if he is an expert. [1].

Another passage in the Tosefta (Baba Kamma 9:3) states: "A skilled physician who is fully licensed and harms a patient is not liable; but if he wounded more than necessary [e.g., did more surgery than necessary, or prescribed a higher dose of medication than necessary], the physician is liable."

Yet another Tosefta passage (Gittin 3:13) states as follows: "A skilled physician who is fully licensed and does harm to the patient—if unintentionally, he is not liable, but if he did so intentionally, he is liable in order to preserve the social order (*tikun olam*)." This is also the conclusion of the code of Jewish law [1].

The last relevant statement in the Tosefta (Makkot 2:5–6) is as follows: "A skilled physician who is licensed and treats a patient but the patient died unintentionally, the physician is exiled." In Jewish law, the penalty for unintentional manslaughter is exile to one of the cities of refuge (Numbers 35:9–29). This punishment is meant to effect atonement by the contrition and regret of the perpetrator of the involuntary manslaughter. Does this rule also apply to a physician whose care of the patient resulted in the inadvertent or unintentional death of the patient? If a duly licensed and well-trained physician treats a patient with very potent medications (e.g., chemotherapeutic drugs) in the proper dosages and manner of administration, and without negligence or mal-intent, and the patient dies as a result of well-known and scientifically recognized side-effects, is the physician liable to be exiled in the same way as a person who unintentionally kills someone by accident? How is medical malpractice or medical negligence defined in Jewish law? Does Jewish law adopt a no-fault standard, which legally exempts a physician only in cases involving accidental harm to patients? Or does Jewish law grant legal immunity in all cases of medical harm or mal-outcome, including those due to negligence on the part of the physician (the total-exemption theory) [2]?

Recent Rabbinic Rulings

Rabbi Yaakov Weiner devotes two chapters in his recent book to the medical accountability of physicians and nurses [3]. Weiner cites a variety of classic Jewish sources pertaining to the subject of medical liability and accountability of physicians, including several codes of Jewish law. Weiner also quotes several talmudic and more recent rabbinic writings, including Rabbi Simon ben Zemach Duran, known as Tashbetz (1361–1444), and Rabbi Moshe Schreiber, known as Chatan Sofer (1763–1839). From these sources, Rabbi Weiner deduces the following conclusions:

An expert physician duly licensed to practice medicine who errs in a diagnosis or treatment because of negligence (e.g., if a surgeon's incision is too deep or if he removes more tissue than necessary or prescribes an excessive dose of medications) is liable for any harm or damage he causes to the patient, because these acts are considered assault and battery. If the patient dies as a result, the physician is banished into exile. Also liable for negligence is an internist who makes a faulty diagnosis, and prescribes the wrong medication or dose resulting in harm or damage to the patient because of the physician's insufficient knowledge or failure to consult with wiser colleagues.

However, a Jewish physician who is fully licensed to practice medicine, and is well trained and knowledgeable in his specialty, who inadvertently or unintentionally harms the patient is fully exempt from liability, because no medical negligence was involved, and the physician used his best efforts and judgment to heal the patient.

Rabbi Weiner illustrates several cases of possible nurse medical liability, such as a nurse who administers medication to a patient upon the orders of a physician. Subsequently the patient suffers harm or damage because the physician erred in his prescription. The nurse is obviously not liable or accountable unless she recognized the error and failed to inform the physician or withhold the medication. Another case quoted by Rabbi Weiner is that of a nurse who administers the wrong medication or dosage resulting in harm to the patient. Since nurses are well trained and knowledgeable about their duties and obligations, such an error on the part of the nurse is considered negligence and she is liable for damages. A third case involving a nurse is the case of a hospital's policy to remove respirators from certain terminally ill patients. If the attending physician orders her to do so, is she obligated to refuse and thereby jeopardize her career, or is she obligated to comply? In Jewish ethics and law, the answer is that if complying means to shorten the patient's life (i.e., active euthanasia), she should refuse to comply irrespective of the implications to her career.

Arthur Jay Silverstein, Jewish attorney, has summarized the subject of physician liability in Jewish law [4]. Silverstein discusses the status and role of the physician and medicine, including the obligation of physicians to heal the sick. In a section entitled "Standards of Conduct," Silverstein defines due care, negligence, gross negligence, and battery, death of the patient, and the patient's waiver of liability.

Silverstein concludes that in delineating the liability of the physician, Jewish law seeks to accommodate three conflicting interests—compensating victims for damages, deterring malpractice, and encouraging physicians to practice medicine. Patients recover damages as a matter of law when the physician is guilty of gross negligence. Even in cases of simple negligence, patients are often compensated by physicians seeking acquittal according to the law of Heaven. During the talmudic period, in the case of the patient's death, physicians were in jeopardy of exile to cities of refuge. Physicians in Jewish law must consult with competent colleagues, when appropriate. A physician must also be licensed to practice by the appropriate licensing authority. Silverstein further concludes that Jewish law struck the proper balance between the interests of the patient, the physician, and society at large [4].

Rabbi Joseph S. Ozarowski discussed the issue of malpractice in an article published in 1987 [5]. He begins by describing the Jewish attitude to healing. He then cites numerous rabbinic sources that deal with the topic of medical liability and medical malpractice. He reiterates the requirements that a Jewish physician must be well trained and skilled as well as fully licensed. Ozarowski cites three different approaches to medical malpractice among the early rabbinic decisors (*Rishonim*). He cites the opinion of Rabbi Shabtai ben Meir Hakohen (1621–1662), known as Schach, Rabbi Simon ben Zemach Duran, known as Tashbetz, cited above by Weiner, and Rabbi Nisson Gerondi, (1320–1380), known as Ran. They all reach similar conclusions, as already discussed in this paper. He also raises the question of rabbinic liability and concludes that a rabbi who engages in correct and authentic rabbinic functions, such as teaching and rendering halachic opinions, would be protected and exempt from liability in Jewish law. A rabbi who provides pastoral counseling and care would be subject to the same rules as similar professionals, provided he has proper training and credentials in this specialty.

Rabbis Ilani and Weinberger wrote an article on "Medical Error and Malpractice" [6]. They discuss cases of drug therapy and surgery, death caused by erroneous administration, injection of a poisonous substance, dentist liability, unwarranted surgery or drug therapy, surgical malpractice, the distinction between malpractice in drug therapy and in surgery, malpractice due to lack of basic medical knowledge, mistaken diagnosis, failure to perform an early examination, insufficient probing of the nature of the illness, reasonable error, insufficient examination of the patient, lack of consideration of medical information provided by the patient's family, and an error due to the physician's laziness in examining the patient. Ilani and Weinberger cite specific rabbinic sources, opinions, and rulings to answer each of the above cases.

Rabbi Isaac Yaakov Weiss [7] discusses the case of a physician who erred and gave the patient the wrong medication, as a result of which the patient died. Rabbi Weiss cites numerous rabbinic classic sources as well as recent rulings from contemporary rabbis. He concludes that the physician should have been more careful; his unintentional error is not excusable, and therefore he is liable for negligence and must suffer the consequences of his act.

Rabbi Joseph Mordechei Baumol [8] discusses the topic of a physician who erred and thereby harmed the patient. Rabbi Baumol concludes that a physician who administers a medication or performs surgery on a patient with a mal-outcome is not liable unless he was negligent in not having sufficient knowledge or skill or was not careful enough in the administration of the therapy, in which case he is liable for malpractice by negligence and is not exonerated for the mal-outcome.

Rabbi C.D. Halevy [9] discusses the case of a dentist whose drill slipped and damaged another tooth in the patient's mouth. If his hand slipped purely by accident (ones gamur), he is not liable for the damage. If the dentist was drilling more than necessary on the diseased tooth, and his hand slipped and the drill injured a neighboring tooth, he is liable for damages because the unnecessary extra drilling on the first tooth is considered negligence and the dentist is liable to pay for the damage he inflicted.

Rabbi Yitzchok Zilberstein [10] discusses several cases of possible medical malpractice with physician and/or dentist liability to pay for damages. He describes cosmetic surgery as an unnecessary procedure in general and prohibits it. He also requires a physician to consult with expert colleagues if there is any doubt about the therapy he plans to administer. Otherwise, the physician is considered negligent and liable for damages if a mal-outcome results from the treatment. Rabbi Zilberstein also cites other cases and precedents in recent rabbinic rulings on the subject.

Rabbi David Lau [11] discusses in detail the liability of a physician for damages if he injures or harms his patient. He reiterates the special status of a physician in Jewish law if he is well trained and licensed, and practices within the scope of his knowledge and skills. He also repeats that a physician is liable for negligence and defines several types of negligence.

Rabbi Zalman Nehemiah Goldberg [12] reviews in detail the topic of physician negligence and cites many classic Jewish sources to support his conclusions. He also states that, although in certain circumstances the skilled and licensed physician who causes harm to a patient inadvertently or accidentally is exempt from payment for damages, he may still be liable to a heavenly court and may wish to atone for the mal-outcome to the patient by paying damages voluntarily.

Rabbi Eliezer Yehudah Waldenberg [13) deals with this subject in at least one volume of his multivolume published responsa.

The most detailed discussion in English of the subject of medical malpractice in Jewish law is the lengthy article by Joshua Fruchter [2]. He compares and contrasts Jewish and American medical malpractice law and examines both the contemporary and ancient sources of the law. Fruchter surveys American and Jewish legal tort principles. He discusses medical malpractice litigation and the American approach to medical malpractice. He reviews the patient-physician relationship, physician's duties and responsibilities, mal-outcome, and errors of judgment. He details American no-fault liability legislation and the Jewish legal approach to medical malpractice. He cites the cardinal principles of the supreme value of human life and the physician's obligation to heal and to save lives. He also discusses the physician's exemption from liability and the various rabbinic opinions on the interpretation of the exemption and its limits. The various exemption theories of Nachmanides, Rabbi Nissin Gerondi, Rabbi Zemach ben Duran (Tashbetz), and Rabbi Eliezer Waldenberg are discussed at length.

Fruchter concludes that the Jewish legal approach to medical malpractice is to protect physicians from undeserved liability by providing explicit exemptions shielding physicians from liability for pure mal-outcome without any negligence. In theory, American law also exempts physicians in cases of mal-outcome or an error in judgment. In practice, however, things are quite different. Fruchter also reiterates the fact that Jewish law stresses that every physician must recognize the limits of his ability and must consult with more experienced physicians in case of doubt. Physicians must approach the treatment of patients with caution and seriousness commensurate with the gravity of their task.

Rabbi Waldenberg, already cited above, in another responsum [14] concludes that if a licensed, well-trained Jewish physician makes an error in judgment, he is exempt from liability. However, if the physician switched medications accidentally or operated on the wrong foot, all rabbinic opinions rule that he is liable for negligence because he was not careful enough. A reasonable mistake or misdiagnosis is a situation where rabbinic opinions may differ. A physician who practices without a license is certainly guilty of malpractice and liable for damages. Physicians in Judaism are totally exempt from mal-outcome but not for malpractice or negligence as defined in Jewish law.

Julius Preuss [15] points out that Jewish law does not recognize double punishment for the same offense. For example, legal punishment (e.g., lashes or exile) and financial compensation for damages cannot both be imposed. One penalty excludes the other. Preuss then summarizes the rules regarding liability of a physician. If he intentionally injures a patient, he is obviously liable. On the other hand, if the injury results from an error on the part of the physician, he is held blameless "because of the public good." If the physician were held liable for every unintentional or accident error, no one would become a doctor. The physician thus is granted an exceptional position. This exemption, however, is limited to a well-trained, fully licensed physician who is not negligent. If a physician injures a patient more than is necessary, negligence has been established and the physician is liable.

Rabbi Immanuel Jakobovits, whose pioneering work [16] gave birth to the field of study known as Jewish medical ethics, points out that Jewish law seeks to steer a middle course between complete exoneration of the physician, leading to recklessness, and subjection of the physician to such rigorous penal sanctions as would make students decide against medical careers and physicians avoid enterprising methods of treatment. The original source for the Jewish regulations and laws of medical malpractice and liability is the Tosefta (see above), which explains that the concession to, or exemption of physicians from pure mal-outcome is "for the sake of the social order." Ordinarily, a human being is always liable to pay full indemnity even for damage done unwittingly and unintentionally. However, a physician is exempt because he has the biblical obligation to heal the sick. The physician, however, may still be held to account before the heavenly tribunal. However, if the physician deliberately causes an injury or is unlicensed, he can be sued for damages. A physician is obviously liable if he was negligent as defined above.

13

Problem Doctors: Is There a Solution?

Problem physicians are those who are substance abusers or whose performance or standard of care is below acceptable levels. It is difficult to measure the quality of physician performance, but systems are being developed to deal with this problem [1]. This essay deals with the problem doctor and what can or should be done.

Discussion

Physician-performance problems are often evident long before a physician enters practice [2]. One explanation of poor performance is that physicians are inundated with paperwork from medical school and residency applications, certification and recertification, continuing medical education, hospital staff appointments, academic medical school appointments, patients' medical records, insurance forms, and much more. Most of this paperwork is considered to be an intrusion on the doctor's time [3].

The hospital credentialing process is one mechanism to address problem physicians [4]. Particularly susceptible to substance abuse are surgeons, anesthesiologists, and emergency medicine specialists because of their easy access to a variety of drugs [5]. Program directors and department heads are often loath to discipline even the most incompetent resident or attending physician [6]. Few hospitals respond adequately to physician-performance failure. Leape and Fronison call on the Federation of State Medical Boards, the American Board of Medical Specialties, and the Joint Commission on the Accreditation of Healthcare Organizations to collaborate on developing better methods for measuring physician performance and to expand programs for helping practitioners who are deficient [1].

A physician who makes an honest error in judgment should not be held liable for any mal-outcome.

However, if the physician is negligent in not consulting with colleagues when appropriate or is inadequately trained in a specific procedure and an untoward outcome results, the physician should be held fully responsible and dealt with accordingly [7]. Physicians generally, but not always, have ethical and moral obligations to disclose their errors to the patient [7]. In addition to honest disclosure and perhaps an apology, under certain circumstances, financial compensation is appropriate [7].

Because of the reimbursement system for physicians' services in the United States, the temptation to be unethical is great, and the slippery slope is becoming smoother [8]. Thompson points out that concern about unethical physicians is nothing new. Fee splitting, legal drug dealers bribing doctors to prescribe their products, and sweetheart deals between doctors and hospitals are as old as the hills [9]. Hr also points out that the American College of Surgeons specifically prohibits the practice of division of fees under any guise whatever.

Medicine is not only an art and a science but includes physician behavior, honesty, and integrity. Most physicians are fully aware of these facts and practice medicine according to the highest professional standards. An occasional exception is a problem doctor, who must be dealt with appropriately. Some doctors are criticized for having a poor bedside manner. Should that be considered a problem that requires disciplinary intervention? Counseling of such a physician would seem to be a more appropriate course of action.

Summary and Conclusions

Most physicians practice medicine according to the highest professional standards, are well trained and experienced, and practice with integrity. The occasional problem physician is usually a substance abuser, or practices unethically by accepting division of fees and bribes from drug companies or by being rude to patients and colleagues or by committing avoidable errors or other unprofessional conduct. These physicians must be appropriately dealt with by the methods already available, such as the credentialing process, or methods yet to be developed. In the meantime, most physicians and patients recognize that medicine is as much an art as a science.

14

Patients' Rights and Caregivers' Rights (Physicians and Nurses)

The United States Constitution bestows the inalienable rights of life, liberty, and the pursuit of happiness upon its citizens. Healthcare is not mentioned at all. In fact, by law, the only individuals in this country who have an absolute right to medical care are prisoners in federal penitentiaries. The average law-abiding citizen has no such right because the legislation was specific in guaranteeing medical care to prisoners in federal penitentiaries. A prisoner who asks to see a doctor or nurse must be so provided. If a federal prisoner has diabetes or other illness, he is guaranteed medical care. In fact, recently a prisoner in a federal penitentiary with chronic renal failure, who was being dialyzed to sustain his life, received a human kidney in a much-publicized transplantation procedure. The ethics or morality of these facts are not the subject of this essay but require dialogue and discussion. The law says that federal prisoners are legally entitled to healthcare, apparently up to and including organ transplantation.

Patients' Rights

On admission to a hospital, a patient receives a package of material usually containing a brochure describing the hospital and its many and varied services, including specialized diagnostic and therapeutic services. The folder also includes a booklet describing the patient's rights, including the Patient's Bill of Rights. Several

105

years ago, there were ten rights, colloquially called the Ten Commandments. These rights have progressively increased, so that they now number twenty, including the most recent right to pain management and pain relief.

In 1991, Congress passed and the president signed the Patient Self-Determination Act, which requires hospitals and private doctors' offices to provide information and forms for the patient to designate a healthcare proxy or surrogate to make medical decisions on behalf of the patient if the latter is incapacitated and cannot make his/her own decisions. Subsequent legislation, including the 1993 Health Security Act, evolved into a patients' charter or Patient's Bill of Rights as the ethical standard of care shifted from paternalism to autonomy and patient self-determination, accompanied by the emergence of managed-care plans and companies, which state that fairness and proportionality must be balanced against patient autonomy and self-determination [1].

The Patient's Bill of Rights is posted in prominent locations in hospitals throughout the United States, usually in English and Spanish. These rights include the right to receive treatment without discrimination as to race, color, religion, sex, national origin, disability, sexual orientation, or source of payment. Patients also have the right to receive considerate and respectful care in a clean and safe environment free of unnecessary restraints. Patients have the right to receive emergency care of it is needed. They have the right to know the name of the physician in charge of their care and the names, positions, and functions of other hospital staff involved in their care. Patients have a right to a no-smoking room unless the hospital is a smoke-free hospital. Patients are entitled to receive complete information about their diagnosis, prognosis, and treatments and all information necessary to give informed consent for any proposed procedure or treatment. This information shall include possible risks and benefits of the procedure or treatment.

New York State's Do Not Resuscitate Law gives patients the right to give informed consent for an order not to resuscitate. Patients also have the right to refuse treatment or test procedure and to be told what effects this may have on their health. They have the right to participate in research or to refuse such participation after being fully informed about the research. In the United States, the protection of the rights of human subjects in research and experimentation has evolved at three levels: professional, public, and private. At the professional level, codes, guidelines and the Patient's Bill of Rights address the issues of protecting the dignity, privacy, and autonomy of individuals who serve as research subjects [2]. The Patient's Bill of Rights also guarantees patient privacy in the hospital and confidentiality of all information and records of the patient's care. The patient has the right to participate in all treatment decisions, including discharge from the hospital. Patients have the right to review their medical records without charge and to receive a copy thereof, for which the hospital may charge a reasonable fee. They have the right to complain about care and services without fear of reprisals. They have the right to make known their wishes regarding organ donation and may document such wishes on a donor card or on the healthcare-proxy form. Finally, patients have the right to receive pain management and palliative care where and when appropriate. Nowhere on the Patient's Bill of Rights is there mention of any patient duties and responsibilities.

United Health Care, a managed-care company headquartered in Atlanta, Georgia, has issued a list of "Customer Rights and Responsibilities." The rights closely follow the Patient's Bill of Rights. Among the patient's responsibilities are the need to keep appointments, to provide information as requested by the physician or other caregivers, follow instructions and guidelines of the physicians and other healthcare professionals, and participate in understanding one's own health problems and the diagnostic and therapeutic approaches suggested by the healthcare givers. These are some of the patient's duties and obligations.

Nurse's Bill of Rights

The American Nurses Association, headquartered in Washington, D.C., has developed a Bill of Rights for Registered Nurses. Seven rights are listed to protect the dignity and autonomy of nurses in the workplace.

1. Nurses have the right to practice in a manner that fulfills their obligations to society and to those who receive nursing care.
2. Nurses have the right to practice in environments that allow them to act in accordance with professional standards and legally authorized scopes of practice.
3. Nurses have the right to work in an environment that supports and facilitates ethical practice in accordance with the code for nurses and its interpretive statements.
4. Nurses have the right to freely and openly advocate for themselves and their patients, without fear of retribution.

5. Nurses have the right to fair compensation for their work, consistent with their knowledge, experience, and professional responsibilities.
6. Nurses have the right to a work in an environment that is safe for themselves and their patients.
7. Nurses have the right to negotiate the conditions of their employment, either as individuals or collectively, in all practice settings.

Physicians' Bill of Rights

The state of California recently passed a Health Care Provider's Act primarily to protect physicians from unscrupulous managed-care companies that unilaterally change manuals, policies, or procedures without the provider's agreement. These practices are prohibited under the California statute. The statute also gives the provider the right to terminate the contract if the parties cannot come to an agreement. Providers also have the right to refuse to accept additional patients, either beyond the contracted number or the reasonable professional judgment of the provider. This provision of the statute is to prevent patient overload, indicating that the Health Care Providers' Bill of Rights also advances a quality-of-care concern. The original bill was amended several times in order to gain support from opposing constituents, including the managed-care companies and healthcare providers, mainly physicians. The primary sponsor of the Bill was the California Medical Association, which expressed general satisfaction with the end result.

To my knowledge, there does not exist a Physician's Bill of Rights similar to the Nurse's Bill of Rights. Shouldn't physicians have the right to expect full cooperation from their patients in terms of providing complete and accurate medical histories and allowing complete physical examinations? Shouldn't physicians have the right to expect that their patients will be compliant with the recommendations and treatment prescribed by the physician? Shouldn't physicians have the right to be appropriately compensated for their services? Shouldn't physicians have the right to expect their patients to change their lifestyle if it is for the purpose of improving or maintaining their health? For example, the physician should have the right to expect the patient, after full discussion and agreement, to lose weight, exercise regularly, stop smoking, and similar beneficial health practices. Perhaps the American Medical Association might undertake to prepare a Physician's Bill of Rights, modeled after the Patient's Bill of Rights and the Nurse's Bill of Rights.

Discussion

The doctor-patient relationship is the cornerstone of medical ethics. Other important principles are patient autonomy and self-determination, benevolence, nonmalificence, and justice. Managed care and managed competition challenge physicians' roles as trust-worthy patient advocates [1]. Fortifying the doctor-patient relationships in managed care would be prudent and has so been legislated in California, as described above. Both doctor and patients want to have strong, personal, values-oriented, trusting relationships.

The Patient's Bill of Rights includes the rights to designate a healthcare proxy and to issue advance directives. The goal of the advanced directive is to realize basic values of human dignity, respect for self-determination, and human life, all of which are perfectly compatible with Catholic moral principles [3].

The right to emergency care is discussed in detail by Robert Baker [4]. He points out that as early as 1886 a proposal was put forth to "draw up . . . a Bill of Rights which shall secure patients from any injustice from the vagaries of science." Nearly a century later, in 1973, the American Hospital Association published a Patient's Bill of Rights. President Clinton's Advisory Commission on Consumer Protection and Quality in the Health Care Industry completed the Patient's Bill of Rights in a 64- page report [5]. The bill also contained a section on patients' responsibilities.

Important considerations of the Patient's Bill of Rights are discussed by Donnell D. Etzwiler [6]. Wendy K. Mariner states that the patients' rights legislation introduced in 1998 is a step in the right direction [7]. However, it fails to include all the rights of patients. This consumer bill of rights, she says, may give people the false impression that their rights as patients are protected when they are not. In a legal review of informed consent, Cheryl K. Smith reminds the reader that in early 1973, the American Hospital Association issued a Patient's Bill of Rights [8]. She adds that this Patient's Bill of Rights has been recognized by courts and incorporated into many state statutes. Both the risks and benefits of medical treatments, she continues, have increased with the forward march of technology. She concludes that patients have the right to choose to participate with the physicians in their own healthcare decision-making, and that the trend toward the reasonable patient standard in informed consent in medical malpractice suits that relied on negligent failure to obtain informed consent reflects a recognition of that right.

Michael Cheng-Tel Tao and Tsung-Po Tsai remind us that one of the rights in the Patient's Bill of Rights is the right to refuse treatment to the extent permitted by law [9]. The situation could be complicated when cultural elements are added to the consideration of who makes the final decision. These authors performed a survey in 2002 in Taiwan, which showed that in a Confucian society, "the family element often determines the course of decision and the patient's autonomy is overlooked." The head of the family, the authors conclude, usually makes the decision, especially when the medical decision has something to do with a life-or-death situation.

Melanie H. Wilson Silver compares patients' rights in England and the United States to the Patients' Charter and the New Jersey Patient Bill of Rights [10].

In England, the government in 1991 introduced a document entitled the Patients' Charter, which mentions a limited number of patients' rights, but unlike its American counterpart, says Silver, it is "neither enforced by statute, externally regulated nor as yet, monitored in an official way." In the United States, federal legislation in the area of patient rights, continues Silver, is concerned with matters of confidentiality, self-determination, and discrimination. In New Jersey, since the early 1970s, many hospitals voluntarily adopted as policy, various versions of the Patient's Bill of Rights [10]. However, it was not until 1989 that laws were enacted by the New Jersey legislature declaring that as a matter of public policy, acute-care hospital patients had certain specific rights. The law also provided for a mechanism to enforce those rights. This law came to be known as the New Jersey Patient Bill of Rights. The author argues that for any Patients Bill of Rights to succeed, it must have a mechanism to ensure enforcement and a system to monitor compliance.

Janice Snider discusses the question of whether a Patient's Bill of Rights should include the right to sue an HMO or other insurance company [11]. She cites a survey of readers in which 84 percent said a Patient's Bill of Rights should include the right to sue.

George Annas reviews the historical development of patients' rights in the 1970s through 1998 [12]. He concludes that a national bill of patients' right must cover all Americans. On the other hand, Annas posits, "health plans must be held accountable for providing the healthcare to their members that they hold themselves out as being able to provide" [12]. He further concludes that Congress should also pass legislation that permits members to sue their health plans directly for harm caused by wrongful acts on the part of the plans. Annas also discusses access to adequate healthcare as a primary goal. His final conclusion is that rights in healthcare are critical, "since without them, citizens may wind up with access to a system that is indifferent to both their suffering and their rights" [12].

Summary and Conclusions

Prior to the 1970s, when the ethical standard of medical practice was paternalism, patients had very few if any rights. In 1973, the American Hospital Association developed and published a Patient's Bill of Rights which has since been widely accepted and adopted and is displayed prominently in most hospitals in the United States. The Patient's Bill of Rights was also recommended to President Clinton in 1998 by a Special Commission he established. Many states have enacted this Patient's Bill of Rights into law. The Bill of Rights is incomplete, however, as it does not include the right of patients to sue their managed-care or other insurance company. Also, there are neither enforcement nor monitoring mechanisms in place. The American Nurses Association has promulgated a bill of rights for registered nurses. There does not exist a physician's bill of rights although California enacted a statute giving physicians certain rights, such as refusing to accept an excessive number of patients to care for if the physician is employed by an HMO, because of patient overload and patient safety. The evolving field of patients' and caregivers' rights is associated with the current era of autonomy and patient self-determination.

PART III
The End of Life

15

The Terri Schiavo Case in Jewish Law

It is axiomatic in Judaism that human life is of supreme value. In order to save a human life, all biblical and rabbinic rules and regulations are temporarily waived. "He who saves one human life," says the Talmud, "is as if he saved a whole world." Euthanasia in any form is condemned as an act of murder; shortening a person's life by even a moment is tantamount to murder. The removal of Terri Schiavo's feeding tube was wrong in that it would inevitably shorten her life and thus constitutes an act of murder. Every human being is entitled to be fed and hydrated until the very end. Thus, the feeding tube should have been reinserted. She was fully alive by classic medical criteria: she was breathing on her own and her heart was beating, even though much of her brain was destroyed.

Autopsy is ordinarily forbidden in Jewish law, based on the biblical prohibitions relating to desecrating the dead, deriving benefit from the dead, and delaying burial of the dead. Furthermore, cremation, which Michael Schiavo had planned for his wife's remains, is the ultimate desecration of a human body created in the image of God and is strictly forbidden in Jewish law. In rare instances, autopsy is not only allowed but mandated in Jewish law. Such a case would be if the results of the autopsy were to be immediately used to save the life of another patient dying of the same illness as the deceased. This was not the case with Terri Schiavo, since she died of starvation and dehydration. An autopsy performed on her would likely not have provided information to immediately save the lives of other vegetative-state patients and would therefore be disallowed in Jewish law. Florida law, however, required an autopsy.

Another principle in Jewish law is that "the law of the land is the law." Thus, we cannot object to the Florida law which allowed the court to accept Michael Schiavo's statement that his wife told him she would not wish to be kept alive by a feeding tube as "clear and convincing evidence" of her wishes. Hence the court ordered the removal of the feeding tube. Although the Florida law is not in accord with Jewish law, we have to accept it as "the law of the land." We and others, however, can and should make strong efforts to have the Florida law changed so that courts in Florida would be empowered to change guardianship from husband to parents and/or siblings in similar future cases, especially when the husband has a fiancée with whom he sired two children during an adulterous relationship. Also tragic in this case is the deep but justified animosity felt by Terri Schiavo's family members toward her infidel husband. May the Lord comfort them in their time of sorrow and bereavement grief.

16

Death by Withdrawal of Nutrition and Hydration: Mercy or Murder?

On October 15, 2003, in Pinnelas Park, Florida, the feeding tube of Terri Schiavo, a 33-year-old severely brain-damaged woman was removed by court order after a ten-year legal battle between her husband and her parents [2]. The expectation was that she would die in a week or ten days. The parents of the patient wanted to care for their daughter and keep her alive in the hospice where she had lived for several years. Her husband said she would rather die. The patient's sister, Suzanne, called the feeding tube removal "judicial homicide." It is not clear whether the patient had written a living will expressing her wish not to live in a chronic vegetative state or had so stated orally to her husband Michael, who claimed that he was carrying out his wife's wishes that she not be kept alive artificially. This seemed to represent clear and convincing evidence of Mrs. Schiavo's wishes, thus allowing the court to order the removal of the feeding tube. Complicating the case was a conflict of interest or bias on the part of the husband because he was engaged to another woman and they had a child together. The family also alleges that the husband, Michael, abused his wife, accusations which have not been substantiated. Michael Schiavo also refused to divorce his wife, fearing that her parents would ignore her wish to die if they became her guardians.

The legislature in the state of Florida quickly passed a law granting the governor the power to override the court, which ordered the removal of the feeding tube. Governor Jeb Bush signed the legislation and promptly overruled the court and ordered the feeding tube to be reinserted. At the time of my writing this essay, the denouement or outcome of this case had not yet occurred. It was expected to go through several appeals before a final determination was made in the unusual right-to-die case of Terri Schiavo.

Many similar right-to-die cases have been discussed and debated over the past three decades, one of the most famous being the case of Nancy Cruzan in Missouri. This unfortunate young woman was in a persistent vegetative state for many years in an institution in Missouri, kept alive with a feeding tube. Her parents petitioned the Supreme Court of Missouri to allow removal of the feeding tube. The case eventually was heard by the U.S. Supreme Court, which sent it back to the Missouri Supreme Court. After many years of Nancy being in a permanent coma, some of her friends came forward and testified that she had told them she would not wish to live like that, hooked up to tubes. On the basis of this "clear and convincing evidence," the Missouri court allowed the removal of the feeding tube. Thirteen days later, Nancy Cruzan died of starvation and dehydration. Many people argued that the withdrawal of the tube was a merciful act, which allowed the patient to die in peace and dignity. Others argued that the removal of the tube represented active euthanasia, which has not yet been universally sanctioned.

Active euthanasia is legally permissible in Holland under certain circumstances. However, opponents of the law point out that some physicians are euthanizing patients without their consent because of "poor quality of life," such as severely handicapped newborns. This was not the original intention of the Dutch legislation legalizing euthanasia. In the United States referenda in several states proposing legalization of euthanasia have been defeated. Only in Oregon is physician-assisted suicide legal, but not active euthanasia. The main reason for patients requesting physician-assisted suicide is not pain and suffering but the desire to be in control of their own destiny.

In the Nancy Cruzan Case, not everybody defended the withdrawal of her feeding tube as a merciful act. A vocal minority considered the withdrawal of the feeding tube an act of murder or active euthanasia, since it was the direct and proximate cause of her death 13 days later. This opposing minority equates the removal of Nancy Cruzan's feeding tube with shooting her in the head. The headshot would kill her instantaneously, and the feeding tube removal resulted in her death two weeks later. Both acts, however, were the direct and proximate cause of her death and should be considered legal murder without justification. Neither act is merciful, but directly causing the death of a person is legal murder. In fact, some years ago in California, two physicians were indicted for murder for withdrawing the feeding tube of a similar terminally ill, noncurable patient. The charges were dismissed and the physicians were exonerated.

One can thus argue both ways. The removal of a feeding tube from a persistent vegetative state patient in persistent coma and from a terminal patient with Alzheimer's disease who cannot bring up secretions and suffers from repeated episodes of pneumonia can both be considered merciful acts in ending the suffering of the patient. But was Nancy Cruzan really suffering? Did she have any physical pain? Was she sentient at all to feel mental pain? No one knows. Certainly her parents, relatives, and friends were suffering, watching her in this condition. The doctors, nurses, and other caregivers may have suffered emotionally in caring for this poor unfortunate patient. The state of Missouri was suffering, because it cost the state $22,000 per year to keep Nancy Cruzan in a nursing home. But was Nancy herself suffering? Did she ever clearly enunciate her autonomous decision not to be kept alive if she were ever in a condition such as a permanent coma? No one knows. Some ethicists and theologians, therefore, argue persuasively that the death of Nancy Cruzan was an act of moral or even legal murder, or legal active euthanasia. It is not ethically or religiously allowed to purchase the relief of the suffering of other people at the cost of taking the life of the patient.

Perhaps the first case involving the removal or withdrawal of life-support medical therapy was the New Jersey case of Karen Ann Quinlan, another unfortunate young woman in a persistent vegetative state. The parents of the patient petitioned the courts in New Jersey to remove the respirator from their daughter so that she could die in peace and dignity. They convinced the New Jersey Supreme Court to allow the removal of the respirator, based on the supposition that would have been the patient's wish. In 1976, the respirator was removed in this landmark case. Surprisingly, the patient continued to breathe on her own without the respirator but remained in her vegetative state of persistent coma. When Mr. Quinlan, the patient's father, was asked at that time "How about removing her feeding tube?" his answer was: "Oh no, that is her life." He obviously felt that it was morally wrong to end her life by withdrawing nutrition and hydration. Every human being is entitled to food and water, no matter how close to death they are. Yet Mr. Quinlan in 1976 would have condoned his daughter's death by the removal of the respirator, a seemingly paradoxical choice.

In 1976 society was not yet ready to take the leap from removing a respirator to withholding or withdrawing nutrition and hydration. Since then, many famous cases have occurred. In Florida, the Court of Appeals ruled that the feeding tube of Helen Corbett could be removed because the right to refuse treatment is protected by both the state and the federal constitution. In California, Elizabeth Bouvia, who was alert and competent, won the right to reject feeding by nasogastric tube. In Massachusetts, Paul Brophy died after his feeding tube was stopped by court order. In New Jersey, the Supreme Court, exactly ten years after the Quinlan case, allowed the removal of a feeding tube from Claire Conroy, determining that such a device should be viewed in the same as other medical and nursing treatments. The same court ordered a nursing home to participate against its will in the removal of the feeding tube of Nancy Cellen Jobes. In New York, an appellate court, in the case of *Delio v. Westchester County Medical Center,* decided that the withdrawal or withholding of nutrition and hydration by artificial means (i.e., feeding tube or intravenously) should be evaluated in the same manner as any other medical procedure, including the use of a respirator or other form of life-support equipment. The court also concluded that where there is clear and convincing evidence that a patient is in a persistent vegetative state but not necessarily terminally ill, and the patient has expressed prior wishes to die with dignity and not be sustained by artificial means, these wishes must be given full consideration. Many other similar court cases have come to similar conclusions.

Thus, an extensive medical literature has emerged in the past two decades supporting the notion that feeding tubes and intravenous lines constitute medical therapy and, when not indicated in a given patient, may be withheld or withdrawn. Prior to that time, the perception of society as well as of the medical profession was that nutrition and hydration by any route or portal of entry are not medical treatments but supportive care no different than skin care, grooming, and bowel and bladder care. Feeding tubes and intravenous lines were considered simple conduits for food and water for patients unable to eat or drink on their own. Food and fluids are universal needs, whereas specific medical or surgical interventions are not. Mr. Quinlan made a sharp distinction between the provision of nutrition and the removal of the respirator from his daughter in

1976, when he responded to the question about removing her feeding tube with the phrase "Oh no, that is her nourishment."

In a landmark statement in March 1986, the American Medical Association's Council on Ethical and Judicial affairs announced that in certain limited circumstances, life-prolonging medical treatment, including "medication and artificially or technologically applied respiration, nutrition or hydration," may be stopped or withheld. There is today nearly universal support in the medical, legal, ethical, and lay professions for this AMA position.

A small minority at the AMA objected, saying, "This is a grievous error because death by starvation, dehydration, volume depletion, or a combination of these is not death from the underlying disease processes and could be considered euthanasia." Others in the minority argued that this development bears the seeds of a great potential abuse, since pulling the tube or pulling the plug is the equivalent of euthanasia, which is illegal in the United States.

I interpret these differences of opinion as hinging on whether feeding tubes and hydration are medical treatments, and thus, when appropriate, may be ethically and legally withheld or withdrawn, or whether, alternatively, feeding tubes and hydration are part-and-parcel of supportive care, such as turning the patient, singing, reading, talking, or just listening to the patient who is dying—general supportive measures that should not be abandoned if doing so would hasten the patient's death.

In the Judaic-Christian system of ethics and values, human life is considered to be of infinite and inestimable value. Therefore, one could argue philosophically that every moment of a person's life is also of supreme value. Furthermore, a person's life and body are not his own property to do with as he wishes. The proprietor of all life, including human life, is none other than God Himself.

My colleague, friend, mentor, and consultant, Rabbi J. David Bleich, visiting professor of law at Yeshiva University's Cardozo Law School, told me that one's personal privilege and responsibility with regard to the human body and human life are similar to the privilege and responsibility of a bailee with regard to a bailment with which he has been entrusted. It is the duty of a bailee who has accepted an object of value for safekeeping to safeguard the bailment and return it to its rightful owner upon demand. Man is but a steward over his human body and is charged with its preservation. He must abide by the limitations placed upon his rights of use and enjoyment [1].

Life with suffering is regarded, in many cases, as preferable to termination of life and with it elimination of suffering. Life accompanied by pain may be preferable to death. It may serve as atonement for the dying person. It may serve to stimulate feelings of compassion and altruism among the family members and caregivers, and recognition of their own mortality. These feelings may facilitate their own fulfillment of the divine plan of creation.

Even when the life of a person on his deathbed seems to be devoid of benefit, meaning, or purpose, the patient retains unique human value by virtue of the role he plays in providing an opportunity for love and compassion. Human life represents a purpose in and of itself; sheer human existence is endowed with moral value.

Many people may disagree with Rabbi Bleich's view, which is based on theological ethics and teachings that may at times appear to be rigorous and have not won acceptance in a secular society. Nevertheless, concludes Rabbi Bleich, an understanding and appreciation of these traditions may result in the tempering of some of the rather extreme views about end-of-life issues, such as active euthanasia and physician-assisted suicide, currently in vogue. If some doubt is engendered in the minds of physicians and other caregivers tending to the needs of the terminally ill, they may take to heart the fact that if they are to err, better to err on the side of life.

My own view is that even if the courts and secular ethicists sanction the withholding or withdrawal of fluids and nutrition from the terminally ill and from chronic vegetative state patients, what is legal and socially acceptable is not always moral and merciful. The patient's or family's right to starve or dehydrate the patient to death does not mean that starvation and/or dehydration are right. The medical literature is divided about whether death by starvation and/or dehydration is more painful and induces more suffering than death with full nutrition and hydration. Finally, legal permissibility by court order to induce death by removing or withholding food and hydration is not necessarily synonymous with moral license to do so.

In October 2003, Wesley J. Smith wrote an article entitled "No Mercy in Florida" about the case of Terri Schiavo and what it portends [3]. He categorically states that the case illustrates how utterly vulnerable people with profound cognitive disabilities have become in this country. Not only are many routinely dehydrated to death, both the conscious and the unconscious, but often the people making the decisions to stop food and water, like Michael

Schiavo in this case, have glaring conflicts of interest. No one would argue that, under the current universally accepted patient-autonomy principle, if Terri Schiavo had orally or in writing previously expressed her wish to have nutrition and hydration withheld or withdrawn if she was ever in a persistent vegetative state or permanent coma, her wishes would be honored without debate.

Wesley Smith [3] quotes the most recent issue of the prestigious medical journal *Critical Care Medicine*. The authors of an article in that journal [4], Robert D. Troug and Walter M. Robinson from Harvard Medical School, urge the adoption of an even more radical policy. They propose the discarding of the "dead donor rule," which requires that vital organ donors be dead before their organs can be procured for transplantation. Troug and Robinson propose that "individuals who desire to donate their organs and who are either neurologically devastated or imminently dying should be allowed to donate their organs without first being declared dead." Such patients may still be considered alive if one refuses to accept brain death as a valid definition of death.

Smith asserts that doctors should only be permitted to procure organs from donors who have been declared dead in the traditional manner, meaning that their hearts have ceased beating without hope of restarting. He then briefly discusses the issue of futile therapy and makes the condemning accusation that "many practitioners of bioethics, medicine and law no longer believe that people like Terri Schiavo are fully human." I strongly disagree with this unsubstantiated statement, which I believe goes too far. Smith concludes his essay by asserting "A nation is judged by the way it heals its most vulnerable citizens." Therefore, there is a lot riding on the Schiavo case.

17

Hospice Care for the Terminally Ill: Help or Hindrance?

A few years ago, a feature article entitled "The Living Will: Help or Hindrance" in the *Archives of Internal Medicine* described in detail the advantages and disadvantages and pitfalls of a living will as written in those days. In 1992, the federal law called the Patient's Self-Determination Act authorized patients to appoint a healthcare proxy to make medical decisions for them if they do not have the capacity to make such decisions for themselves. Physicians and hospitals are obligated to inform their patients of their right to appoint a healthcare-proxy decision maker and must provide patients with the appropriate forms to make their wishes known.

Hospice care for the terminally ill can take place in a hospital setting, a special hospice unit, or even in the patient's home environment. Hospice care ideally provides terminally ill, incurable, nontreatable patients with the best psychosocial, emotional, and spiritual care during their last few hours, days, or weeks of life. One essential component of such care is relief of physical pain and mental suffering. The science of pharmacological and occasional surgical pain relief has reached a level of sophistication such that healthcare givers are cognizant of the fact that pain in terminally ill dying patients can be very severe and even excruciating and requires potent agents, including narcotics or combination of drugs (so-called cocktails) which may need to be administered by continuous infusion. No dying patient should suffer physical pain without potent analgesic intervention.

Most hospices have rules and regulations whereby the patient must have an expected life expectancy of six months or less to be eligible for admission. Most hospices provide only comfort care, and many do not administer antibiotics or blood transfusions.

One of the most sensitive and controversial issues is the provision or withholding of fluids and nutrition. The medical literature is divided as to whether terminal hydration and nutrition make the patient more uncomfortable or not. Different studies have found different results, so the controversy is not yet resolved.

If the patient requests that fluids and nutrition be withheld, one should listen to the patient, providing he/she is making an autonomous informed consent. However, hospices whose routine policy is to withhold fluids and nutrition can be criticized due to the fact that every human being, even near the end of life, is entitled to receive the minimal supportive care of life-sustaining fluids and nutrition. Withholding such fluids and nutrition will probably hasten death, which may be an objectionable action to those who believe that only God gives and takes life, and that patients and/or caregivers have no right to interfere with the divine plan or will. On the other hand, dying patients wracked in pain and suffering should have the right to plead with God to put an end to their suffering.

Does this right extend as far as physician-assisted dying or physician-assisted suicide? Many would argue both ways, with cogent reasons to answer yes to this question. Others would argue just as cogently that no patient has the right to terminate his life prematurely, since man was created in the image of God and is instructed to care for his body and soul until God takes it back. A person must eat and drink to be healthy in order to serve God and mankind and must seek healing from a physician when ill. Intentionally shortening one's life or hastening one's death is objectionable in many religious and philosophical systems.

On October 15, 2001, at the Royal Society of Medicine's Conference on Ethical Dilemmas at the Beginning and End of Life, I made a motion which prompted considerable discussion. For the sake of argument and to initiate the discussion, I titled my motion "That life must be prolonged by all possible medical and technological means."

I argued that this motion was based on the premise that human life is of infinite and inestimable value. Therefore, every moment of human life is also of infinite value. Furthermore, a person's life and body are not his own property to do with as he wishes. The proprietor of all life, including human life, is none other than God Himself.

One's personal privilege and responsibility with regard to the human body and human life are similar to the privilege and responsibility of a bailee with regard to a bailment with which he has been entrusted. It is the duty of a bailee who has accepted an object of value for safekeeping to safeguard the bailment and return it to its rightful owner upon demand. Man is but a steward over his human body and is charged with its preservation. He must abide by the limitations placed upon his rights of use and enjoyment.

Life with suffering is regarded, in many cases, as preferable to termination of life and with it elimination of suffering. Life accompanied by pain may be preferable to death. It may serve as atonement for the dying person. It may serve to stimulate feelings of compassion and altruism among the family members and caregivers, and recognition of their own mortality. These feelings may facilitate their own fulfillment of the divine plan of creation.

Even when the life of a person on his deathbed seems to be devoid of benefit, meaning, or purpose, the patient retains unique human value by virtue of the role he plays in providing an opportunity for love and compassion. Human life represents a purpose in and of itself; sheer human existence is endowed with moral value.

The alleviation of physical and/or mental pain may require aggressive pain-relief treatment. Palliation of pain and suffering whenever possible is mandatory. When the dual goals of avoidance of pain and preservation of life come into conflict, one should recognize the paramount value and sanctity of life and, accordingly, assign priority to the preservation of life. Human life is not a good to be preserved as a condition of other values but an absolute, basic, and precious good in its own stead. The obligation to preserve life is commensurately all-encompassing.

Man's interest in his body and his life are subservient to the interest of his Creator. When ill, a human being is obliged to seek a cure in order to sustain life. Never is man called upon to determine whether or not life is worth living—this is a question over which God is the sole arbiter. An individual close to death or suffering from an incurable terminal illness may not have the capacity to serve God in the active sense. Nevertheless, his very existence constitutes an act of divine service.

There is also a long judicial history of the government's compelling interest in the preservation of the life of each and every one of its citizens. The legal term "compelling state interest" is equivalent to the theological term "sanctity of life." The preservation of human life is a moral value that takes precedence over virtually all other values.

In the context of the suffering associated with a debilitating terminal illness, the patient, even while discharging his obligations as a bailee, is fully entitled to beseech God to terminate those responsibilities. The patient may pray to God to reclaim His bailment, that is, the life entrusted to man. While dutifully taking his prescribed medication, the patient may pray that the medication not prolong his life. The ultimate decision, however, is God's, and God's alone.

In discharging his responsibility with regard to prolongation of life, the physician must make use of all possible medical and technological resources available. However, the physician is not obligated to employ procedures that are themselves hazardous in nature and may foreshorten the life of the patient. Nor is either the physician or the patient obligated to employ experimental therapies.

Theological ethics and teachings may at times appear to be rigorous and fail to win acceptance in a secular society. Nevertheless, an understanding and appreciation of these traditions may result in the tempering of some of the rather extreme views about end-of-life issues, such as active euthanasia and physician-assisted suicide, currently in vogue. If some doubt is engendered in the minds of physicians and other caregivers tending to the needs of the terminally ill, they may take to heart the words of Judge Skelly Wright, that if they are to err, better to err on the side of life.

18

Futile Care for the Terminally Ill: It May Be Legal, But Is It Ethical or Morally Justifiable?

Medical futility is a very difficult if not impossible term to define precisely. It all resides in the eye of the beholder. If a patient with terminal, incurable nonreversible Alzheimer's disease is close to the end, the physicians and other caregivers may feel it is futile to hydrate or nourish the patient and may recommend withholding or withdrawing the feeding tube and IV hydration. The medical literature has conflicting reports about whether starvation and/or dehydration makes a terminally ill dying patient more comfortable or less comfortable. If such a patient suffers a cardiopulmonary arrest, the physicians and other medical staff will probably feel that it is futile or fruitless to attempt cardiopulmonary resuscitation measures, because they would serve no useful purpose. On the other hand, the family may feel that such attempts are worthwhile and not fruitless. If blood circulation and respiration, albeit with mechanical assistance, can be reestablished even for a few minutes or more, the patient's next of kin may feel that to be a worthwhile result. They can spend a little more time with their loved one before the final, irreversible terminal event occurs.

There may also be disagreements among the medical staff and the family of a patient about whether or not certain "standard" medical interventions are futile in this particular patient. If a terminally ill Alzheimer's patient develops pneumonia, is it appropriate to treat it with antibiotics, or is such therapy futile and without merit and should be withheld so that nature can take its course? If such a patient develops a hemorrhage, should transfusion therapy be given, or is that futile, since it serves no useful purpose and will not change the fatal outcome?

The family may argue that antibiotics and/or transfusion therapy should be given to treat these intercurrent happenings as if they are not related to the underlying disease. Even some medical staff may agree with this viewpoint. However, suppose the Alzheimer's patient now suffers from repeated respiratory infections, cannot bring up secretions, and is very uncomfortable and short of breath and dyspneic. Is it now time to withhold antibiotics, since this episode of pneumonia is not an independent occurrence but part-and-parcel of the terminal phase of the patient's disease and life?

Many medical staff and even ethicists would argue that antibiotics at this late stage of the disease are not indicated and in fact are futile and fruitless, because they will serve no useful purpose. Yet the family may insist that everything be done, including the administration of antibiotics, respiratory support if necessary, and certainly hydration and nutrition which every human being is entitled to until the very end, since life is precious and every moment of life is precious.

It is obvious that all comfort measures must be given to every terminally ill patient who is suffering from physical pain, or mental or spiritual pain. The science of pain management (physical and mental) is now a well-understand science and is mostly practiced appropriately, depending on the situation. A patient with terminal cancer in severe physical pain may need much more than a four-hourly dose of narcotic analgesic. The patient may need a continuous infusion of a cocktail of several drugs. Ideally, the patient should control the flow of the infusion and self-regulate the pain-relief medication. Studies have shown that patients who control their own pain-medication administration utilize less total narcotics than do patients who have to request pain relief as needed.

Certain situations are such that cardiopulmonary resuscitation measures are not futile and should be attempted with great vigor. For example, if a near-drowning victim is extracted from a lake and is hypothermic with no pulse or spontaneous respiration and even has a flat encephalogram showing all the usual signs and symptoms of death, every attempt at cardiopulmonary resuscitation should be made, because many such patients can be revived and may live normally for many years, often with no or very minimal neurologic sequelae. So too if a person is struck by lightning and has all the appearances of being dead (no pulse, no spontaneous breathing or movement, coma, flat EEG, absent calorics, etc.), every attempt at cardiopulmonary resuscitation should be made, because there is a reasonable chance that they may be successful and return the patient to sentient life.

Other situations are clearly futile, and CPR attempts are inappropriate, ineffective, fruitless, and without useful purpose. For example, a young woman dying of widespread metastases from breast or ovarian cancer should be categorized as "Do Not Resuscitate" (DNR). Most often the physicians have already spoken to the patient and explained to her the futility of CPR, even including possible adverse effects from the CPR (e.g., fractured ribs). If the patient or family refuses to sign a DNR order, two physicians can document in the chart why CPR would be futile and therefore not attempted. If the patient and/or family insist that if CPR can even only temporarily reestablish cardiopulmonary function, it is not futile but worthwhile, because every moment of life is worthwhile, even when very close to death, the medical staff should and will honor the request not to attempt CPR.

Many end-of-life decisions involve the issue of quality of life. If a person is in a persistent vegetative state or permanent coma with no hope of waking up from that coma, the family, as in the Nancy Cruzan case in Missouri, may argue that the quality of life of the patient is very poor. Not only does the family sign a DNR order, but it may also request that no heroic or extraordinary measures be applied to artificially prolong the patient's life. The family may argue that antibiotics for infections or transfusion for hemorrhage should not be given because they are futile and would not change the outcome of the persistent vegetative state. In the case of Nancy Cruzan, the parents successfully petitioned the Supreme Court of Missouri to allow the removal of the patient's feeding tube in order to let her die in dignity. Two weeks later, Nancy Cruzan was dead. Legal and ethical scholars applauded the court's decision. Lone dissenters argued that removing the feeding tube was an act of murder or manslaughter, because that was the direct and proximate cause of her death.

When it comes to quality-of-life decisions, I believe that only the patient can decide what quality of life is acceptable and tolerable, not the family or other surrogate, including the medical staff, unless it is clearly in the patient's interest to act or not act in a certain way. If there is clear and convincing evidence of what the patient's wishes are, either by an earlier oral or written declaration or a living will, then the patient's wishes should certainly be followed.

The issues of medical futility and the implementation of CPR or DNR are complicated topics and must be evaluated and adjudicated on an individual basis, depending on the specific circumstances of each case. No two cases are identical, and it is therefore difficult to develop broad guidelines for a decision about death and dying and medical futility. Each case must be individualized, and all the medical and surrounding circumstances taken into account. The patient's wishes should always be honored and followed, unless there are cogent and compelling reasons to do otherwise. Pain and suffering must be relieved to the very end. This includes both physical pain and mental suffering. The clergy and social work services are underutilized helpful resources in most settings where a patient is dying. The same applies to family and friends comforting the dying in any possible manner. Doing so is an absolute obligation upon every human being on behalf of another dying human being, since we were all created in the image of God. Whether terminal hydration and nutrition are part of that obligation is a matter of dispute among legal, medical, and spiritual experts and the lay public, where opinions are divided.

19

Human Research in Critically Ill Patients in an ICU or Emergency Room Setting

Human research and clinical trials and the ethics of human experimentation have changed dramatically since the immoral experiments of the Nazi doctors in World War II, especially the notorious and barbaric hypothermia experiments in which innocent Jews, gypsies, and others were cast into ice vats to study the method and rapidity of death as the victims became hypothermic and died a gruesome and tortured death. These unethical studies were performed by the Germans to learn how to save German pilots who were shot down in the frigid North Sea. The postwar Nuremberg trials were followed by the Nuremberg Code in 1946 and numerous other codes and declarations on the ethical conduct of human research. These include the Helsinki Declaration of 1964, the National Research Act of 1974, the Belmont Report of 1979, and many others [1].

The present essay is concerned with resuscitation research and research in critically ill patients, mostly in an ICU or emergency room setting. In resuscitation research, there is an inevitable trade-off between minimizing patient risk to that which is inherent in research regarding therapies for life-threatening conditions and still doing research that ultimately benefits all subsequent victims of the variety of emergency studied [1]. Federal regulation of clinical resuscitation research and the ongoing issues in implementation are detailed by Bircher in his paper on the subject [1].

Research in critically ill patients has the potential to violate the subjects' rights because often they are unable to give informed consent [2]. There is a problem of surrogate consent for research in critically ill patients [2]. Nevertheless, investigators have the option and responsibility to create solutions that can foster the implementation of research in the critically ill patient while maintaining the patient's rights and welfare [2].

Some transitional obstacles to research in critical care units are discussed by Morgenweck [3]. He concludes that permitting innovation is necessary for the advancement of medicine, but innovations must be monitored. Williams and Haywood describe the ethical challenges for clinician-investigators in critical care research on patients with advance directives or do-not-resuscitate status [4]. They postulate that critical care research involving patients with advance directives or do-not-resuscitate status is not only possible, it is desirable. Doing so is just, respects patient autonomy, and results in study populations that better reflect the clinical populations in all respects which should enhance the validity of the research. Clinical investigators must be vigilant and mindful of the conflicts of interest present in their dual role. A patient's decision to participate in research on the critically ill does not relieve the clinician-investigators of the obligation to serve the human research subject's interests, even when doing so involves limiting or withdrawing the patient from the research protocol.

Some authors question whether the concept of informed consent is applicable to clinical research involving critically ill patients [5]. Others are concerned about enrolling the uninsured in clinical trials [6]. These authors make recommendations for how investigators can both protect the uninsured research participants and provide the uninsured with fair access to research in their recruitment and enrollment strategies. They conclude that investigators should not only seek to enroll and recruit all research subjects, including the uninsured, in as fair a way as possible, but that investigators and their institutions should take responsibility for their role in defining what research pursuits and scientific advances are medically and socially valuable.

Kahn and Mastroianni propose that we can and should improve on the ethics of clinical research [7]. They highlight three related and recurring issues in the ethics of clinical research: the quality of informed consent, the (mis) perceptions of research subjects, and the importance of the subjects' overarching trust in researchers, institutions, and the research process [7].

Recent Developments

The World Medical Association has promulgated a fifth revision of the Declaration of Helsinki which strives to strike a balance between ensuring high ethical standards and retaining sufficient sensitivity to local circumstances, especially in developing-world research, to avoid thwarting research with bureaucracy [8]. Tollman asserts that fair partnerships support clinical research [8]. Bastion discusses the gains and losses for the rights of consumer and research participants [8]. Doll concludes that research will be impeded [8]. Hirsch and Guess conclude that some clauses in the revised Declaration of Helsinki will hinder the development of new drugs and vaccines [8].

To impose the protection of human participants in research, the federal government has mandated education and training in bioethics and issues relevant to human research. Rosenbaum states that little is known about whether these efforts actually improve the protection of human subjects [9]. He reviews the history of ethics education in research leading up to the 2000 federal mandate. He then explores ethics education and its evaluation in the biological sciences and medicine, and describes the previous successes and failures of these efforts. He concludes that by having a clear understanding of the specific objectives, strengths, and limitations of an educational intervention, educators can design programs that may have an increased likelihood of improving the protection of human research participants.

It is not uncommon that conflicts of interest arise in human subjects. This fact is detailed by Groegh and Barnes, who assert that the integrity of our research relies on the development of a transparent system to identify, minimize, and manage conflict without stifling the scientific curiosity of investigators, and on allowing investigators the personal and financial rewards associated with their work. They state that federal regulations identify rudimentary conflicts of interest on the part of individual investigators, but the regulations have many gaps. The current debate on the subject of conflict of interest in medical research has broadened our understanding of these conflicts and, rightfully, has identified institutional conflicts as a concern. Standards on how to identify, manage, and eradicate conflicts are rapidly evolving with increased governmental oversight and stricter standards likely.

Another subject of dispute is whether consent should be needed for using leftover body material for scientific purposes [11]. Roberts offers and illustrates a framework for voluntarism in clinical and research consent decisions [12], focusing on four domains of potential influence: (1) developmental factors, (2) illness-related considerations, (3) psychological issues and cultural and religions values, and (4) external features and pressures. He concludes that improved understanding of voluntarism will help in our efforts to fulfill the principle of respect for persons in clinical care and research [12].

Finally, since strict codes and regulations governing clinical research are in place to protect patients, the nursing perspective should be mentioned. Nurses must strike a balance between providing optimal care to patients and advancing medical knowledge [13]. Clinical investigators must recognize that the nurse is vital to the success of clinical research and also has the right and responsibility to question suspected research misconduct. If a nurse is only slightly familiar with the research protocol, she may not realize that her involvement can be crucial to the success of a clinical trial.

Conclusion

Clinical research on the critically ill is associated with all the issues that pertain to all clinical research: the need for informed consent and respect for the patient's autonomy, possible conflict of interest, and other concerns as described in this paper. The latest revision of the Declaration of Helsinki and the federal mandate to educate clinical researchers in ethics and clinical trials are attempts to promote these goals and enhance the outcome of clinical research in an appropriate environment where researchers are not unduly impeded in their work and patient subjects are maximally protected. Research in children is also an important topic about which I have written elsewhere [14].

20

Organ Transplantation and Jewish Law

In the Bible (Exodus 15:26) God clearly states that He is the healer of the sick. Nevertheless, the rabbis in the Talmud (Baba Kamma 85a) interpret another biblical passage (Exodus 21:19) to mean that God grants human physicians a divine license to heal the sick as His agents or messengers. Moses Maimonides considers the healing of the sick to be a positive biblical commandment. He states that the precept of returning a lost object to its rightful owner (Deuteronomy 22:2) includes the healing of the sick; in other words, if a doctor is able to restore a patient's "lost" health, he is obligated to do so. Failure or refusal to heal the sick is a violation of the negative biblical commandment of "not standing idly by the blood of one's fellow human being" (Leviticus 19:16).

Patients have the responsibility and obligation to seek healing when they are sick, based on several biblical commandments (Deuteronomy 4:15 and 22:8). Man does not have full title over his body and life. He must eat and drink and live a healthy lifestyle in order to sustain himself and must seek healing when ill.

Another cardinal principle in Jewish law is the sanctity and infinite value of human life. In order to save a human life that is in imminent danger, all biblical and rabbinic laws except the cardinal three (idolatry, murder, and forbidden sexual relations, such as incest or adultery) are suspended for the overriding consideration of saving a human life. Since the value of human life is nearly absolute and supreme, even the Sabbath or the Day of Atonement (Yom Kippur) may be desecrated, and all other rules and regulations are waived temporarily in order to save a human life. The

137

Talmud states that he who saves one life is as if he saved a whole world (Sanhedrin 37a).

While much of the secular ethical system is based on rights (e.g., the right to die, the right to refuse therapy, the right to abortion), Judaism is an ethical system based on duties and responsibilities. The late chief rabbi of Great Britain, Lord Immanuel Jakobovits, eloquently articulated the Jewish view as follows [1]:

> Now in Judaism we know of no intrinsic rights. Indeed, there is no word for rights in the very language of the Hebrew Bible and in the classic sources of Jewish law. In Judaism, we speak of human duties, not human rights, of obligations, not entitlement. The Decalogue is a list of Ten Commandments, not a Bill of Human Rights.

Organ Transplantation

The attitude of Judaism toward organ transplantation has always been a positive one, based on the concept of saving lives—that is, the lives of recipients dying of organ failure. Thus, heart, lung, kidney, liver, and other life-saving organ transplantation is not only permitted in Judaism but is mandated, based on the supreme value of human life. All legal considerations and prohibitions are set aside for the overriding goal of saving the life of the recipient. These legal concerns, especially regarding the donor, include the possible desecration of the donor, deriving benefit from the donor, delaying the burial of the donor, and obtaining permission or consent from the donor and/or the donor's family. The only critical issue is the establishment of the death of the donor. If an organ is removed from a donor, and that surgical procedure hastens the donor's death, it would be considered an act of murder in Judaism (one of the three cardinal sins cited earlier). There is currently a discussion and difference of opinion among rabbinic authorities as to whether total brain death (i.e., absence of spontaneous respiration) is an acceptable definition of death or whether cardiac standstill is also required [2].

Eye transplantation (i.e., corneal transplants) is also permissible in Judaism, based on the concept that a blind person's life is in danger in that he may step in front of a bus or truck and be killed or fall down a flight of stairs and be killed [3].

In regard to kidney transplantation, the Jewish issue is whether an altruistic donor with two kidneys is allowed or required to donate one of his kidneys to save the life of a patient dying of kidney failure, or is prohibited from doing so because of the risk to the donor of the surgery, including general anesthesia, and the risk of being left with only one kidney. The answer adopted by most rabbinic authorities is that if the danger to the donor is much less than the danger to the recipient without the organ, the donor is permitted but not required to donate the organ. If the risk to the donor is minimal, as in bone marrow transplantation, the majority of rabbinic opinion would be to require the donor to donate bone marrow to save the life of his fellow man [4].

When it someday becomes possible to use animal organs for transplantation into humans (xenotransplantation), Judaism would certainly allow it because of the overriding consideration of saving human lives. After the Lebanon incursion by Israel to eliminate terrorism emanating from Lebanon, the Israeli rabbinate allowed the obtaining and storage of human skin from deceased people for transplantation to burn victims or others who require such transplantation to save their lives [5].

Because of the growing shortage of donor organs for transplantation, it is important for the Jewish community to be aware of the preceding discussion and to be ready and prepared to donate an organ to save the life of one's fellow man. In fact, Rabbi Moshe Feinstein, one of the greatest rabbinic authorities of the twentieth century, said that it is a mitzvah (commandment or meritorious act) to donate an organ, although doing so is not one of the 613 biblical commandments.

One final question concerns the permissibility or lack thereof of compensating organ donors. The rulings of most rabbinic authorities indicate that financial compensation is permitted in Jewish law. However, the family must not withhold a cadaver organ because remuneration is refused or not available. The family has no property rights or estate rights to the body of their relative. It is forbidden to let someone die (i.e., the potential recipient dying of organ failure) because one receives no payment to save him [6].

Summary and Conclusion

The attitude of Judaism toward healing the sick has always been a positive one. A physician is obligated to heal and is given divine license to do so. Physicians must be well trained and licensed in their discipline. A patient is also obligated to seek healing, because one must be healthy in order to serve God by doing His will in the service of mankind. A second cardinal principle in Jewish medical ethics is the supreme value of human life. The preservation of life takes precedence over all biblical and rabbinic commandments, rules, and regulations except three: murder, idolatry, and forbidden sexual relations, such as incest or adultery.

Based on these principles, it follows that organ transplantation is permissible if not mandatory in order to save the life of a patient dying of organ failure. If there is significant risk to the donor in donating a "spare" organ, he is not obligated but is permitted to do so. Compensation for organ donation is permissible but not encouraged in Judaism. Altruism should be the motivation for donating organs for transplantation. Xenotransplantation (i.e., transplanting animal organs into humans), when it becomes scientifically and medically feasible, would be permissible in Jewish law. The storage of organs such as skin, corneas, and bones in organ banks is permissible so that these stored organs can later be used to save lives. When science and technology eventually make the cloning of organs possible, such organs will certainly be sanctioned for transplantation for life-saving purposes.

Epilogue

The Jewish tradition, which dates back to Mount Sinai, is perhaps the longest unbroken tradition in biomedical ethics that is still followed by its adherents. Throughout the millennia, Judaism and medicine have marched hand in hand, as allies not as rivals. The mainstream of Jewish thought and tradition places an enormous value on human life and health, has given human beings an obligation to preserve life and health, and encourages recognized medical therapy with faith in God, the healer of the sick. Jewish law is eminently qualified to apply its reasoned, pragmatic rules of morality to the practice of medicine.

21

Payment for Organ Donors

In Judaism, a physician is given divine license to heal the sick, based on the talmudic interpretation (Baba Kamma 85a) of the biblical phrase *and heal he should heal* (Exodus 21:19). In fact, according to Maimonides (Mishnah commentary on Nedarim 4:4), it is an obligation for the physician to heal the sick, induce remission of illness, and prolong life, based on the biblical commandment of restoring a lost object to its rightful owner (Deuteronomy 22:2), which includes the loss of one's health which the physician may have the ability to restore. Furthermore, continues Maimonides (*Mishneh Torah*, Hilchot Rotzeach 1:14), if a physician refuses or declines to care for the sick, with resultant negative consequences to the patient, the physician is guilty of violating the negative biblical commandment of standing idly by the blood of one's fellow man (Leviticus 19:16).

In Judaism, the patient, when ill, is required to seek healing from a physician, based on many biblical and rabbinic admonitions, such as *take ye therefore good heed unto yourselves* (Deuteronomy 4:15) and *take heed to thyself and take care of thy life* (ibid. 4:9).

The multifaceted problem of organ transplantation in Jewish law, including the use of pig organs for transplantation into humans, is discussed at length elsewhere [1–3].

Statement of the Problem

Human organ transplantation began nearly a century ago. There has been and continues to be a shortage of organ donations to

141

satisfy the needs of all patients who need the replacement of one or more diseased organs. Over 60,000 people die every year while waiting for an organ transplant, such as a kidney, heart, liver, heart-lung, pancreas, or lung transplantation [4]. In spite of intensive efforts and major initiatives to increase the supply of organs, the number of donors available annually remains virtually unchanged. This article deals with the Jewish legal considerations in providing financial compensation to organ donors to encourage them to donate a "spare" organ, such as a kidney, bone marrow, or part of a liver. Is altruism the only acceptable course of action in Judaism in organ donation from live and/or deceased donors? Is payment for an organ allowed or prohibited?

In the secular world, cash rewards for organs have been proposed in the United States and elsewhere, although the 1984 National Organ Transplantation Act prohibits donor compensation or selling of human organs. Although payment for organ donation has traditionally been viewed as anathema by many people, numerous suggestions to increase organ donation include cash rewards or other forms of monetary donor compensation, such as payment of funeral expenses, a cash award to the estate of the donor, a cash award to the charity of the donor's or family's choice, or a limited low-cost life insurance policy redeemable on the donation of organs by the deceased policy holder [5].

Proponents of donor compensation argue that the current system of altruism alone is insufficient to meet the demand and need for organ donors. Proponents also point to the long-standing practice of payment for blood and blood products, for human sperm, and recently for human eggs [6]. Further in favor of compensating organ donors is the opinion that it is morally wrong to let thousands of patients die for lack of donor organs [7]. Opponents of payment for organ donors argue that payment undermines the altruistic consent process, encourages a black market of covert payments for organs, exploits the poor, who may feel obligated to sell their organs in order to feed their families, and raises the issue of the commodification of human organs, which will be bought and sold like any other commodity [8]. Others argue that compensating organ donors and/or their families assumes that the body is dissociable from the self and can be treated like property, and since the "person" is no longer there, who owns the material body, and how much may they profit from its disposition [9]?

Many rabbinic authorities have addressed the issue of compensating organ donors in Jewish law over the past decade, as detailed in this chapter. The relevant Jewish legal questions include the following: Does a live organ donor violate the biblical prohibition against self-wounding? Does an organ donor own his own body, and does he have the right or obligation to donate an organ to save another person's life? Does an organ donor who receives compensation for the organ violate the prohibition of receiving payment for the fulfillment of a biblical commandment? There are talmudic precedents and examples of selling body parts, but not in the context of organ donation in the medical therapeutic sense. For example, the Talmud (Nedarin 65b) discusses the sale of one's hair to provide one's family with food. Elsewhere, (Yerushalmi Shabbat 6:1), the Talmud states that the wife of Rabbi Akiba sold her hair braids to help support them.

Prohibition of Payment for Fulfilling a Commandment

In Jewish law, it is forbidden to receive financial compensation for fulfilling a commandment (mitzvah) or performing a meritorious act. Physicians, teachers, and judges are considered, respectively, to be fulfilling the biblical commandments of healing, teaching, and judging, and are thus not entitled to receive payment for their services. Jews must emulate God; just as He heals, teaches, and judges without compensation, so must we. The codes of Jewish law authored by Jacob ben Asher (1260–1343) [10] and Joseph Karo (1488–1575) [11] rule that a physician may only receive compensation for his trouble and his loss of time. Nowadays, however, physicians, teachers, and judges do not have another occupation, as they did in talmudic times, and they are thus fully occupied with their professions, and therefore are entitled to receive full compensation for their services [12].

The Obligation to Save Life

Is an organ donor or his family permitted to request and/or accept financial compensation for the organ donation since the organ is being used to fulfill the commandment of saving a life (i.e., the recipient's life)?

The Talmud (Sanhedrin 73a) states that if a man sees his neighbor drowning or being mauled by beasts or being attacked by robbers, he is obligated to try to save his neighbor's life. This talmudic ruling was codified as normative Jewish Law by Moses Maimonides (1138–1204) [13].

In fact, the saving of life takes precedence over all other biblical and rabbinic laws except the cardinal three: idolatry, murder, and forbidden sexual relations, such as adultery or incest. Even the Sabbath or the Day of Atonement (Yom Kippur) may be desecrated in order to save a human life. The Talmud (Sanhedrin 37a) states that he who saves a life is as if he saved a whole world.

Ownership of One's Body and Soul

There is a difference of opinion among modern rabbinic authorities as to whether man is master over his money and other material possessions as well as his body and/or soul. Does not God own all of man and give him His body and soul and possessions on loan to use but not to abuse? Can a person donate part of his body to a needy recipient? Does Jewish law sanction or require organ donations? The answer to the latter question is a resounding yes [1–3]. Nevertheless man is charged with the preservation and health maintenance of his body. Some rabbis, including Shlomo Zevin, write that man does not have full title over his body [14]. Therefore a person has no right to wound himself or commit suicide or otherwise denigrate his body, which belongs to God. Rabbi Shaul Yisraeli writes that a person has certain rights over his body in partnership with God [15]. Further discussion in some detail about one's ownership of one's body and soul is found in a series of articles dealing with financial compensation for organ donation [16–24].

Prohibitions Against Self-Wounding and Self-Endangerment

In Jewish law we are commanded to diligently watch over our souls (Deuteronomy 4:15) and to take good care of our life (ibid. 4:9). Based on these and other biblical precepts, such as the prohibition of wantonly destroying anything, including trees as well as one's body (suicide is also prohibited as a form of self-mutilation), all rabbinic opinions prohibit self-wounding and self-endangerment. If so, how is a live organ donor permitted to undergo the surgery and anesthesia and other postoperative complications and possible side-effects? The answer lies in the widely discussed question as to whether Judaism allows, mandates, or prohibits a person to undertake a small danger in order to rescue a fellow man who is in very serious or life-threatening danger.

Normative Jewish law, to which most rabbinic authorities subscribe, holds that it is permissible but not mandatory for a person to undergo a small risk or to subject himself to minor danger in order to save the life of a fellow man. Thus, organ donation from live donors, including blood, bone marrow, skin, one kidney, and even part of the liver, is permissible provided the risk to the donor is small [1–3] and the risk to the recipient without the organ donation is maximal, including possible death.

Payment for Organ Donation

It would seem from the preceding discussion that payment for organ donation should not be allowed in Judaism because the donor is performing a meritorious act or fulfilling a biblical commandment (mitzvah). In fact, the opposite is true. There is no prohibition for the donor or donor's family to receive financial compensation. Rabbi Mordechai Halperin offers several reasons for this conclusion [25]. A physician is entitled to be compensated for his time, effort, and expertise. Similarly, a live organ donor is allowed to receive payment for his pain (physical) and suffering (mental) in giving up his organ (e.g., kidney or bone marrow). A second reason is so as not to discourage organ donation. Finally, there is a great difference between a physician, who is biblically mandated to heal the sick, and an organ donor, who is allowed but not required to undertake the risks, albeit small and few, involved in organ donation. If the physician is allowed to receive compensation for his required services, certainly an organ donor is allowed to receive payment if he voluntarily chooses to donate. Halperin concludes that the general prohibition against receiving payment for the performance of a mitzvah does not in any way prevent the donor from requesting and receiving payment for his organ. Since he is fulfilling the mitzvah, he gets full credit for doing so in spite of being paid for his organ. The question of what constitutes a reasonable fee and what is an excessive fee is discussed elsewhere [12].

In his *Encyclopedia of Jewish Medical Ethics* [3], Rabbi Dr. Avraham Steinberg cites Rabbi Moshe Zev Zarger, who rules that one should not take money for donating blood, but if payment was agreed in advance, it must be paid [26]. Rabbi Moshe Feinstein permits a blood donor to receive compensation for his blood even though it is not needed urgently to save a person's life [27]. His reasoning is based on the fact that the prohibition of intentionally wounding oneself is not involved, since blood drawing is essentially a painless and harmless procedure. Furthermore, bloodletting was practiced for centuries as a therapeutic measure. Hence, there is no reason to prohibit or disallow a blood donor from asking for and receiving financial compensation.

Rabbi Moshe Tendler states that the Jewish point of view raises no objection to payment for organ donations, and that a donor deserves remuneration for his loss of earning power while in the hospital [28], besides his pain and suffering and the risk of the procedure. However, Tendler expresses concern that remuneration might be used as a coercive force if great sums of money are offered.

Rabbi Dr. Abraham S. Abraham quotes Rabbi Shlomo Zalman Auerbach, who permits the payment of money to blood donors because the blood will be used for seriously ill patients [29]. In regard to kidney donation, Abraham arrives at the same conclusion [30], namely, that payment to the donor is permissible because he has no absolute obligation to donate the kidney and is therefore entitled to compensation even if his entire motivation is for the money, because the recipient's life is either saved or prolonged by the transplant. Abraham further quotes Rabbi Auerbach, who asserts that even if the donor is extremely poor or wishes to pay off his debts, since he knows that his donated kidney will benefit the recipient, the donor not only receives payment for his kidney or bone marrow, but also full credit for having performed a meritorious act. Rabbi Auerbach's views are also stated in his own writings [22].

Dr. Abraham raises the question of the deceased patient's' kidneys or other organs being transplanted into needy recipients dying of organ failure [30]. The issue involves the biblical prohibition against deriving benefit from the dead [31]. Thus, it would seem that it is forbidden to receive payment for donating one's deceased relative's organs for transplantation. However, both Rabbi Abraham and Rabbi Auerbach nevertheless permit it.

Rabbi Eliezer Yehuda Waldenberg allows payment to relatives of the deceased for the donation of the deceased's organs because the recipient's life would thereby be saved, since the relative's consent is needed to provide the life-saving organ(s) [32]. Furthermore, continues Waldenberg, for a variety of technical Jewish legal considerations, the prohibition against deriving benefit from the dead is not applicable.

Rabbi Yakov Weiner discusses at length the selling of organs, including the prohibition against self-wounding, which includes suicide, the ultimate form of self-wounding [33]. He concludes that one may sell his organs to save another person's life if there is no or only minimal risk to the donor. The prohibition against wounding oneself does not apply because the selling of the organ is considered to be a great need to save life, and the saving of life is a commandment (mitzvah) that suspends all others except the cardinal three of idolatry, murder, and forbidden sexual relations such as incest and adultery.

Rabbi Mordechai Halperin also concludes that there is no prohibition for a kidney donor to receive financial compensation if the kidney is transplanted to prolong the recipient's life [18]. The same applies if the kidney may not prolong the recipient's life but rather may improve the quality of his life, since prevention of suffering is defined as a great need and the prohibition against self-wounding does not apply [18].

Rabbi Shaul Yisraeli discusses the issue of organ transplantation as well as the subject of paying donors [24]. He concludes that there is no reason in Jewish law for an organ donor to request and receive financial compensation for the part of his body to be transplanted, including blood donations. However, only the donor and not the family is entitled to such payment, because of the donor's pain and suffering and loss of time or income from his job.

Rabbi Avraham Sharman reviews the subject of financial payment to organ donors [23]. He discusses the prohibition against self-wounding, ownership of one's body, the obligation to fulfill commandments without compensation, the duty to save life, and other related subjects. He quotes and agrees with Rabbi Shlomo Zalman Auerbach that it is permissible for a blood or other organ donor to be paid, because the purpose of the donation is to fulfill a biblical commandment (i.e., saving a human life).

Dr. Michael Vigoda wrote a lengthy article entitled "Live Organ Donations and Payment for Them" [16]. He discusses the prohibitions against wounding oneself and/or putting one's life in danger. He asserts that these prohibitions are waived because of the overriding consideration of saving a life (i.e., the recipient's). He cites numerous modern rabbinic authorities and concludes from their remarks that most rabbis permit the selling of organs from a live donor for transplantation into a needy recipient because of the rule that saving a life takes precedence over all other biblical and rabbinic commandments (save the cardinal three cited previously). Financial compensation to the donor does not preclude him from wounding himself even if there is some danger to the donor in doing so. Vigoda also cites a single rabbinic view that prohibits this practice and only allows altruistic donation of organs but not the selling of organs for financial compensation. In a lengthy appendix to his article, Vigoda discusses the obligation of a person to donate a nonvital organ to save the life of another person.

Rabbi Zalman Nechemiah Goldberg, son-in-law of the late Rabbi Shlomo Zalman Auerbach, discusses the laws governing the acquisition of a kidney from a donor by the recipient [22]. He also discusses ownership of one's body and concludes that it is not proper for a person to sell one of his organs to a fellow man.

Israeli Chief Rabbi Yisrael Meir Lau wrote an article entitled "The Selling of Organs for Transplantation" [20]. He discusses at length the topics of ownership of one's body and soul, the obligation to bury an organ removed from a living being, the prohibition of deriving benefit from the deceased, and the voluntary selling of an organ and the recipient's obligation to pay for it if so agreed to. Rabbi Lau concludes that "there is no question that all biblical and rabbinic concerns and laws are set aside in a life-saving situation, such as a recipient dying of organ failure except for the cardinal three." He cites other rabbinic authorities who agree with him, including former Chief Rabbi of Israel Ovadiah Yosef in his famous multivolume work *Responsa Yabia Omer.*

In his article on selling organs, Rabbi Shmuel Rabbinowitz [19] discusses the various legal, social, ethnical, and halachic issues involved in the sale of organs. He concludes that it is permissible but not mandatory to donate a kidney if the risk to the donor is small. He also reiterates that all biblical and rabbinic laws except the cardinal three are waived in order to save a human life. Thus, for a dangerously ill recipient, it is permissible to ask for and receive financial compensation for the organ donation.

Rabbi Dr. Abraham Steinberg discusses the ethical and halachic considerations in organ transplantation [3 and 21] from both live and deceased donors. He briefly presents the Christian and Islamic views on this subject as well as the social and secular ramifications and concerns, including the possible exploitation of the poor. He concludes with a series of practical recommendations, such as that there should be no relationship between the potential donor and the transplant team. He cites various rabbinic authorities who have written and spoken out on the sale of organs for transplantation

[3, 20, 24, 34] and agrees with them that it is permissible to receive payment for an organ because the purpose is to save the life of the recipient, and all Jewish laws are set aside for the overriding consideration of saving a life.

A very recent article by Grazi and Wolowelsky [35] reviews many of the considerations discussed above and suggests that a series of pragmatic systems be developed and implemented so that potential vendors and donors are properly informed and not exploited. They still prefer the altruistic method of organ donation without compensation, but agree that Jewish law does not prohibit such compensation.

These authors quote former Israeli Chief Rabbi Shlomo Goren [36], who wrote that donation of a kidney in consideration of financial reward does not change its positive characteristic of saving the recipient's life. He further wrote that there is no Jewish legal basis on which to prohibit a person from donating a kidney for financial gain, "inasmuch as this reflects an agreement between the donor and the recipient."

Rabbi Abraham Sharman wrote an article entitled "Organ Donation for the Sake of Financial Profit" [23] in which he discusses the various halachic issues involved, including the prohibition of self-wounding, ownership of one's body, and the circumstances, such as danger to life, which permit the suspension of these considerations and prohibitions. He quotes the opinions of Rabbis Feinstein, Auerbach, Elchanan Wasserman, and others, and implies that he agrees with their verdicts that financial compensation to organ donors is permissible because the purpose is to fulfill the commandment of saving a life.

Dr. Chava Tabankin authored an article about the sale of a kidney from a living donor for transplantation according to Jewish and current Israeli law [17]. He concludes that under specific conditions it is permissible in Jewish law to sell a kidney from a living donor. He also concludes that even according to Israeli societal and legal edicts, many arguments support the permissibility of payment for the donation of organs in view of the mental and physical suffering the donor may experience for many years. He also discusses the opinion of those who are opposed to the sale of organs for a variety of ethical and other reasons.

Summary and Conclusions

A cardinal principle in Judaism is that the value of human life is supreme. Hence, in order to save a human life, all biblical and rabbinic laws and regulations are temporarily suspended. Organ transplantation is a multifaceted topic in Judaism, involving many legal questions regarding the donor. The prohibitions against desecrating the dead, deriving benefit from the dead, delaying burial of the dead, and others are waived because of the overriding consideration of saving the life of the recipient. Other issues include the need (or lack thereof) for permission from the donor or next of kin for organ transplantation and the legal status of the donor buried without the organs now functioning in the recipient. These and other questions are answered in detailed essays on this subject [1–3]. The consensus of nearly all rabbinic authorities is that cadaver organ transplantation is permissible, desirable, and perhaps even mandatory to save the lives of people dying of organ failure, provided the donor is deceased at the time the organ is removed for transplantation.

The present essay deals exclusively with the issue of payment to donors or their families for the organs, in part to encourage organ donation from live donors as well as from cadaver organs. The Jewish legal and moral issues involved in financial compensation for organ donation include the prohibitions against self-wounding and self-endangerment, the prohibition against receiving payment for the performance or fulfillment of a commandment (mitzvah), the fact that humans are not total masters over their own bodies and souls, which are gifts from God on temporary loan to preserve, hallow, and care for in dignity and holiness, the possibility of exploiting the poor, and other considerations. The preponderance of rabbinic opinion is that all the above concerns and considerations are set aside because of the overriding principle that saving human life takes precedence over all other biblical and rabbinic commandments except the cardinal three of idolatry, murder, and forbidden sexual relations, such as incest or adultery. Therefore, financial compensation to a live organ donor for a "spare" organ, such as a kidney or bone marrow, is permitted in Jewish law. However, the family of the deceased must not withhold a cadaver organ because remuneration is refused or unavailable. The family has no property rights or estate rights over the body of their deceased relative. It is an obligation on the family to donate the deceased's organs to save one or more human lives. It is forbidden to let someone die because one is not financially remunerated to save him. The Talmud clearly states, "He who saves one life is as if he saved an entire world" (Sanhedrin 37a).

PART IV
Miscellaneous Topics

22

Ethical Dilemmas of an Observant Jewish Physician Working in a Secular Society

When the Albert Einstein College of Medicine of Yeshiva University began preparing to admit its first class of students in September 1955, many members of the faculty had serious concerns and reservations as to whether observant Jewish graduates of Yeshiva College would fully comply with all the rules and regulations of the new medical school, the first under Jewish auspices. Some of the faculty were concerned that the observant Jewish students might not dissect their cadavers as part of the anatomy and pathology courses because of Jewish concerns prohibiting the desecration of the dead, prohibiting the derivation of benefit from the dead, and the religious requirement to promptly bury the dead. Other members of the faculty voiced concerns about whether the observant Jewish students would work on the Sabbath or Jewish holidays in the hospital during the third and fourth years when students are clinical clerks and thus part of the medical team caring for patients. In fact my interviewer asked me that specific question. I responded that I would be there and do everything necessary for the proper care of my patients according to standard and accepted good medical practice. I explained to the interviewer that I was not only divinely licensed to become a physician and practice medicine but was also divinely mandated to heal the sick after receiving appropriate training, that is, the medical school and post-doctoral residency of my choice, and after receiving appropriate licensure from the municipal or governmental authorities to practice medicine.

My interviewer must have been satisfied with my answer, because I was accepted as a member of the first class. One of my close friends who graduated college with me as the only summa cum laude in the class was interviewed by the chairman of the Department of Pathology, who asked him, "Will you request an autopsy on a patient of yours who dies?" He unexpectedly answered no. His admission to the medical school was delayed and required the personal intervention of Dr. Samuel Belkin, then president of Yeshiva University, to clarify the applicant's answer. He was finally admitted, excelled throughout the four years of medical school, and went on to become a prominent neurosurgeon.

Throughout the four years of medical school, the students of the first class at the Albert Einstein College of Medicine were faced with numerous religious and moral questions regarding the physician's license and obligation to heal, procreation and sexuality including abortion, contraception, sperm procurement and analysis, artificial insemination, induction of labor, sterilization procedures in men and women, and many more. Questions involving issues of death and dying included informing the critically ill patient, euthanasia, the definition of death in Jewish law, autopsy, embalming, burial of organs removed at surgery, and many more. Other questions concerned hazardous therapy and human experimentation, mental health, dentistry, and a series of miscellaneous topics.

By far, most questions concerned the practice of medicine on the Sabbath by a medical student or by a physician. All these questions were posed to Rabbi Moshe Feinstein, who answered them with sensitivity, compassion, and concern for the medical students. All the answers or responsa provided by Rabbi Feinstein were collected and published in a book that is still very popular among Jewish medical students entitled *Practical Medical Halachah* [2].

The Jewish contribution to medical ethics began with the pioneering, now classic book by the late chief Rabbi of the British Commonwealth of nations entitled Jewish Medical Ethics [3], which has since been followed by numerous scholarly treatises and books [4–29], culminating in the recent publication of a multi-volume *Encyclopedia of Jewish Medical Ethics* [30].

For over a hundred years in New York City, it was very difficult for a Jewish college graduate to gain admittance to medical school. It was also very difficult for Jewish physicians to obtain post-doctoral specialty training, and even more difficult for Jewish physicians to obtain staff privileges at most hospitals. These facts led to the creation of the Mount Sinai Hospital in New York, followed by the creation of the other New York Jewish Federation hospitals. The problem was greatly alleviated if not eliminated with the opening of Yeshiva University's Albert Einstein College of Medicine, which resulted in the other New York medical schools accepting Jewish men and women college graduates to their medical schools and hospitals.

A prominent observant Danish obstetrician/gynecologist has described in some detail the problems he has encountered in his career in practicing in a non-Jewish society guided by secular medical ethics [1]. He describes the problem of a Jewish physician or nurse who refuses to participate in the performance of abortions, inseminations, and other procedures that may be contrary to his/her religious convictions. He also details his personal problems with employment in a hospital, and promotion to a more senior position. He eventually became chairman of the department. He describes the personal solutions he used to overcome his problems as an observant Jewish physician working in a non-Jewish secular society.

Jewish and Secular Approaches to Medical Ethics

The differences between the secular and Jewish approaches to medical ethics are detailed by Avraham Steinberg [31]. He points out that several radical scientific, philosophical, and social changes over the past several decades have overwhelmingly influenced the shaping of current secular medical ethics, and he exemplifies each of these changes. Of most significant importance is the philosophical shift in the physician–patient relationship from the primacy of beneficence and paternalism to the primacy of autonomy. This concept stresses rights of privacy and individual liberty, patient autonomous decision-making and self-determination. Our medical system of care has shifted from the physician-oriented model to the patient-oriented model. The secular ethical system nowadays emphasizes patient rights. Patients have the right to a doctor. Patients have the right to know their diagnosis and prognosis, and the reason why the physician is recommending certain diagnostic tests and therapeutic interventions. Patients have the right to be told about alternative options, and what the outcome is likely to be if they refuse to follow the doctor's recommendations. Patients have a right to abortion, a right to assisted suicide (in the state of

Oregon), the right to appoint a healthcare proxy for a time in which they are unable to make health care decisions for themselves. Few people who advocate the principle of autonomy and patents' rights speak of patients' duties and/or obligations.

Much of the secular ethical system is based on rights; Judaism is an ethical system based on duties and responsibilities. Judaism requires patients to do whatever is proper in order to be healthy. It is an obligation in Judaism to be healthy. One should not smoke; one should eat properly and not excessively. One should exercise regularly, sleep adequately, only engage in proper and legitimate sex, and lead an overall healthy lifestyle. These are just some of the legal and moral duties, obligations, and imperatives in Judaism [32]. The limited autonomy of the patient in Jewish law is discussed in some detail by Shimon Glick [33]. The late Chief Rabbi of the British Commonwealth of Nations, Lord Immanuel Jakobovits, eloquently articulates the Jewish view as follows:

> Now in Judaism we know of no intrinsic rights. Indeed there is no word for rights in the very language of the Hebrew Bible and of the classic sources of Jewish law. In the moral vocabulary of the Jewish discipline of life we speak of human duties, not of human rights, of obligations, not entitlements. The Decalogue is a list of Ten Commandments, not a Bill of Human Rights [34].

Case Study

An Observant Jewish Physician's Personal Experience in the Era of Autonomy and Patient Self-Determination and Decision-Making

A 46-year-old woman was brought to the emergency room comatose after she ran her car into a tree. Resuscitative measures were attempted. She was intubated, a nasogastric feeding tube inserted, nasal oxygen applied, and a respirator used to support her breathing. The family related that six months earlier, the woman had watched her husband die of advanced lung cancer while he was attached to life-support equipment. The woman firmly told her children and other family members that she did not want to die like that, "hooked up to tubes and machines." The patient was admitted to the medical service and given appropriate care, including nutrition by nasogastric tube and hydration by intravenous infusion. She remained comatose.

Two days later, as director of the Department of Medicine, I received a phone call from the hospital's lawyer saying that the family had obtained a court order to remove the respirator, based on the clear and convincing evidence of her previously expressed wishes to the family. I told the lawyer he was welcome to come to the hospital to carry out the court order, to which he replied, "But I am an attorney, not a physician." I told him that it does not require a physician to turn off a respirator and I would be happy to show him the switch to turn it off. He refused. I spoke to the family that had obtained the court order and suggested that they carry out the order and I would show them how to turn off the control switch. They too refused.

The hospital's attorney insisted that it was my responsibility to disconnect the respirator. I told him that the patient might wake up from her coma any day and recover with some or no neurological sequelae. "If I remove the respirator now," I said, "and if she dies as a result, I will have shortened her life and committed an act of moral murder, since my religious beliefs prohibit the performance of an act that might shorten a person's life." The lawyer insisted that if I was not willing to carry out the court order, it was my responsibility to find a physician on my staff who would be willing to do so. I canvassed my entire house staff and my entire attending staff, and no one was willing to disconnect the respirator.

I solved the dilemma by referring the problem to the hospital's medical director, who found a physician in the Department of Neurology who was willing to comply with the court order. When he disconnected the respirator, the patient began breathing on her own just as Karen Ann Quinlan did in 1976 in that landmark case where the New Jersey Supreme Court granted her parents' petition to remove her respirator so that she could die in dignity rather than remain indefinitely in a persistent vegetative state.

The next morning I received another telephone call from the hospital's attorney, saying that the family had now obtained a second court order to remove the feeding tube. I again told him that he was welcome to come to the hospital to do so and I would show him how. Again he said, "I am an attorney, and not a physician." I explained to him that withdrawing nutrition from the patient would cause her to starve to death, and I could not be the one to commit moral murder by shortening her life by starvation. We continued to discuss the matter.

The next morning when I arrived in the patient's room, I found the nasogastric tube on the floor. The nurses denied having removed it. The house staff denied having removed it. The family denied having removed it. We were all surprised but decided not to reinsert it because of the court order.

In secular medical ethics and in Catholic medical ethics, there is no moral or legal difference between withholding and withdrawing a feeding tube. In Jewish medical ethics, there is a moral difference. Passively omitting to do something (known in Hebrew as *shev ve'al taaseh*) is morally acceptable under certain circumstances such as medical futility. The act of removing the feeding tube (known in Hebrew as *kum va'aseh* or *maaseh beyadayim*) is prohibited if it shortens the patient's life. This problem solved itself because the feeding tube was mysteriously found on the floor of the patient's room and was not reinserted to comply with the court order.

The next morning I received another phone call from the hospital's attorney saying that the family had obtained another court order to remove the nasal oxygen. I explained to him that the oxygen was purely a comfort measure to ease her breathing and was not a specific medical therapy. I spoke to the family and convinced them of this fact, and they allowed the continuation of the nasal oxygen.

The final telephone call from the hospital's attorney came two days later. He said that the family had obtained an additional court order to remove the intravenous infusion that was hydrating the patient, who was still comatose but breathing on her own. I pondered long and hard about this quandary. Is the act of removing the intravenous line an act of shortening the patent's life and therefore morally forbidden in the Jewish ethical system? I resolved the matter by telling the house staff that when the current infusion ended, they were to passively not hang up another bag of fluids (*shev ve'al taaseh*). They followed my instructions, and subsequently the nurses removed the needle from the patient's vein. The patient lived for 49 days without any nutrition or hydration until her heart and breathing stopped and she was declared dead. This lengthy period without food and water is comparable to the length of time it took for Irish prisoners some years ago who went on a hunger strike to fast to their death.

Such cases are obviously uncommon, and most observant Jewish physicians practicing in a secular medical society are rarely, if ever, faced with such problems. Guidance is easily available from the multitude of books now available in English on Jewish medical ethics [2–31].

Informing the Patient of a Fatal Illness

There are significant differences between the Jewish and secular views about telling the patient "everything" even if it is very bad news. Disclosure of information to patients has drastically changed in the past few decades in the secular ethical system.

This was the era of paternalism. Since the 1960s, opinion on the role of disclosure has changed rapidly in the United States, stimulated by the patients' rights movement and the rise of bioethics. The current climate supports honest and complete disclosure of information. In 1972, the board of trustees of the American Hospital Association affirmed a Patient's Bill of Rights which states that patients have the right to obtain from their physician complete current information concerning his diagnosis, treatment, and prognosis in terms they can be reasonably expected to understand [10]. Bioethics now favors full disclosure as a means of respecting patient autonomy [11]. The American College of Physicians *Ethics Manual* states that disclosure to patients is a fundamental ethical requirement [12]. The era of patient autonomy ended the traditional pattern of withholding information, which was characteristic of the previous era of paternalism.

The Jewish view toward full disclosure of a fatal illness to a patient, and especially a patient who is terminally ill, is in general a negative one because of the fear that the patient may give up hope, suffer severe mental anguish (*tiruf hadaat*), become despondent, and die sooner than otherwise. Shortening a patient's life is strictly forbidden because Judaism espouses the concept that God-given life is sacred, even only a short period thereof. Disclosure should be conveyed in the context of optimism. The most positive outlook should be imparted to the patient. Disclosure must be imparted with compassion, sensitivity, and hope, thus giving the patient an opportunity to "set his house in order" and recite the confessional penitent prayer known as *Viduy*.

Medical Confidentiality and Patient Privacy Rights

Another area in modern medical practice to which the observant Jewish physician must pay great attention is the subject of medical confidentiality and patient privacy rights. Recent legislation passed by the U.S. Congress and signed into law by the president requires all physicians to comply with the new HIPAA rules governing medical privacy and patient confidentiality. The new mandatory standards protect individuals' medical records and other health information. Patients now have much more control over their health information. Safeguards are built into the new rules, and penalties can be imposed on physicians who fail to protect the privacy of health information. Observant Jewish physicians and all other physicians are scrambling to comply with the new HIPAA rules and regulations. A fundamental Jewish ethical principle states that "the law of the land is the law." Therefore, all physicians, including observant Jewish physicians, must comply with the law.

The Jewish view on confidentiality is described in detail elsewhere [35–41].

Conclusion

The attitude toward healing in Judaism has always been a positive one. A physician is obligated to heal and is given divine license to do so. A physician must be well trained and licensed in his discipline. A physician must apply his skills for the benefit of the patient and be careful not to do harm. Thus, the ethical principles of beneficence and nonmaleficence are deeply rooted in Judaism. A patient is obligated to seek healing because one must be healthy in order to serve the Lord by doing His will in the service of mankind.

A second cardinal principle of Judaism is the infinite value of human life. The preservation of life takes precedence over all biblical and rabbinic commandments except three: murder, idolatry and forbidden sexual relations, such as incest or adultery. The Talmud states that all lives are equal because one person's blood is not redder than that of another person (Pesachim 25b).

Preventive medicine is a centerpiece of the Jewish system. The Jewish view toward the practice of medicine emphasizes prevention over treatment. Prevention of danger and thereby the preservation of life and health are biblical mandates. One must observe rules of personal hygiene, such as hand washing before eating. Diet, exercise, sex, and bodily functions must all be properly tended to. Preventive medical services and patient responsibilities are fully consonant with Judaism. Thus, emphases on prevention of illness and on personal responsibility are deeply rooted in Judaic teaching and tradition.

With regard to the Internet, Judaism views any new technology or scientific advance with favor if it is used for the betterment of mankind, such as the prevention and treatment of illness. Harnessing of the natural sciences is not considered an encroachment upon divine prerogatives. On the contrary, God gave us dominion over the world to use nature to subdue the earth (Genesis 1:28) by transforming its secrets into products and technology to benefit mankind. The Internet is a wonderful tool to accomplish this purpose, with some caveats as discussed elsewhere.

These principles of Judaism guide the Jewish physician in the practice of medicine. As new Jewish bioethical questions arise, rabbinic decisors will provide answers based on the expert medical and technical information provided by physicians and scientists. Such answers must be consonant with the physician's ability to practice medicine, using the most up-to-date advances in medical science and biomedical technology. However, the answers must also remain true to traditional Judaic teachings as transmitted by God to Moses and the children of Israel.

23

Managed Care: A Jewish View

Universal access to health care is a moral imperative based in part on traditional Judeo-Christian ethics. Thus, society owes every patient health care, with the gold standard of medical practice being the best interest of the patient. Physicians should be advocates for their patients before they consider their own self-interest, autonomy, income, and other prerogatives.

The optimal goals of American managed care are to provide universal coverage and universal access to healthcare for all Americans at a cost the country can afford. However, some consider the term "managed care"' to be a euphemism for cost containment and rationing. Under a fee-for-service system the incentives stimulate physicians to do more, while in contrast, under managed care the incentives restrain the physician to do less.

The effects of these restraints on the quality of patient care are, as yet, unknown, because outcome data are, as yet, sparse. In some institutions, quality of care is being redefined not as excellence of care, but as minimal acceptable care. It seems that the controlled use of resources to reduce the cost of medical care may be desirable and helpful, but over-management can also lead to a decrease in quality.

Clearly, managed care and managed competition are cost-driven and not care-driven phenomena. I submit that physicians working in a managed care system must remain advocates for their patients because "the physician is, inescapably, a moral accomplice if harm is done to the patient" [1]. Thus, the physician has an ethical imperative to appeal against unjust rules and regulations about the restrictions of technology and consultation if the patient clearly needs these resources. The physician must always recommend and do what is best for the patient and must not become a functionary of the system. Although the physician-patient relationship under managed care may be somewhat distorted, the patient's interests can and must be safeguarded. Patients should not view their provider as a case manager or a gatekeeper but as a caring and concerned physician who works under certain restrictions dictated by social values and cost considerations.

This essay deals with a Jewish view of several of the major moral issues involved in the health care reform debate, and particularly the ethical concerns surrounding managed care. These include medical gatekeeping and the physician's obligation to heal, preventive medicine and patient responsibility, society's obligation to provide healthcare, and finally, rationing and priorities in Judaism. Classic Jewish sources such as the Bible and the Talmud as well as more recent rabbinic pronouncements are cited to illustrate the Jewish legal and moral position on these issues.

Medical Gatekeeping and the Physicians' Obligation to Heal

Under managed care, the primary physician who manages the patient's medical care is expected to control costs by serving as a gatekeeper to limit access to specialists and to expensive technology. Medical gatekeeping, according to Pellegrino, a medical ethicist, can be described as being of three types: one is morally mandatory, one is morally questionable, and one is morally indefensible [2]. The first of these is traditional gatekeeping, in which the physician recommends tests, treatments and consultations that are appropriate, effective, and beneficial to the patient. According to Pellegrino, the physician should use "diagnostic elegance and therapeutic parsimony." This is the way to practice good medicine.

In the morally questionable, negative form of gatekeeping, the physician is pressured to restrict the use of tests, treatments and consultations, particularly those which are very expensive. The third form of medical gatekeeping, which Pellegrino characterizes as morally indefensible, is positive gatekeeping, in which the physician increases access to medical services to enhance profits for himself and/or his employer.

In the Jewish tradition, a physician is given specific divine license to practice medicine. The biblical verse *and heal he shall heal* (Exodus 21:19) is interpreted by the talmudic sages as teaching us that God grants the physician authorization to heal (Baba Kamma 85a). In Jewish law, a physician is not merely allowed to practice medicine but is in fact commanded to do so if he has chosen to become a physician. This biblical mandate is based upon two scriptural precepts. *And thou shalt restore it to him* (Deuteronomy 22:2) refers to the restoration of lost property; Moses Maimonides, in his commentary on the Mishnah, states that "it is obligatory from the Torah for the physician to heal the sick, and this is included in the explanation of the scriptural phrase *and thou shalt restore it to him*, meaning to heal his body" [3]. Thus, Maimonides and the Talmud (Nedarim 38b) both state that the law of restoration also includes the restoration of the health of one's fellow man. If a person has "lost his health" and the physician is able to restore it, he is obligated to do so.

The second scriptural mandate for the physician to heal is based on the phrase *neither shalt thou stand idly by the blood of thy neighbor* (Leviticus 19:16). The passage refers to the duties of human beings to their fellow men and of the moral principles which the sages expound and apply to every phase of civil and criminal law. If one stands idly by and allows one's fellow man to die without offering help, one is guilty of transgressing this precept. A physician who refuses to heal, thereby resulting in suffering and/or death of the patient, is also guilty of transgressing this commandment.

Thus, permission for the physician to heal is granted in the Bible from the phrase *and heal he shall heal.* Some scholars, notably Maimonides, claim that healing the sick is not only allowed but is actually obligatory. Rabbi Joseph Karo, in his code of Jewish law, combines both thoughts: "The Torah gave permission to the physician to heal; moreover, this is a religious precept and it is included in the category of saving life; and if he withholds his services, it is considered as shedding blood" [4].

If one asks why God granted physicians license and even a mandate to heal the sick, one can offer the following explanation. A cardinal principle of Judaism is that human life is of infinite value. The preservation of human life takes precedence over all commandments in the Bible except three: idolatry, murder and forbidden sexual relations. Life's value is absolute and supreme. In order to preserve a human life, the Sabbath and even the Day of Atonement may be desecrated, and all other rules and laws save the aforementioned three are suspended for the overriding consideration of saving a human life. "He who saves one life is as if he saved a whole world" (Sanhedrin 37a). Even a few moments of life are worthwhile. Judaism is a "right-to-life" religion. The obligation to save lives is an individual as well as a communal obligation. Certainly a physician, who has knowledge and expertise far beyond that of a lay person, is obligated to use his medical skills to heal the sick and thereby to prolong and preserve life. Physicians must apply their skills for the benefit of the patient and be careful not to cause harm. Thus, the ethical principles of beneficence and nonmaleficence are deeply rooted in Judaism.

Jewish law also requires a physician to be well trained and licensed by the local authorities [4]. An unlicensed physician is liable to pay compensation to the patient for unintentional errors or side-effects. A negligent physician is obviously culpable even if he is licensed. However, he is not liable for misjudgments or side effects or a bad outcome if he acted responsibly. This topic is discussed extensively elsewhere [5]. Judaism protects physicians from undeserved liability but stresses that the physician must recognize the limits of his ability and demands that physicians consult with more experienced colleagues in situations of doubt.

The topic of physicians' fees is also beyond the scope of this essay and is discussed in detail elsewhere [6]. Briefly, physicians are entitled to reasonable fees and compensation for their services. In talmudic times, when physicians, rabbis, teachers, and judges served the community on a part-time basis only and had other occupations and trades, their compensation was limited to lost time and effort. Nowadays, however, when physicians have no other occupation, they can charge for their expert medical knowledge and receive full compensation. Excessive fees are discouraged but are not prohibited if the patient agrees to the fee in advance. Indigent patients should be treated for a reduced fee or for no fee at all. These principles are applicable both to a salaried physician as well as to a physician in private practice who charges fee-for-service.

The foregoing Judaic principles require that physicians practicing under a managed care system must continue to place the interests of their patients first and must advocate for any care they believe will materially benefit their patients. Frugality should not be allowed to lead to less than appropriate care. Efforts to contain costs should not place patients' welfare at risk. Physicians must continue to practice good medicine, eliminate what is unnecessary, and be conscious of the need to contain costs. Physicians must also practice within the areas in which they are credentialed and do so in the best interests of their patients, not of themselves nor of those who employ them.

Preventive Medicine and Patient Responsibility

Preventive medical services represent a major component of managed care. Such an approach is fully consonant with Jewish tradition, because preventive medicine has been the centerpiece of the Jewish system for more than two thousand years. The Jewish view emphasizes prevention rather than treatment.

An entire chapter in Moses Maimonides' famous *Code of Jewish Law* is devoted to hygienic and medical prescriptions for healthy living and for the prevention of illness [7]. Among the many subjects discussed are normal bodily excretory functions, recommended times for eating, amounts and types of food to be consumed, beverage imbibition, exercise, sleep habits, cathartics, climatic and weather effects on eating habits, detrimental and beneficial foods, fruits, meats, vegetables, bathing, bloodletting, sexual intercourse, and domicile.

The maintenance of one's health requires Jews to avoid harmful foods and activities and to prevent danger wherever possible. This principle is exemplified by the precept of building a parapet on one's roof (Deuteronomy 22:8). One must also be concerned about ecological and environmental factors, such as clean air and sunshine, which may impact upon one's health. One must observe rules of personal hygiene such as hand washing before eating. Diet, exercise, sex, and bodily functions must all be tended to as outlined by Maimonides. He concludes his exposition as follows:

> *I guarantee anyone who conducts himself according to the directions we have laid down that he will not be afflicted with illness all the days of his life until he ages greatly and expires. He will not require a physician, and his body will be complete and remain healthy all his life unless his body was defective from the beginning of his creation, or unless he became accustomed to one of the bad habits from the onset of his youth, or unless the plague of pestilence or the plague of drought comes onto the world [8].*

Maimonides thus cites exceptions to the goal of preventing rather than treating illness. Genetic diseases and certain epidemics cannot be prevented. For this reason, the final paragraph in Maimonides' chapter on the regimen of health states that a person should not reside in a city that does not have a physician. A similar pronouncement is found in the Talmud (Sanhedrin 17b).

If, in spite of all the above, a person becomes ill, healing from a human physician is mandated in the Torah and does not constitute lack of faith in the true Divine Healer. On the contrary, it is forbidden to rely on miracles or on Providence alone. One must do whatever one can to restore health and to maintain life.

Numerous talmudic citations support the position that not only allows but requires the patient to seek medical aid when sick. We are told that he who is in pain should go to a physician (Baba Kamma 46b). Furthermore, if one is bitten by a snake, one may call a physician even if it means desecrating the Sabbath, because all restrictions are set aside in case of possible danger to human life (Yoma 83b). Similarly, if one's eye becomes afflicted on the Sabbath, one may prepare and apply medication thereto, even on the Sabbath (Abodah Zarah 28b). When Rabbi Judah the Prince, compiler of the Mishnah, contracted an eye disease, his physician, Samuel Yarchina'ah, cured it by placing a vial of chemicals under the rabbi's pillow so that the powerful vapors would penetrate the eye (Baba Metzia 85b).

The Bible also tells us to *take heed to thyself, and take care of thy life* (Deuteronomy 4:9) and *take good care of your lives* (Deuteronomy 4:15). Thus, it is clear that a patient is obligated to care for his health and life. Man does not have full title over his body and life. He is the steward who is responsible for dignifying and preserving that life. He must eat and drink to sustain himself and must seek healing when he is sick.

In the United States, citizens are endowed with a variety of legal rights. People have the right to die, the right to refuse treatment, the right not to be resuscitated, the right to abortion, and many other rights. Rarely does one hear about responsibilities and obligations of citizens. Judaism requires everyone to do what is proper in order to be healthy. It is an obligation in Judaism to be healthy. Hence, one should accept appropriate medical advice. One should not smoke, one should eat properly and not excessively, exercise regularly, sleep adequately, only engage in proper and legitimate sexual activities and, overall, lead a healthy life. These are moral obligations and legal imperatives in Judaism.

Thus, while much of the modern secular ethical system is based on rights, Judaism is an ethical system based on duties and responsibilities. Rabbi Jakobovits eloquently articulates the Jewish view as follows:

> Now, in Judaism we know of no intrinsic rights. Indeed, there is no word for rights in the very language of the Hebrew Bible and of the classic sources of Jewish law. In the moral vocabulary of the Jewish discipline of life we speak of human duties, not of human rights, of obligations, not entitlement. The Decalogue is a list of Ten Commandments, not a Bill of Human Rights [9].

This personal responsibility concept of Judaism, although several thousand years old, is as valid today as it was when Moses received it on Mount Sinai.

Society's Obligation to Provide Healthcare

Mackler describes the traditional Jewish understanding of *tzedakah*, which he interprets as justice and support for the needy, especially as related to the provision of medical care [10]. The concept of *tzedakah*, usually translated as "charity" or "almsgiving," is found throughout the Bible, from the instructions regarding the corners of one's field, gleanings, and forgotten produce which are to be left for the poor (Leviticus 19:9–10, Deuteronomy 24:19–22) to the tithe which is to be given to the poor (Deuteronomy 14:28–29, 26:12–15), from the freeing of slaves and cancellation of debts in the sabbatical year to the return of the land to its original owner in the jubilee year (Leviticus 25, Deuteronomy 15).

Charity (*tzedakah*) is an attribute of God Himself, who executes justice (*tzedakah*) for orphans and widows, and who loves the stranger and gives him food and clothing (Deuteronomy 10:17–18). A person who gives charity emulates, or walks after, the Lord (Deuteronomy 13: 5). Charity to the poor is equated with lending to the Lord, a good deed for which He will repay the giver (Proverbs 19:17).

In talmudic and rabbinic literature, the term *tzedakah* is used in the sense of helping the needy with gifts. The rabbis view "charity not as a favor to the poor but [as] something to which they have a right, and the donor an obligation" [11]. In the Talmud it is said that *tzedakah* is as important as all the other commandments put together (Baba Bathra 9a) and that *tzedakah* is greater than all the

Temple sacrifices (Sukkah 49b). Giving *tzedakah* hastens redemption (Baba Bathra 10a), ensures the giver with wise, wealthy, and learned children (Baba Bathra 19b), and atones for sin (Baba Bathra 9b).

The laws of charity, including those pertaining to the giver, the recipient, the amount to be given, the manner of dispensing it and various general laws, are scattered throughout the Talmud and codified by Rabbi Joseph Karo in his *Shulchan Aruch* [12] and by Moses Maimonides in his *Mishneh Torah* [13]. The highest degree of *tzedakah*, according to Maimonides, is to give a poor person a gift or a loan, or to go into business with him, or to find him work, so that the poor person is not dependent on others [14].

Extrapolating from the general requirements of *tzedakah*, one can conclude that the Jewish view of justice requires "the provision of a 'decent minimum' of health care, sufficient to meet the needs of each member of society" [10]. Society's obligations to protect the health and welfare of its citizens are exemplified in Judaism in numerous contexts. For example, the Talmud asserts that captives should not be ransomed for more than their value, to prevent abuse (Gittin 2:6), either so that captors should not be encouraged to seize more captives and make excessive ransom demands, or so as not to impoverish the community. Yet, captives must be redeemed as a societal obligation because the kidnap victim's life is considered to be in danger. Since Jewish society has a fundamental obligation to save lives, it must certainly provide for proper medical care for all its citizens, regardless of age, income or social status.

As part of their religious duty to care for the sick, many Jewish communities in the past engaged communal physicians and established hospitals and other medical facilities. Specialized care was organized during plagues and epidemics. Special associations were formed for health care and later became *bikkur cholim*, or "visiting the sick," societies which paid for physicians, pharmacists, midwives, hospital attendants, and the like. These societies sometimes had expanded duties and responsibilities, including the provision of free loans, sponsorship of circumcision celebrations, medical care in childbirth and related necessities [15].

In more recent times, Rabbi Immanuel Jakobovits writes that the financial needs of the sick have significant claim on communal resources [16]. Rabbi Eliezer Waldenberg discusses various ways that society can discharge its obligation to ensure the provision of health care [17]. He states that supporting hospitals financially is a very praiseworthy act because one thereby helps to save many lives

[18]. He also quotes a prominent rabbi who lauds the establishment by the Jewish community of an old age home which contributes to the prolongation of the life of its residents. Rabbi Moshe Feinstein refers to a community obligation to raise funds for a patient even if the treatment is very expensive because the saving of lives takes precedence over all other commandments except the cardinal three (idolatry, murder and forbidden sexual relations) [19].

Society must also be concerned not only for the welfare of all its citizens in the present but also for future generations. This thesis is illustrated in the Talmud in a situation in which the water supply of town A is situated on top of a hill (Nedarim 80b). Town B, located at the bottom of the hill, cannot obtain water unless the townspeople of town A do not water their flocks and/or launder their clothes. Rabbi Jose rules that the townspeople from town A at the top of the hill take precedence over those of town B. Although the immediate danger from lack of water is to the people of town B, the long-term danger from not washing one's body and clothes to the people of town A overrides the immediate needs of the people of town B at the bottom of the hill. The talmudic sage and physician Samuel explains that scabs of the head caused by not washing can lead to blindness, that scabs arising through the wearing of unlaundered garments can cause madness, and that scabs due to neglect of the body can cause boils and ulcers (Nedarim 81a). Thus, we have clear evidence that society must be concerned about future generations and long-term planning.

Another example of society's obligation to public health, even if individual rights have to be sacrificed, is passive smoking. Judaism requires society to negate a person's right to smoke in the presence of others to protect the latter from the harmful effects of passive smoking. Rabbi Feinstein clearly and definitely prohibits passive smoking [20]. Rabbi Waldenberg also rules that a smoker can be prevented from doing so in public if any nonsmoker is bothered by the smoke or might become ill as a result of the passive smoking [21]. From all the foregoing, one can conclude that in Judaism:

> *Society has the responsibility to ensure that needed medical care is provided to those who would otherwise be unable to receive it, as society has the responsibility to ensure that all basic needs of the poor are met. Medical care for potentially life-threatening conditions justifies extraordinary expenditures, and represents an urgent obligation of society [10].*

Rationing and Priorities in Judaism

Healthcare reform is being driven in part by the need to control costs. Organ transplantation, hemodialysis, sophisticated cardiac and other surgery, *in vitro* fertilization and other reproductive technologies, magnetic resonance imaging and other advanced diagnostic tools are all very costly. The care of small premature babies, patients with AIDS, and elderly patients with chronic physical or mental disabilities is extremely expensive. We can no longer afford to pay for everything for everybody. Despite the varied and extensive health technology available nowadays, including a multitude of diagnostic and therapeutic modalities, not all needs can be met.

The allocation or rationing of scarce medical resources, however, is not always a problem of financial allocation. Immediate triage in a hospital emergency room or intensive care unit (ICU) may require decisions involving scarcity of personnel, instrumentation, machines, or specialized beds or equipment. The physician in an emergency room is faced with life-and-death decisions related to the emerging scarcity of ICU beds and/or dialysis machines. Which patient is to be admitted to the last available bed? Which patient is chosen to be dialysed if all cannot be dialysed? Who takes precedence over whom? May one remove a patient from a dialysis machine to dialyse another, more seriously ill patient? May one discharge a patient who needs ICU care from an ICU in order to make room for a more critically ill patient?

The classic talmudic source which discusses priorities (i.e., rationing) teaches that a man takes precedence over a woman in matters concerning the saving of life because he has more commandments to fulfill (Horayot 3:7). A woman takes precedence over a man in respect of clothing because her shame is greater if she must wear shabby clothing. A woman also takes precedence over a man in ransoming them from captivity because she may be raped by her captors. When both are exposed to immoral degradation, however, the man's ransom takes precedence as follows: if a man and his father and his teacher were kidnapped, his ransom takes precedence over his teacher, and his teacher takes precedence over his father, while his mother takes precedence over all of them. A scholar takes precedence over a king of Israel, for if a scholar dies there is no one to replace him, while if a king of Israel dies, all Israel are eligible for kingship. A king takes precedence over a high priest, and a high priest takes precedence over a prophet (Horayot 13a).

It seems from this talmudic discussion that Judaism considers religious status, personal dignity, social worth, and even inherited station in life as factors which determine priorities and precedences in the allocation of ransom money or other scarce resources. Yet such an approach is in direct contrast to the cardinal Jewish principle that one may not sacrifice one human life to save another human life (Sanhedrin 72b, Oholot 7:6). The reason, as cited in the Talmud, is that one person's blood is not redder than the blood of another (Pesachim 25b), indicating that all lives are of equal value. The infinite value of human life disallows the sacrificing of one life to save another, because all lives are of equal value. This rule implies that no qualitative distinctions should be made between people. But the Talmud passage cited above lists orders of precedences based on social worth, religious status, and personal dignity! How can these two approaches be reconciled?

A classic example of 'lifeboat ethics' is described in the Talmud (Baba Metzia 62a) in regard to two people traveling in the desert far from civilization, with only one having a canteen of water. If both drink the water, they will both die, but if only one drinks, he can reach civilization but the other will die. Ben Petura rules that it is better that both should drink and die rather than one behold his companion's death. But Rabbi Akiba rules that only the one who owns the canteen drinks, because the biblical verse *that thy brother may live with thee* (Leviticus 25:36) means that "thy life takes precedence over his life." Rabbi Akiba's reasoning seems to be self-evident. A person is obligated to save his fellow man's life if the latter is drowning or mauled by beasts or attacked by robbers (Sanhedrin 73a) [22]. If one fails to do so, one violates the biblical precept *Thou shalt not stand idly by the blood of thy neighbor.* This injunction is not applicable when one's own life would be endangered in the attempt to save one's fellow man. One's neighbor's life is secondary to one's own when both are at stake, because "his blood is no redder than yours." The final legal ruling in the case of the single canteen of water is in accordance with the opinion of Rabbi Akiba.

How are these classic biblical and talmudic sources applied to modern medical situations involving triage, the allocation of scarce medical resources, and rationing? Which patients should be seen, and in what order of priority in an emergency room or in a doctor's office? Rabbi Yitzchok Zilberstein supports the principle of "first come, first served," but allows for exceptions when waste of precious time and/or resources might otherwise result [23]. Patients should be seen in the order that they present themselves to the doctor or hospital. An orphan, widow, or seriously ill patient, however, may be seen out of order. Thus, social status at times may play a role. A patient who offers to pay more to be seen first should not be given preferential consideration purely for financial reasons.

Rabbi Moshe Feinstein was asked about two patients who needed a scarce medicine or treatment, the supply of which only sufficed for one patient [24]. Although the first patient would obtain palliation from the medicine, his life expectancy would remain short (*chayeh sha'ah*). The second patient might survive without the medicine, but if he received it he could look forward to extended survival (*chayeh olam*). Feinstein ruled that if neither patient had yet been prescribed the medicine, the choice was up to the physicians: whoever they judge has a better chance of recovery. However, if the treatment had been initiated on one of the two patients, it is forbidden to discontinue it and give it to the other patient. Once either patient receives the treatment, he now "owns" the treatment, and his life takes precedence over all others because his blood is no less red than that of the other person.

Rabbi Eliezer Waldenberg cites sources which rule that a potentially curable patient should be given a scarce medicine or treatment rather than a patient whose disease may be controlled but only temporarily [25]. Another case cited by Rabbi Waldenberg is that of a scarce medicine sufficient for only one of two patients. If one of the patients owns it, he may take it and try to save his life. If neither owns it, it should be given to the more critically ill patient. If both are critically ill and neither owns it, the medicine should be divided equally, because it will prolong both their lives for a while, and perhaps both can survive by divine intervention [25].

What is the Jewish approach when many patients arrive for care simultaneously and all cases are of equal medical urgency? There is no "first come, first served" principle to implement. Such a situation may be encountered in an emergency room or a hospital, or during an epidemic or on a battlefield. Which patient takes precedence over which other? Who is cared for first? Who receives the scarce medicine or treatment or ICU bed or dialysis machine or physician's attention? An outbreak of meningitis in Jerusalem occurred in 1948 when the supply of penicillin was extremely limited. Chief Rabbi Isaac Herzog inquired of Rabbi Feinstein about which children should receive the life-saving antibiotic. Feinstein instructed Herzog to treat the patients in the order they entered the ward. The reasoning for this ruling was based on the "first come, first served" principle modified to mean "first encountered, first served."

What happens if patients in an emergency room or clinic or doctor's office push themselves to the front of the line? Rabbi Feinstein objects to "crashing the line" because of the psychological trauma sustained by a patient waiting for a long time who sees another being cared for first [24]. The problem of prioritization thus applies not only to patients in mortal danger but also to situations in which two or more patients present simultaneously for medical care.

Several responses from the Holocaust literature deal with the allocation of scarce resources [26]. The most illustrative example deals with the question of whether a Jew may save his own life by causing the death of a fellow Jew. In September 1941, in the Kovno ghetto, the German commandant ordered the Jewish council of elders to distribute among the laborers 5,000 white permit cards to allow them and their families to remain in the ghetto. The remaining thousands of Jews were to be annihilated. Rabbi Oshry was asked whether the council of elders was allowed to obey the commandant's orders to distribute the cards. Every card given to a laborer automatically spelled a death sentence for another laborer. Could they choose one life over another? The second question posed to Rabbi Oshry was whether it was permissible for a Jew to grab a white card to save his life, for by doing so he was sending another Jew and his family to their death.

Rabbi Oshry ruled that it was the duty of the communal leaders to save as many people as possible by issuing the white cards. The council of elders had to take courage and distribute the cards in any way they saw fit to save as many people as possible. As to the second question, he stated that it would initially seem that no Jew is ever allowed to do anything that places another Jew's life in danger. Nevertheless, Rabbi Oshry ruled that according to the principle outlined in the answer to the first question, in a case of danger to a community one must save whoever can be saved. Therefore, each laborer was entitled to do whatever he could to save his life and the lives of his family.

Are the criteria used by society to ration services and to determine the allocation of scarce resources different from those used by individuals in the conduct of their private lives? Are the ethical standards different for society and for individuals? Rabbi Moshe Tendler states that "societal ethics are more than individual ethics. Whereas individual ethics must be taken into account in societal decisions, there is more to society than the individuals in it" [27].

Support for this position can be found in several classic Jewish sources. The Talmud states that captives should not be ransomed for more than their value to prevent abuses (Gittin 2:6). The reason for this decree is so that kidnappers should not be encouraged to seize more people and make excessive ransom demands and/or so as not to impoverish the community. If society had to pay large sums of money to ransom kidnap victims, that money could not be allocated to other pressing societal needs. The Talmud continues as follows: "Come and hear: Levi ben Darga ransomed his daughter for 13,000 dinari of gold" (Gittin 45a), which shows that an individual is allowed to pay exorbitant fees if he wishes, and the reason why society may not spend large sums of money to redeem captives is to protect the community. Thus it is clear that a man is allowed and perhaps obligated to ransom his wife or daughter for a very large amount of money. The Talmud's underlying point is that "no one can establish an ethical principle that compels society to pay any price to redeem a captive, and society can survive such an ethical decision to forego ransoming someone. . . . Here you see a clear distinction between a societal ethical decision and a private ethical decision. Society needs money for other expenditures" [27].

Summary and Conclusion

The attitude toward healing in Judaism has always been a positive one. A physician is obligated to heal and is given divine license to do so. A physician must be well trained and licensed in his or her discipline. Physicians must apply their skills for the benefit of the patient and be careful not to do harm. Thus, the ethical principles of beneficence and nonmaleficence are deeply rooted in Judaism. A patient is also obligated to seek healing, because one must be healthy in order to serve the Lord by doing His will in the service of mankind.

A second cardinal principle of Judaism is the infinite value of human life. The preservation of life takes precedence over all biblical and rabbinic commandments except three: idolatry, murder, and forbidden sexual relations, such as incest or adultery. The Talmud states that all lives are equal because one person's blood is not redder than that of another person.

Because of this principle, one may not sacrifice one life to save another life. Furthermore, asserts the Talmud, he who saves one life is as if he saved an entire world. Thus, because of the equal and infinite value of all human beings, Judaism supports equal access and universal access to healthcare and other social services as a matter of justice.

Classic Jewish sources deal with the situation in which resources are insufficient to satisfy all essential needs and difficult decisions about allocations have to be made. The Talmud describes the case of two people in a desert with only one pitcher of water; the ruling here clearly indicates that there is no distinction between people and that everyone is of equal value. Elsewhere, however, the Talmud considers religious status, personal dignity, and social worth as determining factors in the allocation of limited financial resources. For example, in ransoming captives, a woman takes precedence over a man because her captors may seduce or rape her. In order to prevent this violation of her dignity, she must be ransomed first. In saving a drowning victim, a scholar takes precedence over an ignoramus because he is difficult to replace. In the distribution of synagogue honors, a priest takes precedence over a Levite, who in turn takes precedence over an Israelite. How does one reconcile the talmudic listing of priorities based on social worth, religious status, and personal dignity with the concept that all lives are equal and there is no distinction between people?

The answer is that in Judaism societal ethical standards differ from those to be used by individuals in the allocation of scarce financial, medical, or other resources. Society may not expend an inordinate amount of its limited resources to redeem captives, although a rich man may pay his entire fortune to ransom his close relative. Clearly, a distinction is made in Judaism between societal ethics and individual ethics.

An individual physician must treat all patients equally, usually on a "first come, first served" basis. The physician must do whatever is necessary to care for the patient, irrespective of cost. The physician should not be involved in rationing at the bedside. The physician's only concern should be the "here and now" of a patient. Society, however, must be concerned about long-term planning and future generations, and can, therefore, make decisions based on considerations of cost or social status. Hence, governmental spending caps are consistent with Judaic teaching.

Preventive medicine is a centerpiece of the Jewish system. The Jewish view toward the practice of medicine emphasizes prevention over treatment. Prevention of danger and thereby the preservation of life and health are biblical mandates. One must observe rules of personal hygiene such as handwashing before eating; dieting, exercise, sex, and bodily functions must all be properly tended to.

Preventive medical services and patient responsibilities also represent cornerstones of managed care. Such an approach is fully consonant with Judaism. Thus, emphasis on prevention of illness, universal access, and universal provision of care, as well as personal responsibility, are deeply rooted in Judaic teaching and tradition.

Specifically in regard to health maintenance organizations, Judaism supports the goals of giving care to everybody, cost containment, and reduction of excessive and sometimes unnecessary diagnostic and therapeutic interventions to allow for more appropriate care and preventive measures and personal health. However, Judaism objects to limitations on the indicated use of the best available technology and to any administrative directives that undermine the physician's ability to properly care for patients. Judaism considers immoral the postponement of necessary acute care, premature hospital discharge, and overzealous gatekeeping regulations. Judaism views as illegal the sacrificing of patient care on the altar of cost containment.

Returning to society's obligations to provide health care for all its citizens, society must also be concerned about future generations and long-term planning. Society must be concerned about the long-term effects of its actions. This is not so for individuals. The doctor in the ICU must make decisions that affect individual patients here and now. The two individuals in the desert with a single pitcher of water have to be concerned with preserving their lives here and now; maybe they will be rescued tomorrow. The allocation of a medicine or treatment to one of two patients if there is not enough for both is a decision needed for the "here and now" care of one or both patients. An individual researcher using radioisotopes is concerned with the immediate safety from radiation of himself and his co-workers. But society has to be concerned with the disposal of nuclear wastes because of the danger to future generations of the radioisotopes used today.

One cannot, however, totally divorce individuals from responsibility to consider future generations in the allocation of resources. Perhaps this point is most beautifully depicted in the talmudic story of the righteous man called Choni who was journeying on the road and saw a man planting a carob tree (Taanit 23a). He asked him, "How long does it take for this tree to bear fruit?" The man replied, "Seventy years." Choni then further asked him, "Are you certain that you will be here another seventy years?" The man replied, "I found ready-grown carob trees in the world; as my fore-fathers planted those for me, so I, too, plant these for my children."

The responsibility of government includes concern for the future, for generations not yet born. In this respect, there is no difference between now and later; they are one and the same. Society differs from the individual in the time scale that it uses for decisions. An individual responds to the problem at hand. Society has a long-term view. Society must deal with its own survival. When society must choose, it must take the future into account as if it were the present. The allocation of public funds has always been and is likely always to be political. Society can and must decide how to allocate its healthcare dollars. Let us hope that it will do so wisely.

24

Therapeutic Efficacy of Laughter in Medicine

Introduction

The Bible states that *A merry heart does good like a medicine* (Proverbs 17:22) and *makes a cheerful countenance* (ibid. 15:13). The Talmud (Berachot 61b) suggests that the spleen produces laughter [1]. In the past two thousand years, humor and laughter have been used therapeutically in a variety of medical and other situations. Randomized controlled clinical trials have not been conducted validating the therapeutic efficacy of laughter. However, benefits have been reported in geriatrics [2], oncology [3–5], critical care [6], psychiatry [7, 8], rehabilitation [9], rheumatology [10], home care [11], palliative care [12], hospice care [13], terminal care [14], and general patient care [15].

Physiology of Laughter

Humor, mirth, and laughter have numerous physiologic effects involving the muscular, respiratory, cardiovascular, endocrine, immune, and central nervous systems [16]. The heart and respiratory rates increase, and the exchange of residual air accelerates, thereby enhancing blood oxygen levels and increasing tissue oxygenation. The body's immune system, including phagocytosis, is improved, thereby helping the body fight infection [17]. Increased catecholamine levels may improve mental function, interpersonal responsiveness, alertness, and memory [16]. Side-effects from laughter are few, but an occasional patient may develop syncope and monocular blindness following hysterical laughter [18].

181

Laughter and Humor in Treating Illness

In addition to physiological benefits, laughter also provides communicative, psychological, and spiritual benefits [12]. Laughter is important in medicine and may enhance conversation between physician and patient. The ability to laugh with a patient is a sign of good rapport. Mutual understanding between patient and doctor when they smile at each other may be more important than the diagnosis or formal treatment [19].

Laughter may help to control pain by distracting attention, reducing tension, changing expectations, and increasing the production of endogenous endorphins [20]. One famous hospitalized patient with ankylosing spondylitis claims that 10 minutes of laughter gave him hours of pain-free sleep [10]. Laughter does not cure any illness but is a coping mechanism for people under stress. Laughter reduces stress, tension, and pain. It is a form of emotional support for patients. Laughter improves the quality of life and helps ill nursing home and rehabilitation center residents recover from illness [21].

The depressed and elderly suicidal can benefit from therapeutic humor by "reviving and awakening their merry hearts" [22]. Humor and laughter may be of particular use in patient education, such as hemodialysis teaching sessions, where patients learn to come to terms with their illness. Humor injected into the teaching sessions may also relieve pressure from the patients' relatives, friends, and colleagues as well as from their healthcare providers [15].

Humor to Reduce Caregivers' Stress

Caregivers, including doctors and nurses, are not immune from the stresses and tensions of caring for seriously or critically ill patients. Laughter and humor facilitate nursing interventions in a variety of clinical settings and may ease the mind and divert attention to pleasant thoughts by both patient and nurse [4]. Introducing the joy of laughter into the high-stress, high-demand work environment of a hospital, especially the operating room (OR) or intensive care unit (ICU), can increase the creativity, productivity, motivation, and morale of nurses working in such locations [23]. Laughter and humor can successfully combat the stress and pressure of the perioperative environment [24]. The use of humor in critical care nursing serves not only as a coping strategy for combating job-related stress for the practitioner but also as a useful and beneficial therapeutic intervention for patients and families. Humor may serve as a "release valve" for ICU team members and facilitate cohesion, relaxation, and more productive work relationships among the ICU nurses [6].

Another area of high stress for doctors and nurses is the emergency department. In such a setting, humor and laughter serve as "the body's instinctive, cognitive, and biologic mechanism for restoring homeostasis and equilibrium" [25]. Laughter restores balance and equilibrium. It dissipates tension, fear, frustration, and other stress, such as "burnout," perhaps by producing biochemical changes in the body, such as decreases in serum growth hormone, cortisol, dopac, and epinephrine levels [26]. Doctors and nurses are increasingly recognizing the importance of humor in reducing stress and promoting feelings of well-being in both patients and themselves as caregivers. Laughter is an often-neglected resource in managing personal and professional stress.

Conclusion

Humor and laughter can be therapeutic for both patient and caregiver. They reduce pain and stress, enhance hope, relieve tension, and stimulate the immune system [27]. Facilitating patients' and families' laughter is an important skill in providing emotional support, which is central to the therapeutic role of caregivers [28]. Laughter provides emotional and physiological benefits to patients and caregivers alike [29].

On a cautionary note, as with any other therapeutic intervention, "there are indications for, limits to, and contraindications for the use of humor" [3]. Like any other skill, the effective use of humor needs to be learned, practiced, and developed as a medical and nursing strategy [30].

However, when properly used and indicated, humor therapy promotes beneficial physiological changes and an overall sense of well-being. It may relieve illness-associated stress. It also serves as "a natural healing component for caregivers" [29] and helps them cope with the stress of their occupation. Humor does not make problems disappear, but it makes them easier to bear [24]. Humor and laughter are good for the body and good for the spirit. The following seems to be good advice for patients and caregivers alike: "Laugh regularly, smile often, and help others to laugh and smile" [11]. In this era of complementary therapies, it seems appropriate that humor and laughter take their place of honor as a supplementary form of the treatment of illness, together with prayer [31] and chicken soup [32].

25

Allocation or Misallocation of Limited Medical Resources

Although America is the richest country in the world and the only superpower, there is not enough money to pay for everything for everybody. The term "allocation of limited medical resources" is really a euphemism for rationing, a word nobody wants to hear. Certain forms of rationing are already in effect in this country. The state of Oregon decided several years ago, with federal government approval, to use its healthcare financial resources to pay primarily for very common medical and surgical conditions that affect the vast majority of the population. Oregon will not pay for very expensive procedures that benefit only a few patients, such as heart, lung, or liver transplants. In New York State, medicaid patients are only entitled to see a clinic physician a certain number of times per year and are restricted to a limited number of visits to a dental clinic. There are millions of Americans who are underinsured or not insured for healthcare coverage, some by choice ("it is too expensive," "I may not need it"), some not by choice (unemployed, lost their job, etc.). The federal government and Congress are now debating expanded healthcare coverage, especially for children who are now uninsured or underinsured and prescription drug coverage for the elderly. All options cannot be implemented because of the enormous cost and the effects these programs may have on the rest of the economy, including the looming budget deficit.

The classic example of the allocation of scarce resources is the issue of hemodialysis, which was first developed and implemented in Seattle, Washington, in about 1950. A single dialysis machine was available, and a committee was appointed to decide which patients would have access to it and which would not. The committee was called the death committee because whoever was not chosen to be dialyzed would certainly die of renal failure. Nowadays, the shortage of dialysis machines has been markedly alleviated and the government pays for most dialysis services under its medicare program.

The problem of limited or scarce medical resources is not limited to money or dialysis machines. At times there are critical shortages of people or medical personnel, such as nurses, technicians, and other healthcare personnel. Many areas of this country have a shortage of practicing obstetricians/gynecologists because of the high price of malpractice insurance forcing some of them to limit their practice or to give it up altogether.

Another example of limited medical resources is intensive care beds for the critically ill. If an ICU admitting resident has one free ICU bed and receives a call from the emergency room that two patients require an ICU bed, a gastrointestinal bleeder in shock and a terminal cancer patient with gram-negative sepsis, the resident will probably decide in favor of donating the bed to the GI bleeder, who has a curable, reversible, and treatable condition. But if the emergency room has a GI bleeder in shock and an acute myocardial infarction patient in shock, and each needs an ICU bed, how does the ICU resident make the decision? Both patients have potentially treatable, reversible, curable conditions. Which patient gets the single available ICU bed? Here the limited or scarce medical resource is the ICU bed.

Even more difficult is the situation where there are no available ICU beds at all. How does the ICU resident decide which patient to discharge from the ICU or move to a regular medical unit? What criteria are equitable, fair, moral, and ethically and medically defensible?

Thus, it is clear that limited or scarce medical resources requiring rationing decisions can involve shortages of equipment, personnel, beds, or other essential hospital assets.

In the classic case of hemodialysis, nephrologists have traditionally selected who gets dialyzed and who does not by a two-stage process. If 20 patients need dialysis and only three machines are available, some patients are often excluded on the basis of age, sex, race, medical condition, ability to pay, and other exclusionary reasons, all of which are of questionable morality. If 10 of the 20 patients have thus been excluded, the nephrologist will then select from the remaining pool of patients depending on their family status (e.g., a woman with six children vs. a bachelor), contribution to society (e.g., a college professor vs. an alcoholic drug addict), or other selection criteria, all of which are just as dubiously unethical as the exclusionary criteria. The decision is often made on purely medical grounds (i.e., the patient with the best chance of success from the dialysis). The only totally equitable way of decision-making is the first-come, first-served principle, which unfortunately is not always followed for a variety of social, medical, administrative, and financial reasons.

Another example of the possible unethical or misallocation of limited resources is the issue of organ transplantation. With the tremendous worldwide shortage of organ donors, thousands of needy recipients die of organ failure for lack of a suitable donor. The reasons for the organ donor shortage and proposed remedies are beyond the scope of this brief discussion, because organ transplantation is a large subject requiring a lengthy treatise. However, in view of the shortage, how are allocation decisions made when an organ becomes available? Who should receive it of all the needy waiting recipients?

For certain organs, arguments can be made to withhold organs from patients who brought their disease and organ failure upon themselves. Should we give a liver transplant to an alcoholic with end-stage liver failure form years of alcohol abuse? Or should the liver be given to a patient with end-stage liver disease or liver cancer from hepatitis virus B or C through no fault of the patient? Should we transplant lungs into patients who developed lung cancer from years of smoking or reserve the lungs for cystic fibrosis patients who have end-stage lung failure through no fault of their own? These are moral and social policy questions that require an extensive dialogue both pro and con. Some guidelines from a special donor organ committee may be useful to guide social policy and perhaps legislation in this very sensitive and emotional topic.

All the aforementioned issues are referred to as microallocation decisions: The nephrologist decides who gets dialyzed and who does not. The ICU resident decides who gets the last ICU bed. The oncologist decides which patient will receive the experimental drug if there is not enough for all the patients who need it. How can these limited resources be enhanced? A departmental director or hospital administrator must decide whether to buy more dialysis machines, hire more nurses, build more ICU beds, or buy more experimental medicine for oncology patients.

Macroallocation decisions are those made by governmental agencies. Once the health budgetary allocations are made for a given fiscal year, the government must decide how to allocate that budget. Should it pay for drugs for senior citizens? Should it operate and fund more diabetes and hypertension screening programs? Should it provide more spaces for substance-abuse patients who wish to become detoxified and give up their evil habit? One might argue that for the price of one B-1 bomber, the government could buy enough hemodialysis machines to satisfy the needs of all patients who require hemodialysis. Such an argument is indeed naive because the government must also provide funds for education, highways, museums, parks, and other social needs.

Furthermore, how are macroallocation decisions made by the government once the health budget has been allocated? Should more well-baby clinics be built and operated? Should more women's health centers be created? How about men's health centers? Who decides? Are physicians and patients consulted? How are decisions made? Are they appropriate in the allocation of limited medical resources including money, people, technology and medical programs? Is the government misallocating some or most of the health budget dollars? How does one decide? What criteria should be used?

Summary and Conclusions

The allocation of scarce or limited resources, medical or otherwise, is a complicated, multifaceted issue associated with many moral and ethical dilemmas. Many systems have been proposed to equitably distribute finite medical resources and to make allocation decisions that are consonant with basic principles of ethics. None are perfect. The criteria used by an individual physician at the bedside or by a department director or hospital administrator may differ from the macroallocation decisions made by large institutions or governmental bodies (federal, state, and local).

Epilogue

Very small premature babies are now kept in neonatal intensive care units for many months to give them a chance at near-normal life but at a cost of up to a million dollars. Is that a proper allocation of our finite medical resources (personnel, equipment, supplies, and other necessities) for premies? Or is such action a misallocation of these resources? Both sides of the argument have positive and negative merit. A final philosophical statement is that every human being created in the image of God has supreme value. It is the obligation of fellow human beings and of society in general to preserve and dignify human life and to care for the total needs of individual citizens to enable them to be healthy and productive members of society. This general principle should help individual physicians to make proper microallocation life-and-death decisions for individual patients and to assist governmental bodies responsible for making macroallocation decisions concerning the short- and long-term needs and priorities of the population as a whole. All such decisions should be guided by the basic ethical principles of beneficence, nonmaleficence, autonomy, and justice.

However, these principles may at times conflict. For example, if the autonomous rights of the patient conflict with the justice appeals of the community, or if beneficence to an individual patient conflicts with the needs of another patient. Can we deny healthcare services or not? By what criteria? (Merit, potential, effort, achievement, age?) These are difficult if not impossible questions to answer, but they pertain to the topic of this commentary on the allocation of limited medical resources, which is meant to raise the sensitivity of the reader to the complexity of the problem and to raise ethical questions that are not easily answered or dealt with.

26

Are the Courts Practicing Medicine?

One author writes that many observers are of the opinion that medicine's aims are for doctors and patients to decide without interference from the state [1]. However, continues the author, government restrictions on the role of medicine are often bitterly disputed, and many reach the U.S. Supreme Court. Abortion, assisted suicide, and rationing of care are among the clinical issues the court has considered, the author points out. The author concludes that in general the court's deference to medical authority often raises disputes among the justices themselves [1].

The influence on medicine and health of the Rehnquist Supreme Court between 1996 and 2005 is discussed by Gostin [2]. Gostin discusses the court's decisions on reproductive rights such as abortion, and on privacy including medical testing and treatment; its tendency to federalism in safety regulation and health insurance; and the future of Supreme Court jurisprudence. The author concludes that the Supreme Court's resolution to federalism may subside with the retirement of Justice O'Connor, its most committed federalist.

William J. Curran reviews court-ordered cesarean sections and discusses several specific cases where the courts intervened. Annas discusses the subject of court-ordered separation of conjoined twins and presents in detail the ramifications in a specific British case of twins Marie and Jodie. He analyzes very precisely the various opinions of the three justices who decided the case [4].

In the opinion of this writer, it seems appropriate for courts to intervene by ordering a transfusion to save the life of a child of

Jehovah's Witnesses. It also seems appropriate for the courts to order observed treatment of patients with tuberculosis or AIDS who refuse to comply with their prescribed medication regimen. I also support court-ordered involuntary commitment to a psychiatric facility when appropriate and indicated to protect the patient and others. I obviously support court-ordered involuntary confinement to a corrections facility for a convicted criminal.

I am certainly doubtful about the appropriateness of all the court-ordered caesarian sections described in the literature to save the baby's life [3]. I also question the appropriateness of the court-ordered separation of the twins Jodie and Marie against the parents' expressed objections, as well as court-ordered separation of other conjoined twins [4]. As a hematologist, I also object to the court-ordered nontreatment of Mr. Saikowicz, who suffered from acute myelocytic leukemia, some years ago in Massachusetts.

In conclusion, there are situations in which court-ordered surgical or medical interventions or noninterventions are medically and morally appropriate. In other situations, such court-ordered decisions are either doubtful or inappropriate. This issue is a very sensitive one and requires continuing dialogue. Perhaps this commentary editorial will stimulate such dialogue.

27

Smoking, Lung Cancer, and the Tobacco Industry: Ethical Considerations

Tobacco use is the largest avoidable cause of illness and death in the United States, responsible for about one in five of all American deaths annually. When people stop smoking permanently, even after years of smoking, the risks are immediately reduced and continue to decrease in the subsequent years of absence.

Williams, Gagne, Ryan, and Deci have proposed an autonomy model to facilitate motivation for smoking cessation. Their model indicates that the autonomy supportive intervention predicts smoking cessation and is an efficacious intervention. When the first Surgeon General's Report on Smoking and Health was released in 1964, smoking was largely viewed as a problem of men's health—so many men were dying from lung cancer and associated diseases that scientists debated whether the lower numbers of female smokers were resistant to the tobacco scourge. But now tobacco use has taken its place as a serious health threat for women and is viewed as a contemporary epidemic in women in the United States and many other countries. Lung cancer incidence has dipped in men but not in women. The risk of tobacco use in women is not disputed. Tobacco has killed 62 million people since the Second World War and will be responsible for the deaths of a further 100 million over the next 20 years. Faced with a disaster of this scale, one may legitimately raise questions about the responsibility of the tobacco industry, which, protected by battalions of lawyers, has remained unvanquished for 40 years.

We can do that in our attitudes about strong national legislation, in our discussions with patients, and in offering support by ourselves and our organizations for an international treaty, The Framework Convention on Tobacco Control (FCTC), which governments are now negotiating is being facilitated by the World Health Organization.

This essay reviews the ethical issues involved in smoking, lung cancer, and the tobacco industry.

Ethical Considerations

The unethical behavior of the tobacco companies in encouraging people to smoke and to remain smokers, and their conflicts of interest and cooperative efforts with the pharmaceutical and other industries are well known. Some writers strongly encourage authors to disclose financial ties with the tobacco industry and question the adequacy of current policies regarding competing interest disclosures and the acceptability of tobacco industry funding for academic research. Smoking is deleterious to health, and the tobacco industry manipulates nicotine, targets children, and buys scientists.

There is no better example of lying by a whole industry, of hypocrisy and a boundless search for profit leading to the greatest global disaster of all time. The Philip Morris Tobacco Company promised "to shut down instantly" if cigarettes were found to be harmful. Now that the company has admitted that "smoking causes lung cancer, heart disease, emphysema, and other serious diseases," when will it keep its promise to stop making cigarettes? After all, a promise is a promise.

The tobacco industry is notorious for its attempts to influence the public health sector. An analysis of millions of industry documents reveals just how successful companies were in enlisting top health experts in tobacco-friendly studies—a tactic that many believe is responsible for the lax antismoking laws. Universities should stay away from the tobacco industry. Dentists who use tobacco may be asked by their patients, "Doc, if you can't stop smoking, why should I?"

This is a real ethical dilemma. Another ethical issue is the effect of the work environment and heavy smoking on the social inequalities in smoking cessation. A large proportion of the social differences in smoking cessation could be explained by differences in work-environment exposures to heavy smoking. Tobacco industry responses to research linking smoking to carcinogenic mutations mirror prior industry efforts to challenge the science linking smoking and lung cancer. The extent of tobacco industry involvement in tumor-suppressor gene research and the potential conflict of interest are such that there is a need for consistent standards for the disclosure and evaluation of such potential conflicts in biomedical research.

Summary and Conclusions

Tobacco consumption is one of the world's greatest preventable health problems. According to the World Health Organization, 1.1 billion people worldwide are addicted to nicotine, with tobacco causing an estimated 4 million premature deaths every year. Smoking-cessation programs of various types, including nicotine replacement, counseling, pharmacotherapy, and others, have met with only partial success. The development of a nicotine-conjugate vaccine suggests that immunization may hold promise for a future therapeutic and preventive strategy for tobacco smoking and nicotine addiction. The adverse effects of smoking include lung cancer, head and neck cancer, bladder and kidney cancer, coronary artery disease and chronic obstructive pulmonary disease (COPD). In the latter case, we can prevent or forestall progress to advanced COPD by considering the following advice: Test your lungs, know your numbers, stay healthy, and enjoy life in a smoke-free environment. The tobacco industry's unethical behavior in encouraging smoking among young and old and its conflicts of interest and other unethical behavior are well known.

Smoking-cessation programs, even those funded by the tobacco industry, are in direct competition with the industry's goal of selling cigarettes. It is therefore recommended that counter-marketing efforts need to be carried out with young and adult smokers. Both groups must be made aware of the benefits of behavioral and pharmacological assistance that can help them quit. Graphic warning labels should replace the ineffective test-based warnings now required on cigarette packs.

Tobacco use is now a serious health threat not only for men but also for women. It is now seen as a contemporary epidemic in women in the United States and many other countries. One can conclude from all the discussion on smoking and lung cancer, the tobacco industry, and ethical considerations that smokers world-wide need professional smoking-cessation support combined with a broad tobacco-control strategy to restrict all tobacco products.

In conclusion, this essay was written in an attempt to stimulate a dialogue on smoking and its adverse effects, smoking-cessation programs, and the ethics of the tobacco industry in promoting its goal of selling cigarettes and sponsoring research and smoking-cessation programs favorable to its financial interests, irrespective of possible conflicts of interest. Let the tobacco companies note that ethics tells us to do well, to do no harm, and to consider the norms of justice, equity, and respect for autonomy and for one's fellow citizens.

Epilogue

In addition to the ethical questions raised in this essay concerning the tobacco industry, there are ethical questions which relate to patients with lung cancer, their physicians, and society in general. Doesn't the patient bear some responsibility for bringing the lung cancer upon himself knowing full well the dangers of smoking? Are physicians obligated to care for patients who are mostly responsible for their own diseases, such as lung cancer from smoking, HIV from drug abuse or homosexual behavior, or other sexually transmitted diseases from promiscuous sexual behavior? The answer, of course, is that physicians are obligated to treat all patients who seek their care. Is society obligated to provide lung transplants for smokers with lung cancer who are partly or fully responsible for their disease? Shouldn't society save such a scarce resource for patients who have end-stage lung disease through no fault of their own, such as patients with cystic fibrosis? These ethical questions involve patient responsibility and obligations, physicians' professional and moral obligations, society's allocation of its limited financial and medical resources, including organs for transplantation, and similar moral, ethical, and philosophical questions of justice, beneficence, nonmaleficience, and equity. The topic is complex, and definitive answers are not easy to come by, but dialogue about these questions is necessary to clarify and perhaps resolve the issues.

28

Bioterrorism: Are We Prepared?

The attacks of September 11, 2001 with the murder of three thousand innocent people changed America's concepts of vulnerability. Physician involvement focused primarily on public health and medical issues related to bioterrorism defense, such as vaccination against smallpox and recognition of inhalation anthrax [1]. The recently published *Encyclopedia of Bioterrorism Defense* [2] provides a discussion of the medical literature that supports the emerging discipline of bioterrorism defense. The encyclopedia is "an information bank, organized alphabetically by topic" [l].

The editors of the encyclopedia recognize the need for the public to have accurate information and therefore provide facts about the aerosol type of microorganism delivery as well as methods to develop protective equipment, vaccines, and detectors. Medical topics such as anthrax, influenza, and ricin, among others, are discussed in separate chapters devoted to these topics. The book reviewer states that the 120 nonmedical topics discussed in the encyclopedia fall into four themes, two of which are descriptions of terrorist organizations such as Hamas and Hizbollah, and discussions of technical terms, such as aerosol and biological stimulant [1].

Relman cites examples of bioterrorism which have caused fear and near-panic among Americans and others. These examples include the potential poisoning of the milk or other food supply with botulinum toxin, the dissemination of smallpox by self-infected terrorists, and the massive release of aerosolized anthrax spores in the subway [3]. He points out that government concern about bioterrorism has led to new federal restrictions on the handling of infectious agents. He also asserts that the logic behind biowarfare programs in the past should not guide future misuses of the life sciences, because the former can be misleading. As science and technology advance, the number of worrisome bioterrorism agents is greatly expanding, argues Relman [3]. Furthermore, the improved packaging, manipulation, and delivery of virulent organisms make the threat of bioterrorism even greater. We should also not underestimate the amount of harm that these bioterrorism agents can inflict on the population [3].

Lo and Katz point out that recent public health emergencies involving anthrax, severe acute respiratory syndrome (SARS), and shortages of influenza vaccine dramatized the need for restrictive public health measures, such as quarantine, isolation, and rationing [4]. These authors then discuss the ethical dilemmas that front-line physicians may face during public health emergencies such as a bioterrorism attack. The physician's primary responsibility during such emergencies, they maintain, is to the public rather than to the individual patient. However, physicians will still need to address the patients' needs and concerns, recognize their changed roles, and work closely with public health officials [4].

Kennedy and Klafter discuss in detail the case of an engineering student who works with explosives and says that he plans to rid the world of nonbelievers. The patient suffers delusions but repeatedly refuses psychiatric treatment [5]. The authors discuss the outcome of this case in that the student was granted a medical leave and placed on academic probation for two months, during which time he returned to his native country to be with his parents. The faculty later dismissed the student from the engineering program, citing poor academic and laboratory performance. The authors conclude the story by saying that his visa expired and renewal was contingent on his enrollment in a full-time academic program [5].

Steinbrook discusses in detail Bio-safety level 4 laboratories where dangerous and exotic agents are studied that cannot be safely studied in other laboratories. These agents include bacteria and viruses that may cause fatal diseases if used as part of a bioterrorism attack [6].

Okie points out that the war on terror has generated ethical and legal dilemmas [7], including the use of aggressive interrogation methods, even bordering on torture. Torture has been absolutely condemned and prohibited by the Bush administration [8]. In a special supplement to the American College of Physicians publication *ACP Observer*, the ACP warns physicians not to wait for confirmation of their suspicions with laboratory findings before reporting a suspected bioterrorism attack. The ACP also issued a guide to chemical terrorism identification and provides the telephone number of the federal Emergency Technical Assistance Chemical and Biological Hotline which is available 24/7. The number is 800-424-8802.

In summary and conclusion, bioterrorism is an ever present threat and danger to the United States and other countries. Preparedness with specific emergency plans should include instructions for first responders, availability of protective equipment, medications, vaccines, and other needed supplies, personnel, and technical assistance. The danger of a bioterrorism attack should not be minimized, because of its potential lethal effects. Medical and public health officials need to be fully informed and educated about the topic of bioterrorism in order to respond promptly, properly, and accurately to an emergency situation if it should occur.

References

Introduction

1. Muntner, S. "Medicine." *Encyclopaedia Judaica*, Jerusalem: Keter, 1971. Vol. 11, cols. 1178–1195.
2. Glick, S. Foreword to *Pioneers in Jewish Medical Ethics* (ed. F. Rosner), Northvale, NJ: Jason Aronson, 1997, pp. xv–xxi.
3. Jakobovits, I. *Jewish Medical Ethics: A Comparative and Historical Study of the Jewish Religious Attitude to Medicine and Its Practice*, New York: Philosophical Library, 1959, p. viii.
4. Rosner, F. Jewish medical ethics. *Journal of Clinical Ethics*, 1995; 6:202–217.
5. Karo, J. *Shulchan Aruch*, Yoreh Deah 336.
6. Fruchter, J. Doctors on trial: A comparison of American and Jewish legal approaches to medical malpractice. *American Journal of Law and Medicine*, 1993; 19:453–495.
7. Rosner, F., and Widroff, J. Physicians' fees in Jewish law. *Jewish Law Annual*, 1997; 12:115–126.
8. Maimonides, M. *Mishneh Torah*, Deot 4:1 ff.
9. Rosner, F. Moses Maimonides and preventive medicine. *Journal of the History of Medicine* 1998, 51:313–324.
10. Jakobovits, I. *The Timely and the Timeless: Jews, Judaism and Society in a Storm-Tossed Decade*, 1989, New York: Bloch, p. 128.
11. Cohen, A.S. On maintaining a professional confidence. *Journal of Halacha and Contemporary Society*, 1984, 7:73–87.
12. Tendler, M.D. Confidentiality: A biblical perspective on rights in conflict. *National Jewish Law Review*, 1989; 4:1–7.

13. Bleich, J.D. Genetic screening. *Tradition,* 2000; 34: 63–87.
14. Bleich, J.D. Rabbinic confidentiality. *Tradition,* 1999; 33:54–87.
15. Steinberg, A. *Encyclopedia of Jewish Medical Ethics (Encyclopedia Talmudit Refuit).* Jerusalem: Schlesinger Institute of the Shaare Zedek Medical Center. Vol. 4, 1994; pp. 613–642.
16. Jakobovits, I. Future trends and currents in Jewish medical ethics. In *Pioneers in Jewish Medical Ethics* (ed. F. Rosner). Northvale, NJ: Jason Aronson, 1997, pp. 231–234.
17. Jakobovits, I. Personal communication. February 23, 1999.

Chapter 1

1. Haan, E.A. Screening for carriers of genetic disease: Points to consider. *Medical Journal of Australia,* 1993; 158:419–421.
2. Council on Ethical and Judicial Affairs, American Medical Association. Ethical issues related to prenatal genetic testing. *Archives of Family Medicine,* 1994; 3:633–642.
3. Council on Ethical and Judicial Affairs. Use of genetic testing by employers. *Journal of the American Medical Association,* 1991; 266:1827–1830.
4. Council on Ethical and Judicial Affairs. Physician participation in genetic testing by health insurance companies. *Reports of the Council on Ethical and Judicial Affairs.* Chicago: American Medical Association 1993; 4(2):174–182.
5. Council on Ethical and Judicial Affairs. Ethical issues in carrier screening of cystic fibrosis and other genetic disorders. *Reports of the Council on Ethical and Judicial Affairs.* Chicago: American Medical Association 1991; 2(2):89–106.
6. Wertz, D.C., Fanos, J.H., and Reilly, P.R. Genetic testing of children and adolescents. Who decides? *Journal of the American Medical Association,* 1994; 272:875–881.
7. Hoffmann, D.E., and Wulfsberg, E.A. Testing children for genetic predispositions; Is it in their best interest? *Journal of Law, Medicine, and Ethics,* 1995; 23:331–344.
8. Struewing, J.P., Abeliovich, D., Peretz, T., et al. The carrier frequency of the *BRCA1* 185delAG mutation is approximately 1 percent in Ashkenazi Jewish individuals. *Nat Genet,* 1995; 11:198–200.
9. FitzGerald, M.G., MacDonald, D.J., Krainer, M., et al. Germ-line *BRCA1* mutations in Jewish and non-Jewish women with early onset breast cancer. *New England Journal of Medicine,* 1996; 334:143–149.

10. Offit, K., Gilewski, T., McGuire, P., et al. Germline *BRCA1* 185delAG mutations in Jewish women with breast cancer. *Lancet*, 1996; 347:1643–1645.
11. Parens, E. Glad and terrified: On the ethics of *BRCA1* and 2 testing. *Cancer Investigation*, 1996; 14:405–411.
12. American Society of Clinical Oncology. Genetic testing for cancer susceptibility. *Journal of Clinical Oncology*, 1996; 14:1730–1736.
13. Collins, F.S. *BRCA1*—lots of mutations, lots of dilemmas. *New England Journal of Medicine*, 1996; 334:186–188.
14. Hubbard, R., and Lewontin, R.C. Pitfalls of genetic testing. *New England Journal of Medicine*, 1996; 334:1192–1194.
15. Lerman, C., and Croyle R. Psychological issues in genetic testing for breast cancer susceptibility. *Annals of Internal Medicine*, 1994; 154:609–616.
16. Weber, B. Breast cancer susceptibility genes: Current challenges and future promises. *Annals of Internal Medicine*, 1996; 124:1088–1090.
17. Flicks, Y. Heredity and environment: Genetics in Jacob's handling of Laban's flock. *Techumin*, 1982; 3:461–472.
18. Rosner, F. *Medicine in the Bible and the Talmud:* 2nd augmented ed. Hoboken, NJ: Ktav and Yeshiva University Press; 1995, pp. 43–49.
19. Jakobovits, I. *Jewish Medical Ethics*. New York: Bloch; 1975, pp. 155–156 and 261–266.
20. Glickman, I. Concerning marriages among relatives permitted according to the Torah. *Noam*, 1969; 12:369–382.
21. Chafuta, A. Concerning the law of consanguineous marriages and [the principle that rules about] danger to life are stricter [than ritual laws]. *Noam*, 1970; 13:83–103.
22. Jung, L. Marriages among relatives. Noam, 1969; 12:314–316.
23. Slonim, Z.D. Concerning marriages among relatives. *Noam*, 1969; 12:317–321.
24. Yisraeli, S. Marriage in a case of serious [genetic] illnesses in the families. *Amud Hayemini*; 1966, 33:311–317.
25. Hershler, M. Genetic engineering in Jewish law. *Halachah Urefuah*, 1981; 2:350–353.
26. Rosner, F. *Maimonides' Introduction to His Commentary on the Mishnah*, Northvale, NJ: Jason Aronson; 1995.
27. Rosner, F. *Modern Medicine and Jewish Ethics*. 2nd ed. Hoboken, NJ, and New York: Ktav and Yeshiva University Press; 1991. pp. 253–369.

28. Feinstein, M. *Responsa Iggrot Moshe,* Even Haezer 4:10. Bnei Brak, 1985.
29. Feinstein, M. Testing to determine the health of a fetus and the prohibition of abortion for Tay-Sachs disease. *Halachah Urefuah* 1980; 1:304–306.
30. Bleich, J.D. *Contemporary Halakhic Problems.* New York: Ktav; 1977, pp. 109–115.
31. Broide, E., Zeigler, M., Eckstein, J., and Bach, G. Screening for carriers of Tay-Sachs disease in the ultra-Orthodox Ashkenazi Jewish community in Israel. *American Journal of Human Genetics* 1993; 47:213–215.
32. Rosner, F. *Modern Medicine and Jewish Ethics.* 2nd ed. Hoboken, NJ, and New York: Ktav and Yeshiva University Press; 1991, pp. 85–121.
33. Hakohen, I.M. *Sefer Chafetz Chayim.* Vilna: Ravarsetz, 1873.
34. Drori, M. Genetic engineering: Preliminary discussion of its legal and halachic aspects. *Techumin,* 1980; 1:280–296.
35. Rabbinowitz, A.Z. Remarks concerning halachic policy and its implication for genetic engineering. *Techumin,* 1981; 2:504–512.
36. Abraham, A.S. *Nishmat Avraham.* 2nd ed. Vol. 4, Choshen Mishpat 425:2. Jerusalem, 1993. pp. 215–218.
37. Steinberg, A. Paternity. *Journal of Halacha and Contemporary Society,* 1994; 27:69–84.
38. Grazi, R.V., and Wolowelsky, J.B. Preimplantation, sex selection and genetic screening in contemporary Jewish law and ethics. *Journal of Assisted Reproduction Genetics,* 1992; 9:318–322.

Chapter 2

1. Kaji, E.H., and Leiden, J.M. Gene and stem cell therapies. *Journal of the American Medical Association* 2001; 285:545–550.
2. Scolding, N. New cells from old. *Lancet* 2001; 357:329–330.
3. Lo, K.C., Chuang, W.W., and Lamb, D.J. Stem cell research: The facts, the myths and the promises. *Journal of Urology* 2003; 170:2453–2458.
4. Rosner, F., and Reichman E. Embryonic stem cell research in Jewish law. *Journal of Halacha and Contemporary Society,* 2002; 43:49–68.

Chapter 3

1. Beecher, H.K. Ethics and clinical research. *New England Journal of Medicine* 1966; 274:1354–1360.
2. Experiments at Willowbrook (Editorial). *Lancet* 1971; 1:1078–1079.
3. Ross, L.F., Newburger, J.W., and Sanders, S.P. Ethical issues in pediatric trials. *American Heart Journal* 2001; 142:233–236
4. National Commission for the Protection of Human Subjects of Biomedical and Behavioral Research. Report and recommendations: Research involving children. Washington, D.C.: U.S. Government Printing Office, 1977.
5. Burns, J.P. Research in children. *Critical Care Medicine* 2003; 31 (Suppl.):5131–5136.
6. Ross, L.F. Do healthy children deserve greater protection in medical research? *Journal of Pediatrics* 2003; 142:108–112
7. Clantz, L.H. Research with children. *American Journal of Law and Medicine* 1998; 24:213–244.
8. Robinson, W.M. Ethical issues in pediatric research. *Journal of Clinical Ethics* 2000; 11:145–150.
9. Grodin, M.A, and Glantz, L.H. (eds.). *Children as Research Subjects: Science, Ethics and Law*. New York: Oxford University Press, 1994.
10. Kopelman, L.M., and Moskop, J.C. (eds.). *Children and Health Care: Moral and Social Issues*. Dordrecht: Kluwer Academic Publishers; 1989.
11. Ross, L.F. *Children, Families and Health Care Decision Making*. New York: Oxford University Press; 1998.
12. Steinbrook, R. Protecting research subjects: The crisis at Johns Hopkins. *New England Journal of Medicine*, 2002; 346:716–720.
13. Kopelman, L.M., in W.I. Reich (ed.), *Encyclopedia of Bioethics*. Rev. ed. New York: Simon & Schuster/Macmillan; 1995. Vol. 1, pp. 357–367.
14. Jakobovits, I. Medical experimentation on humans in Jewish law. Reprinted in *Jewish Bioethics* (ed. Rosner, F., and Bleich, J.D.). New York: Sanhedrin Press; 1979, pp. 377–383.
15. Avraham Steinberg, *Encyclopedia of Jewish Medical Ethics* (trans. F. Rosner). New York and Jerusalem: Feldheim. Vol. 2, pp. 520–535.

16. Miller, F.G., Wendler, D., and Wilford, B. Do the federal regulations allow placebo-controlled trials in children? *Journal of Pediatrics*, 2003; 142:102–107.
17. Rosner, F. *Animal Experimentation: Biomedical Ethics and Jewish Law.* Hoboken, NJ: Ktav, 2001, pp. 413–433.

Chapter 4

1. Radford, T. Korean scientists clone 30 human embryos. *British Medical Journal*, 2004; 328:421.
2. Yamamoto, K.R. Bankrolling stem-cell research with California dollars. *New England Journal of Medicine*, 2004; 351:1711–1713.
3. Spar, D. The business of stem cells. *New England Journal of Medicine* 2004; 351:211–213.
4. Cheshire, E.P., Pellegrino, E.D., Bevington, L.K., Ben Mitchell, C., Jones, N.L., Fitzgerald, K.T., and Koop, C.E. Stem cell research: Why medicine should reject human cloning. *Mayo Clinic Proceedings,* 2003; 78:1010–1018.
5. Landry, D.W., and Zucker, H.A. Embryonic death and the creation of human embryonic stem cells. *Journal of Clinical Investigation,* 2004; 114:1184–1186.
6. McHugh, P.R. Zygote and "clonote"—The ethical use of embryonic stem cells. *New England Journal of Medicine,* 2004; 351:209–211.
7. Fischbach, G.D, and Fischback, R.L. Stem cells: Science, policy, and ethics. *Journal of Clinical Investigation,* 2004; 114:1364–1370.
8. Jaenisch, R. Human cloning—The science and ethics of nuclear transplantation. *New England Journal of Medicine,* 2004; 351:2787–2791.
9. Vastaq, B. Human embryos cloned for stem cells. Work not seen as leap toward reproductive cloning. *Journal of the American Medical Association,* 2004; 291:1185–1186.
10. Anonymous. Facts versus ideology in the cloning debate. *Lancet,* 2004; 363:581.
11. Caulfied, T. Scientific freedom and research cloning: Can a ban be justified? *Lancet,* 2004; 364:124–126.
12. Spurgeon, B. France bans reproductive and therapeutic cloning. *British Medical Journal,* 2004; 239:130.
13. Tauer, C.A. International policy failures: Cloning and stem cell research. *Lancet,* 2004; 364:209–214.

14. Mayor, S. Claim of human reproductive cloning provokes calls for international ban. *British Medical Journal*, 2004; 328:185.
15. Daley, G.Q. Cloning and stem cells—Handicapping the political and scientific debates. *New England Journal of Medicine*, 2003; 349:211–212.
16. Tanne, J.H. American Medical Association approves stem cell research. *British Medical Journal*, 2003; 326:1417.
17. Blackburn, E. Bioethics and the political distortion of biomedical science. *New England Journal of Medicine*, 2004; 350:1379–1380.
18. Dyer, O. Scottish researchers apply for license for human cloning. *British Medical Journal*, 2004; 329:820.
19. Koralage, N. Creator of Dolly the sheep applies for therapeutic cloning license. *British Medical Journal*, 2004; 328:1036.
20. Wilmut, I. Human cells from cloned embryos in research and therapy. *British Medical Journal*, 2004; 328:415–416.
21. Drazen, J.M. Legislative myopia on stem cells. *New England Journal of Medicine*, 2003; 349:300.
22. Phinister, E.G, and Drazen, J.M. Two fillips for human embryonic stem cells. *New England Journal of Medicine*, 2004; 350:1351–1352.
23. Van Harsdorf, R., Poole-Wilson, P.A., and Dietz, R. Regenerative capacity of the myocardium: Implications for treatment of heart failure. *Lancet*, 2004; 363:1306–1313.
24. Hadaway, B. Embryonic stem cell research finally regulated. *Canadian Medical Association Journal*, 2004; 170:1086.
25. Gunderman, R.B. The science and ethics of cloning: What physicians need to know. *Radiology*, 2003; 229:638–640.
26. Guenin, L.M. The morality of unenabled embryo use—Arguments that work and arguments that don't. *Mayo Clinic Proceedings*, 2004; 79:801–808.
27. Birmingham, K. The move to preserve therapeutic cloning. *Journal of Clinical Investigation*, 2003; 112:1600–1601.
28. Wilson, J.F. How cloning could change medicine. *Annals of Internal Medicine*, 2003; 139:535–538.
29. Hu, Y., and LaBaer, J. Tracking gene-disease relationships for high throughput functional studies. *Surgery*, 2004; 136:504–510.
30. Allegrucci, C., Denning, C., Priddle, H., and Young, L. Stem-cell consequences of embryo epigenetic defects. *Lancet*, 2004; 364:206–208.

Chapter 5

1. Conjoined twins. In *Bioethical Dilemmas: A Jewish Perspective* (ed. J.D. Bleich). Hoboken, NJ: Ktav, 1998, pp. 283–328.
2. Kohli, N. Ethical issues surrounding separation of conjoined twins. *Journal of the Louisiana State Medical Society*, 2001; 152 (11): 559–564.
3. Drake, D.C. The twins decision: One must die so one can live. *Philadelphia Inquirer*, Oct. 16, 1977, pp. 1A and 14A–15A.
4. Annas, G.J. The Siamese twins: Killing one to save the other. *Hastings Center Report*, 1987; No. 2, 17:27–29.
5. Moraczewski, A.S. Against the separation of Jodie and Mary, *Ethics Medics*, 2001; 26 (6): 1–2.
6. Aborin, S. Brave new ethics: How far would you go to save a child? *Ladies' Home Journal* 2001. March:118 (3:134, 136–137, 191).
7. Therrien, M. Did the principle of double effect justify the separation of Jodie and Mary? *National Catholic Bioethics Quarterly*, 2001; 1 (3): 417–427.
8. Lathovic, M.S., and Nelson, T.A. A Catholic moral perspective on the separation of the conjoined twins Jodie and Mary: A survey and critique. *National Catholic Bioethics Quarterly*, 2001; 1 (4):1–30.
9. Abraham Steinberg, *Encyclopedia of Jewish Medical Ethics* (trans. F. Rosner). Jerusalem and New York: Feldheim, 2003. Vol. 3, pp.1106-1111.
10. Watt, H. Conjoined twins: Separation as mutilation. *Medical Law Review*, 2001; 9:237–245.
11. Baritun, Y.M. One or two? An examination of the recent case of the conjoined twins from Malta. *Journal of Medicine and Philosophy*, 2003; 28, No. 1: 27–44.
12. Huxtable, R. The Court of Appeal and conjoined twins: Condemning the unworthy life? *Bulletin of Medical Ethics*, 2000; Oct.:13–18.
13. Crowley, C. The conjoined twins and the units of rationality in applied ethics *Bioethics*, 2003; 17:71–87.
14. McCullough, L.B. Going against the grain: In praise of contrarian clinical ethics. *Journal of Medicine and Philosophy*, 2003; 28, No 1:3–7.
15. Appel, J.M. Ethics: English High Court orders separation of conjoined twins. *Journal of Law, Medicine and Ethics*, 2000; 28(3):312–313.

16. Maynous, R.O. Conjoined twins: Whose best interest should prevail: An argument for separation. *Pediatric Nursing,* 2002; 28 (5):525–529.

17. Dickens, B.M., and Cook, R.J. The management of severely malformed newborn infants: The case of conjoined twins. *International Journal of Gynecology and Obstetrics,* 2001; 1:69–75.

18. Imposed separation of conjoined twins: Moral hubris by the English courts (editorial). *Journal of Medical Ethics,* 2001; 27:3–4.

19. Separation of conjoined twins (editorial). *Lancet,* 2000; 234:953.

20. London, AJ. The Maltese conjoined twins: Two views of their separation. *Hastings Center Report,* 2001; 31 (1): 48–49.

21. Paris, J.J., and Elias Jonas, A.C. "Do we murder Mary to save Jodie?" An ethical analysis of the separation of the Maltese conjoined twins. *Postgraduate Medicine Journal,* 2001; 77 (911):593–598.

22. Thomasma, D.C., Muraskas, J., Marhall, P.A., Myers, J., Tomich, P., and O'Neill, J.A., Jr. The ethics of caring for conjoined twins. The Lakeberg twins. *Hastings Center Report,* 1996; 26, No. 4: 4–12.

23. Annas, G.J. Conjoined twins: The limits of law at the limits of life. *New England Journal of Medicine,* 2001; 344 (14):104–1108.

Chapter 6

1. Lebacqz, K. Difference or defect? Intersexuality and the politics of difference. *Annual of the Society of Christian Ethics,* 1997; 17:213–219.

2. Chase, C. Rethinking treatment for ambiguous genitalia. *Pediatric Nursing,* 1999; 25:451–455.

3. Money, J., Devore, H., and Norman, B.F. Gender identity and gender transposition: Longitudinal outcome study of 32 male hermaphrodites assigned as girls. *Journal of Sexual and Marital Therapy,* 1986; 12:165–181.

4. Money, J., and Ehrbardt, A.A. *Man and Woman, Boy and Girl.* Baltimore: John Hopkins University Press, 1972.

5. Money, J., and Tucker, P. *Sexual Signatures: On Being a Man or Woman.* Boston: Little, Brown, 1975.

6. Diamond, M., and Eigmundson, H.K. Sex reassignment at birth: A long-term review and clinical implications. *Archives of Pediatric and Adolescent Medicine,* 1997; 150:298–304.

7. Diamond, M., and Eigmundson, H.K. Management of intersexuality: Guidelines for dealing with persons with ambiguous genitalia. *Archives of Pediatric and Adolescent Medicine,* 1997; 151:1046–1050.

8. Colajinto, J. The true story of John/Joan. *Rolling Stone,* 1997; Dec. 11:54–73, 92–97.

9. Beh, H.G., and Dian, M. An emerging ethical and medical dilemma: Should physicians perform sex assignment on infants with ambiguous genitalia? *Michigan Gender and Law,* 2000; 7:1–63.

10. Minto, C.L., Liao, L.M. Woodhouse, C.R.J., Ransley, P.G., and Creighton, S.M. The effect of clitoral surgery on sexual outcome in individuals who have intersex conditions with ambiguous genitalia: A cross-sectional study. *Lancet,* 361:1251–1257.

11. Dreger, A.D. "Ambiguous sex"—or ambivalent medicine? Ethical issues in the treatment of intersexuality. *Center Report,* 1998; May/June:24–35.

12. Daaboul, J., and Trader, J. Ethics and the management of the patient with intersex: A middle way. *Journal of Pediatric Endocrinology and Metabolism,* 2001; 14:1575–1583.

13. Kessler, S.J. *Lessons from the Intersexed.* New Brunswick, NJ: Rutgers University Press, 1998.

14. Kipnisk, K., and Diamond, M. Pediatric ethics and the surgical reassignment of sex. *Journal of Clinical Ethics,* 1998; 9:398–410.

15. Diamond, M. Pediatric management of ambiguous and traumatized genitalia. *Journal of Urology,* 1999; 162:1021–1028.

Chapter 7

1. Jakobovits, I. *Jewish Medical Ethics.* New York: Bloch, 1975, p. 227.

2. Chavel, C.D. *Kitve Rabbenu Moshe ben Nahman.* Jerusalem: Mossad Harav Kook; 1964, pp. 44–45.

3. Halevi, C.D. Tashlum sekhar harofe' behalachah. In *Torah Shebe'al Peh* (ed. Y. Rafael). Jerusalem: Mossad Harav Kook, 1976, pp. 29–37.

4. Steinberg, A. Bedin sekhar harofe. *Sefer Assia,* 5736/1976, p. 279.

5. Yisraeli, S. Sekhar harofe. *Hatorah Vehamedinah*, 5715–16 (1955–56); 7–8:299–300.
6. Ibn Tova, A. *Hut Hameshulosh*, Pt. 4. Lemberg, 1891, responsum 20.
7. Fleckeles, E. *Responsa Teshuvah Me'Ahavah*, Pt. 3. Yoreh Deah 408.
8. Zilberstein, Y. Sekhar harofe behalachah. *Sefer Assia*, 1986; 5:24–29.
9. Shoshan, A. Refuah, chirugiah uterufot beMidrash Rabbah. *Koroth*, 1975/5735; 6, nos. 9–10:588.

Chapter 8

1. Bleich, J.D. *Judaism and Healing*. New York: Ktav, 1981, pp. 34–36.
2. Bleich, J.D. *Bioethical Dilemmas: A Jewish Perspective*. Hoboken, NJ: Ktav, 1998. pp. 148–159, 190–192.
3. Bleich, J.D. Genetic screening. *Tradition*, 2000; 34:63–87.
4. Chalmers, J., and Muir. R. Patient privacy and confidentiality. *British Medical Journal*, 2003; 348:1486–1490.
5. Clayton, P.D. Confidentiality and medical information. *Annals of Emergency Medicine*, 2001; 38:312–316.
6. Cohen, A.S. On maintaining a professional confidence. *Journal of Halacha and Contemporary Society*, 1984; 7:73–87.
7. Committee on Confidentiality. American Psychiatric Association guidelines on confidentiality. *American Journal of Psychiatry*, 1987; 144:1522–1527.
8. Hoppszalbein, S., and Hughes, L. HIPAA: The patient privacy challenge. *Hospital Health Net*, 2002; 76:37–43.
9. Josefson, D. US sets national standards for patient privacy. *British Medical Journal*, 2001; 322:8.
10. Rennert, S. *AIDS/HIV and Confidentiality: Model Policy and Procedures*. Washington, DC: American Bar Association, 1982.
11. Russell, J. Confidentiality of patient's information must be guaranteed. *British Medical Journal*, 2003; 327:812.
12. Steinberg, A. *Encyclopedia of Jewish Medical Ethics* (trans. F. Rosner). Jerusalem: Feldheim, 2003, Vol. 1, pp. 229–235.
13. Tendler, M.D. Confidentiality: A biblical perspective on rights in conflict. *National Jewish Law Review*, 1989; 1–7.
14. Winslade, W. *Confidentiality. Encyclopedia of Bioethics* (ed. W.T. Reich), rev. ed. New York: Macmillan, 1995. Vol. 1, pp. 451–459.

15. Rosner, F. *Biomedical Ethics and Jewish Law.* Hoboken, NJ: Ktav, 2001.

Chapter 9

1. Levine, E.M. The constitutionality of court ordered cesarean surgery: A threshold question. *Albany Law Journal of Science and Technology,* 1994; 4:229–309.
2. Rensting, S.C. The temptation to twin medical recommendations into judicial orders: Consideration of court ordered surgery for pregnant women. *Georgia State University Law Review,* 1994; 10:615–689.
3. Flannery, M.T. Court ordered prenatal intervention: A final means to the end of gestational substance abuse. *Journal of Family Law,* 1991–1992; 30:519–604.
4. Elkins, T.E., Brown, D., Barclay, M., and Anderson, H.F. Maternal fetal conflict: A study of physician concerns in court ordered cesarean sections. *Journal of Clinical Ethics,* 1990; 1:316–319.
5. Ouellette, A. A new medical technology: A chance to reexamine court-ordered medical procedures during pregnancy. *Albany Law Review,* 1994; 57:927–960.
6. Curran, W.J. Court ordered cesarean sections receive judicial defeat. *New England Journal of Medicine,* 1990; 323:489–492.
7. Pacheco, D.A., Copel, J.A., Robbin, J.C., Holden, A.R., and Curran W.J. Court ordered cesarean sections. *New England Journal of Medicine,* 1991; 324:272–273.
8. Leavine, B.A. Court ordered cesareans: Can a pregnant woman refuse? *Houston Law Review,* 1992; 29:185–218.
9. Stanyer, B.T. Court ordered cesarean sections: An example of the dangers of judicial involvement in medical decision making. *Gonzaga Law Review,* 1992–1993; 28:121–140.
10. Brenner, B., and Burnett, R. Court ordered obstetric intervention: A commentary. *New Zealand Medical Journal,* 1995; 108:431–432.
11. Stern, K. Court ordered cesarean sections: In whose interests? *Modern Law Review,* 1993; 56:238–243.
12. Rowan, C. Court ordered cesarean sections: In whose interests? *Nursing Ethics,* 1998; 5:542–544.
13. Morgan-Stern, P.S. Court ordered cesarean sections: Round II. *Healthspan,* 1990; 7(6):10–11.

14. Kitzinger, S. Kitzinger's letter from Europe: Court ordered cesarean sections in the United Kingdom. *Birth*, 1998; 25:202–203.
15. Beech, B.A. Court ordered cesarean sections are discouraging women from seeking obstetric care. *British Medical Journal*, 1997; 314:1908.
16. Lindgren, K. Maternal fetal conflict: Court ordered cesarean sections. *Journal of Obstetric, Gynecologic, and Neonatal Nursing*, 1996; 25:653–656.
17. Cahill, H.A. Orwellian scenario: Court ordered cesarean section and women's autonomy. *Nursing Ethics*, 1999; 6:494–505.
18. Annas, G.J. Conjoined twins: The limits of law at the limits of life. *New England Journal of Medicine*, 2001; 344:1104–1108.
19. Dyer, C. Trusts face damage after forcing women to have cesareans. *British Medical Journal*, 1998; 316:1480.
20. Rosner, F. The ethics of separating Siamese twins. See chapter 5 in this volume.

Chapter 10

1. Bleich, J.D.. *Judaism and Healing: Halakhic Perspectives.* Hoboken, NJ: Ktav, 1981, p. 19.
2. Whitney, S.N., McGuire, A..L., and McCullough, L.B. A typology of shared decision-making, informed consent, and simple consent. *Annals of Internal Medicine*, 2003; 140:54–59.
3. Schneiderman, L.J., Kaplan, R.M., Pearlman, R.A., and Teetzel, H. Do physicians' own preferences for life-sustaining treatment influence their perceptions of patients' preferences? *Journal of Clinical Ethics*, 1993; 4:28.
4. Blendon, R.J., Aiken, L.H., Freeman, H.E., and Corey, C.R. Access to medical care for black and white Americans: A matter of continuing concern. *Journal of the American Medical Association*, 1989; 261:278.
5. Quillte, B.H. Physician recommendations and patient autonomy: Finding a balance between physician power and patient choice. *Annals of Internal Medicine*, 1996; 125:763.
6. Savulescu, J. No consent should be needed for using leftover body material for scientific purposes: Against. *British Medical Journal*, 2002; 325:648–651.
7. Van Dienst, P.J. No consent should be needed for using leftover body material for scientific purposes: For. *British Medical Journal*, 2002; 325:648–651.

8. Rosner, F. Research and/or training on the newly dead: The Jewish perspective. *Mount Sinai Journal of Medicine*, 1997; 64:120–124.

9. DeVita, M.A, Nicclair, M., Swanson, D., Valenta, C., and Schold, C. Research involving the newly dead: An institutional response. *Critical Care Medicine*, 2003, 31(5 Suppl.):5385–5390.

10. Rosner, F. Research and training on the newly dead. *Archives of Pathology and Laboratory Medicine*, 1997; 121:1029.

11. Bircher, N.G. Resuscitation research and consent: Ethical and practical issues. *Critical Care Medicine*, 2003; 31(5 Suppl.):5379–5384.

12. Warner, E.A., Walker, R.M., and Friedman, P.D. Should informed consent be required for laboratory testing for drugs of abuse in medical settings? *American Journal of Medicine*, 2003; 115:54–58.

13. Zawistowski, C.A., and Frader, J.E. Ethical problems in pediatric critical care: Consent. *Critical Care Medicine*, 2003; 31(1 Suppl.):5407–5410.

14. Bigatello, L.M., George, E., and Hurford, W.E. Ethical considerations for research in critically ill patients. *Critical Care Medicine*, 2003; 31(3 Suppl.):5178–5181.

15. Luce, J.M. Is the concept of informed consent applicable to clinical research involving critically ill patients? *Critical Care Medicine*, 2003; 31(3 Suppl.):5153–160.

16. Rosner, F. The ethics of randomized clinical trials. *American Journal of Medicine*, 1987; 82:283–290.

17. Arnold, R.M, and Kellum, J. Moral justifications for surrogate decision-making in the intensive care unit: Implications and limitations. *Critical Care Medicine*, 2003; 31(Suppl.):5347–5353.

18. Roberts, L.W. Informed consent and the capacity for voluntarism. *American Journal of Psychiatry*, 2002; 159:705–712.

19. Kapp, M.B. Evidence based medicine and informed consent. *Academic Medicine*, 2002; 77:1199–1200.

20. Bridson, J., Hammond. C., Leach, A., and Chester, M.R. Making consent patient centered. *British Medical Journal*, 2003; 327:1159–1161.

21. Weddle, M., and Koskotails, P. Adolescent substance abuse confidentiality and consent. *Pediatric Clinics of North America*, 2002; 49:301–315.

22. Jenkins, K., and Baker A.B. Consent and anesthetic risk. *Anesthesia*, 2003; 58:760–774.

23. White, S.M., and Baldwin, T.J. Consent for anesthesia. *Anesthesia*, 2003; 58:760–774.
24. Skene, L., and Smallwood, R. Informed consent: Lessons from Australia. *British Medical Journal*, 2002; 324:39–41.
25. Reich, W.T. *Encyclopedia of Bioethics*. New York: Simon & Schuster; 1995. Vol. 3, pp. 1232–1270.
26. Ibid., pp. 1232–1238.
27. Ibid., pp. 1238–1241.
28. Ibid., pp. 1241–1250.
29. Ibid., pp. 1250–1256.
30. Ibid., pp. 1256–1265.
31. Ibid., pp. 1265–1270.
32. Avraham Steinberg, *Encyclopedia of Jewish Medical Ethics* (trans. F. Rosner). Jerusalem and New York: Feldheim; 2003. Vol. 2, pp. 545–560.

Chapter 11

1. Rosner, F. Emotional care of the cancer patient: To tell or not to tell. *New York State Journal of Medicine*, 1974; 74:1467–1469.
2. Bleich, J.D. *Bioethical Dilemmas: A Jewish Perspective*. Hoboken, NJ: Ktav, 1998, pp. 27–59.
3. Jakobovits I. *Jewish Medical Ethics*. New York: Bloch, 1975, p. 120.
4. Lavit, G.J. Truth-telling to patients with terminal diagnoses. *Journal of Halacha and Contemporary Society*, 1998; 15:94–124.
5. Wixon, B. Therapeutic deception: A comparison of halacha and American law. *Journal of Legal Medicine*, 1992; 13:77–97.
6. Avraham Steinberg, *Encyclopedia of Jewish Medical Ethics* (trans. F. Rosner). Jerusalem and New York: Feldheim, 2003. Vol. 1, pp. 317–328.
7. Bleich, J.D. *Judaism and Healing: Halachic Perspectives*. New York: Ktav, 1981, pp 27–33.
8. Brown, K.H. Information disclosure: Attitudes toward truth-telling. In *Encyclopedia of Bioethics* (ed. W.T. Reich), rev. ed. New York: Simon & Schuster/Macmillan, 1995. Vol. 3, pp. 1221–1224.
9. Jameton, A. Information disclosure: Ethical issues. In *Encyclopedia of Bioethics* (ed. W.T. Reich), rev. ed. New York: Macmillan; 1995. Vol. 3, pp. 1225–1232.

10. Lee, A.L., and Jacobs, G. Workshop airs patient's rights. *Hospitals*, 1973; 47:39–43.
11. Katz, J. *The Silent World of Doctor and Patient.* New York: Free Press, 1984.
12. *American College of Physicians Ethics Manual,* 3rd ed. *Annals of Internal Medicine,* 1992; 117:947–960.

Chapter 12

1. Karo, J. *Shulchan Aruch,* Yoreh Deah 336:1.
2. Fruchter, J. Doctors on trial: A comparison of American and Jewish legal approaches to medical malpractice. *American Journal of Law and Medicine,* 1993; 19:453–495.
3. Weiner, Y. *Ye Shall Surely Heal: Medical Ethics from a Halachic Perspective.* Jerusalem: Jerusalem Center for Research, 1995, pp. 202–224.
4. Silverstein, A.J. Liability of the physician in Jewish law. *Israel Law Review,* 1975; 10:378–388.
5. Ozarowski, J.S. Malpractice. *Journal of Halacha and Contemporary Society,* 1987; 14:111–127.
6. Hani, Z., and Weinberger, Y. Medical error and malpractice. Jewish Medical Ethics, 2001; 4:41–45.
7. Weiss, I.Y. *Responsa Minchat Yitzchak* 104–105.
8. Baumol, J.M. In *Emek Halachah* (ed. A. Steinberg). Jerusalem: Schlesinger Institute, 1986. Pt. 2, pp. 135–138.
9. Halevy, C.D. *Responsa Shevet Halevi,* Yoreh Deah 151.
10. Zilberstein, Y. In *Emek Halachah* (ed. A. Steinberg). Jerusalem: Schlesinger Institute, 1986, pp. 124–137.
11. Lau, D. *Techumin,* 1974; 16:187–197.
12. Goldberg, Z.N. *Techumin* 1977; 19:317–322.
13. Waldenberg, E.Y. *Responsa Tzitz Eliezer,* Vol. 5, Ramat Rachel 23.
14. Waldenberg, E.Y. *Responsa Tzitz Eliezer,* Vol 4, no. 13.
15. Preuss, J. *Biblical and Talmudic Medicine* (trans. F. Rosner). New York: Hebrew Publishing Co., 1978, pp. 27–31.
16. Jakobovits, I. *Jewish Medical Ethics.* New York: Bloch, 1955, pp. 217–221.

Chapter 13

1. Leape, L.L., and Fromson, J.A. Problem doctors: Is there a system level solution? *Annals of Internal Medicine*, 2006; 144:107–115.
2. Papadakio, M.A., Teherani, A., Banach, M.A., Knettler, T.R., Partner, S.L., Stern, D.T., et al. Disciplinary action by medical boards and prior behavior in medical school. *New England Journal of Medicine*, 2005; 353:2673–2682.
3. Krasner, J. Plan would tie co-payments to doctors' ranking. *Boston Globe*, Jan. 27, 2006; A1.
4. Gifford, D.R., Crausman, R.S., and McIntyre, B.W. Problem doctors: Is there a system-level solution? (Letter). *Annals of Internal Medicine*, 2006; 144:862–863.
5. Gold, M.S, and Frost Pineda, K. (Letter). *Annals of Internal Medicine*, 2006; 145:861.
6. Kahn, D.M. (Letter). *Annals of Internal Medicine*, 2006; 145:861. *Physician Executive* 2005; March/April:38–39.
7. Rosner, F., Berger, J.T., Kark, P., Potash, J., and Bennett, A.J. for the Committee on Bioethical Issues of the Medical Society of the State of New York. *Archives of Internal Medicine*, 2000; 24 (60):2089–2092.
8. Thompson, R.E. The temptation to be unethical is greater and the slippery slope is smoother than ever before. *The Physician Executive* 2005, March–April.
9. Thompson, R.E. Lantern of Diogenes: Is "honest physician" a 21st century oxymoron? *Physician Executive*, 2005; March/April:36–37.

Chapter 14

1. La Puma, J. Anticipated changes in the doctor-patient relationship in the managed care and managed competition of the Health Security Act of 1993. *Archives of Family Medicine*, 1994; 3:665–671.
2. Oddi, L.F., and Cassidy, V.R., Nursing research in the United States: The protection of human subjects. *International Journal of Nursing Studies*, 1990; 27 (1):21–33.
3. Haniel, R.P., Advance directives compatible with Catholic moral principles. *Health Progress*, 1988; 69 (3):36–40, 88.
4. Baker, R. American independence and the right to emergency care. *Journal of the American Medical Association*, 1999; 9:859–869.

5. Marwick C. Bill of Rights for Patients sent to Clinton. *Journal of the American Medical Association*, 1998; 279 (1);7–8.
6. Etzwiler, D.D. Important considerations of the Patient's Bill of Rights. *Diabetes Educator*, 2002; 28 (1):18, 20.
7. Mariner, W.K. Hollywood with patient rights in managed care. *Journal of the American Medical Association*, 1999; 281 (9):861.
8. Smith, C.K. Legal review: Informed consent—a shift from paternalism to self-determination? *Topics in Health Record Management*, 1990; 1:71–75.
9. Tai, M.C.E., and Tesai, T.P. Who makes the decision? Patient's autonomy vs. paternalism in a Confucian society. *Croatian Medical Journal*, 2003; 44:558–661.
10. Silver, M.H.W. Patients' rights in England and the United States of America: The Patient's Charter and the New Jersey Patient Bill of Rights: A comparison. *Journal of Medical Ethics*, 1997 (4):213–220.
11. Snider, J. Question of the mouth. Should a patients' bill of rights include the right to sue an HMO or other insurance company? *Journal of the American Dental Association*, 2001 May; 132 (5):596.
13. Annas, G.A. National bill of patients' rights. *New England Journal of Medicine*, 1998; 338 (10):695–699.

Chapter 16

1. Bleich, J.D. 2002, personal communication.
2. Stacy, M. *New York Sun*, Oct, 16, 2003, p. 5.
3. Smith, W.J., No mercy in Florida. The horrifying case of Terri Schiavo, and what it portends. *Weekly Standard*, Oct. 20, 2003:22–23.
4. Troug, R.D., and Robinson, W.M. Role of brain death and the dead donor rule: The ethics of organ transplantation. *Critical Care Medicine*, 2003; 31 (9):2391–2396.

Chapter 19

1. Birchner, N.E. Resuscitation research and consent: Ethical and practical issues. *Critical Care Medicine*, 2003; 31 (Suppl. 5):5379–5384.
2. Bigatello, L.M., George, E., and Hurford, W.E. Ethical considerations for research in critically ill patients. *Critical Care Medicine*, 2003; 31 (Suppl. 3): 5178–5177.

3. Morgenweck, C.J. Innovation to research: Some transitional obstacles in critical care units. *Critical Care Medicine*, 2003; 31 (Suppl. 3): 5172–5177.

4. Williams, M.A., and Haywood, C., Jr. Critical care research on patients with advance directives or do-not-resuscitate status. Ethical challenges for clinician investigators. *Critical Care Medicine*, 2003; 31 (Suppl. 3):5167–5171.

5. Luce, J.M. Is the concept of informed consent applicable to clinical research involving critically ill patients? *Critical Care Medicine*, 2003; 31 (Suppl. 3): 5153–5160.

6. Pace, C., Miller, F.G., and Davis, M. Enrolling the uninsured in clinical trials: An ethical perspective. *Critical Care Medicine*, 2003; 31 (Suppl. 3):5121–5125.

7. Kahn, J.P., and Mastroianni, A.C. Compliance to conscience. We can and should improve on the ethics of clinical research. *Archives of Internal Medicine*, 2001; 161:925–928.

8. Tollman, S.M., Bastian, H., Doll, R., Hirsch, L.J., and Guess, H.A., What are the effects of the fifth revision of the Declaration of Helsinki? Fair partnerships. *British Medical Journal*, 2001; 323:1419–1423.

9. Rosenbaum, R. Educating researchers: Ethics and the protection of human research participants. *Critical Care Medicine*, 2003; 31 (Suppl. 3);5161–5166.

10. Groeger, J.S., and Barnes, M. Conflict of interest in human subjects research. *Critical Care Medicine*, 2003; 31 (Suppl. 3):5137–5142.

11. Van Diest, P.J., and Savvulescu, J. Education and debate: For and against. No consent should be needed for using leftover body material for scientific purposes. *British Medical Journal*, 2002; 325:649–651.

12. Roberts, L.W. Informed consent and the capacity for voluntarism. *American Journal of Psychiatry*, 2002; 159 (5):705–712.

13. Karigan, M. Ethics in clinical research: Nursing perspective. *American Journal of Nursing*, 2001; 101 (9):26–31.

14. Rosner, F. Medical research in children: Ethical Issues. See Chapter 3 in this volume.

Chapter 20

1. Jakobovits, I. *The Timely and The Timeless: Jews, Judaism and Society in a Storm-Tossed Decade*. New York: Bloch, 1989, p. 128.

2. Rosner, F. *Biomedical Ethics and Jewish Law.* Hoboken, NJ: Ktav, 2001, pp. 287–301.
3. Unterman, I.Y. *Shevet Miyehudah.* Jerusalem: Mossad Harav Kook, 1955, pp. 313–322.
4. Rosner, op. cit., pp. 313–333.
5. Ibid., pp. 355–365.
6. Rosner, F. Compensating organ donors and Jewish law. *Mount Sinai Journal of Medicine,* 62 (2):167–170.

Chapter 21

1. Rosner, F. *Biomedical Ethics and Jewish Law.* Hoboken, NJ: Ktav, 2001, pp. 313–366.
2. Jakobovits, I. *Jewish Medical Ethics.* New York Bloch, 1975, pp. 285–291
3. Steinberg, A. *Encyclopedia of Jewish Medical Ethics.* Jerusalem: Schlesinger Institute at the Shaare Zedek Medical Center, 1991. Vol. 2, pp. 191–244 (Hebrew).
4. Evans R.W. The potential supply of organ donors: An assessment of the efficiency of organ procurement efforts in the United States. *Journal of the American Medical Association,* 1992, 267:239–246.
5. Kilter, D.S., Hogan, M.M., Thukral, V.K., et al. Incentives for organ donation? *Lancet,* 1991; 238: 1441–1443.
6. Capron, A.M. Whose child is this? *Hastings Center Report,* 1991; 21:37–38.
7. Caplan, A.L. Sounding board: Ethical and policy issues in the procurement of cadaver organs for transplantation. *Human Organ Transplantation,* 1987; 272, 275.
8. Pellegrino, E.D. Families' self interest and the cadaver's organs: What price consent? *Journal of the American Medical Association,* 1991; 265:1305–1306.
9. Joralemon, D., and Cox, P., Body values: The case against compensating for transplant organs. *Hastings Center Report,* 2003; 33:27–33.
10. Jacob ben Asher. *Tur Shulchan Aruch,* Yoreh Deah 336.
11. Karo, J. *Shulhan Aruch,* Yoreh Deah 336.
12. Rosner, F., and Widroff, J. Physician's fees in Jewish law. *Jewish Law Annual,* 1997; 12:115-126.
13. Maimonides, M. *Mishneh Torah,* Hilchot Rotzeach 1:14.
14. Zevin, S.J. *Le'Or Hahalachah,* pp. 318 ff., and *Halachah Urefuah,* 1981; 2: 93–100 (Hebrew).

15. Yisraeli, S. *Hatorah ve Hamedinah*, 5713–14; 5–6:106 ff., and *Amud Hayemini* 16:16 ff. (Hebrew).
16. Vigoda, M. Live organ donation and commerce in organs. *Assia*, 2003; 18 (3–4):5–24 (Hebrew).
17. Tabankin, H. Topics in the sale of kidneys from live donors in Israeli and Jewish Law. *Assia*, 1999; 16 (3–4):74–92 (Hebrew).
18. Halperin, M. Selling tissues and organs. *B'Or HaTorah*, 1993; 8:45–55.
19. Rabbinowitz, S. Commerce in organs. *Assia*, 1998, 15 (1–2):58–64 (Hebrew).
20. Lau, Y.M. Selling of organs for transplantation. *Techumin* 18:25–136 (Hebrew).
21. Steinberg, A. Ethical and halachic perspectives in organ donation. In *Kovetz Hatzionit Hadatit* (ed. S. Raz). Jerusalem, 2001, pp. 417–441 (Hebrew).
22. Goldberg, Z.N., The sale of kidneys. *Ateret Shlomo*. (Hebrew).
23. Sharman, A. Donation of organs for financial compensation. *Techumin*, 2000; 20:353–362 (Hebrew).
24. Yisraeli, S. Kidney donations from live donors: Danger to the donor and financial compensation to the donor. *Assia*, 1997; 15 (1–2): 5–8 (Hebrew).
25. Halperin, M. Organ transplantation in Jewish law. *Assia*, 1989; 12 (1–2): 34–61 (Hebrew).
26. Zarger, M.Z. *Responsa Vayeslev Moshe* 1:93 and 94.
27. Feinstein, M. *Responsa Iggrot Moshe*, Choshen Mishpat 1:103.
28. Tendler, M.D. Rabbinic comment: Transplantation surgery. *Mount Sinai Journal of Medicine*, 1984; 51:54–57.
29. Abraham, A.S., *Nishmat Abraham*. Jerusalem: Feldheim, 1995, Yoreh Deah 349:3.
30. Ibid., Choshen Mishpat 420:31.
31. Avodah Zarah 29a, Sanhedrin 48b, and elsewhere in the codes of Jewish law and rabbinic responsa literature.
32. Waldenberg, E.Y., quoted in *Nishmat Abraham*, Choshen Mishpat 420:31, p. 222 (Hebrew).
33. Weiner, Y. *Ye Shall Surely Heal: Medical Ethics from a Halachic Perspective*. Jerusalem: Jerusalem Center for Research, 2000, pp. 14–161.
34. Goren, S. *Torat Harefuah*. Jerusalem, 2001, pp. 127 ff. (Hebrew).
35. Grazi, R.V., and Wolowelsky, J.B. Nonaltruistic kidney donations in contemporary Jewish law and ethics. *Transplantation*, 2003; 75:250–252.

36. Goren, S.H. *Torat Harefuah.* Jerusalem, 2000, pp. 147 ff. (Hebrew).

Chapter 22

1. Goldstein, H. An observant Jewish physician in a non-Jewish society. In *Selected Topics in Jewish Medical Ethics* (ed. F. Rosner, H. Goldstein, and E. Reichman). Denmark: Hojers Forlag, 2003, pp. 127–133.
2. Rosner, F., and Tendler, M.D. (eds.). *Practical Medical Halachah.* 3rd rev ed. 1990. Hoboken, NJ: Ktav, 1990; reprinted by Jason Aronson, Northvale, NJ, 1997.
3. Jakobovits, I. *Jewish Medical Ethics: A Comparative and Historical Study of the Jewish Religious Attitude to Medicine and Its Practice.* New York: Bloch, 1959.
4. Rosner, F., and Bleich, J.D. (eds.). *Jewish Bioethics.* New York: Sanhedrin Press, 1979. Reprinted by Jason Aronson, Northvale, NJ, 2000.
5. Rosner, F. *Biomedical Ethics and Jewish Law.* Hoboken, NJ: Ktav, 2001.
6. Rosner, F. *Medicine and Jewish Law,* Northvale, NJ: Jason Aronson, 1990.
7. Rosner, F. *Medicine and Jewish Law,* Vol. 2, Northvale, NJ; Jason Aronson. Bleich, J.D. *Bioethical Dilemmas: A Jewish Perspective,* Hoboken, NJ: Ktav, 1998.
8. Schulman, N.E. *Jewish Answers to Medical Ethics Questions: Questions and Answers from the Medical Ethics Department of the Office of the Chief Rabbi of Great Britain.* Northvale, NJ: Jason Aronson, 1998.
9. Kellner, M.M. *Contemporary Jewish Ethics,* New York: Sanhedrin Press, 1978.
10. Rosner, F., and Feldman, D.M. *Compendium on Medical Ethics: Jewish Moral, Ethical and Religious Principles in Medical Practice,* 6th ed. New York: Federation of Jewish Philanthropies, 1984.
11. Meier, L. *Jewish Values in Bioethics,* New York: Human Sciences Press, 1986.
12. Meier, L. *Jewish Values in Health and Medicine.* Lanham, MD: University Press of America, 1991.
13. Grazi, R.V. *Be Fruitful and Multiply. Fertility Therapy and the Jewish Tradition.* Jerusalem: Genesis Press, 1994.

14. Koenigsberg, M. *Halachah and Medicine Today*. Jerusalem: Feldheim. 1997.
15. Feldman, E., and Wolowelsky, J.B. *Jewish Law and New Reproductive Technologies*. Hoboken, NJ: Ktav. 1997.
16. Weiner, Y. *Ye Shall Surely Heal: Medical Ethics from a Halachic Perspective*. Jerusalem: Jerusalem Center for Research, 1995.
17. Feldman, D.M. *Health and Medicine in the Jewish Tradition*. New York: Crossroad Press, 1988.
18. Jakobovits, I. *Jewish Law Faces Modern Problems*. New York: Yeshiva University Press 1965.
19. Feldman, D.M. *Marital Relations, Birth Control and Abortion in Jewish Law*. New York: New York University Press, 1968. Schocken paperback reprint, 1974 and 1975.
20. Levin, F. *Halacha, Medical Science and Technology: Perspectives on Contemporary Halacha Issues*. New York: Moznaim Press, 1987.
21. Steinberg, A. *Jewish Medical Law, Compiled and Edited from "The Tzitz Eliezer."* Jerusalem: Gepri, 1980.
22. Bleich, J.D. *Judaism and Healing: Halachic Perspectives*. Hoboken, NJ: Ktav, 1981.
23. Abraham, S.A. *Medical Halachah for Everyone*. Jerusalem: Feldheim, 1980.
24. Abraham, S.A. *The Comprehensive Guide to Medical Halachah*. Jerusalem: Feldheim, 1990.
25. Rosner, F., Garbasch, C., and Goldstein, H. (eds.). *Medicine, Ethics and Jewish Law*, Holte, Denmark: Paedagogisk Psykologisk.
26. Rosner, F., Garbasch C., and Goldstein H. (eds.). *Selected Topics in Jewish Medical Ethics*. Thisted, Denmark; Hojers. Halperin, M., and Fink, D. (eds.). *Proceedings of the First International Colloquium on Medicine, Ethics and Jewish Law, July 1993*. Jerusalem: Falk Shlesinger Institute at the Shaare Zedek Medical Center, 1996.
27. Halperin, M., and Fink, D. (eds.). *Proceedings of the Second International Colloquium on Medicine, Ethics and Jewish Law, July 1996*. Jerusalem: Shlesinger Institute at the Shaare Zedek Medical Center, 1996.
28. Steinberg, A. *Encyclopedia of Jewish Medical Ethics* (trans. F. Rosner). Jerusalem: Feldheim, 2003.
29. Steinberg, A. Medical ethics: Secular and Jewish approaches. In *Medicine and Jewish Law* (ed. F. Rosner). Northvale, NJ: Jason Aronson, 1990.

30. Rosner, F. Judaism and medicine—Jewish medical ethics. *Young Israel Viewpoint*, 2002; 44, no. 3.
31. Glitz, S. The autonomy of the patient in Jewish ethics. In *Selected Topics in Jewish Medical Ethics*. Thisted, Denmark: Hojers, 2003, pp. 90–99.
32. Jakobovits, I. *The Timely and the Timeless: Judaism and Society in a Storm-Tossed Decade*. New York: Bloch, 1989, p.128.
33. Cohen, A.S. On maintaining a professional confidence. *Journal of Halacha and Contemporary Society*, 1984; 7:73–87.
34. Tendler, M.D. Confidentiality: A biblical perspective, rights in conflict. *National Jewish Law Review*, 1989; 4;1–7.
35. Bleich, J.D. Genetic screening. *Tradition*, 2000; 34:63–87.
36. Bleich, J.D. Rabbinic confidentiality. *Tradition*, 1999; 33:54–87.
37. Bleich, J.D. *Judaism and Healing*. New York: Ktav, 1981, pp. 34–36.
38. Bleich, J.D. *Bioethical Dilemmas: A Jewish Perspective*. Hoboken, NJ: Ktav, 1998, pp. 148–159 and 190–192.
39. Steinberg, A. *Encyclopedia of Jewish Medical Ethics* (trans. F. Rosner). New York and Jerusalem: Feldheim, 2003. Vol. 1, pp. 224–235.
40. Rosner, F. Jewish medical ethics. *Journal of Clinical Ethics*, 1995; 6: 202–217.

Chapter 23

1. Pellegrino, E.D. Managed care and managed competition: Some ethical reflections. *Calyx*, 1994; 4:1–5.
2. Pellegrino, E.D. Rationing health care: The ethics of medical gatekeeping. *Journal of Contemporary Health Law and Policy*, 1986; 2:23–45.
3. Maimonides, M. Mishnah Commentary on Nedarim 4: 4.
4. Karo, J. *Shulchan Aruch*, Yoreh Deah 336.
5. Fruchter, J. Doctors on trial: A comparison of American and Jewish legal approaches to medical malpractice. *American Journal of Law and Medicine*, 1993; 19:453–495.
6. Rosner. F., and Widroff, J. Physicians' fees in Jewish Law. *Jewish Law Annual*, 1998; 12.
7. Maimonides, M. *Mishneh Torah*, Deot 4.
8. Ibid., Deot 4:20.
9. Jakobovits, I. *The Timely and the Timeless: Jews, Judaism and Society in a Storm-Tossed Decade*. New York: Bloch, 1989, p. 128.

10. Mackler, A.L. Judaism, justice and access to health care. *Kennedy Institute of Ethics Journal*, 1991; 1:143–161
11. *Encyclopaedia Judaica.* Jerusalem: Keter, 1972; s.v. Charity, Vol. 5:338–353.
12. Karo, J. *Shulchan Aruch*, Yoreh Deah 248–259.
13. Maimonides, M. *Mishneh Torah*, Mattenot Aniyim 1–10.
14. Ibid. 10:7.
15. *Encyclopaedia Judaica.* Jerusalem: Keter, 1972; s.v. Sick care, communal, Vol. 14, 1498–1499
16. Jakobovits, I. *Jewish Medical Ethics.* New York: Bloch, 1959, pp. 106–109.
17. Waldenberg, E.Y. *Responsa Tzitz Eliezer.* Vol. 5, Ramat Rachel, pp. 31–32.
18. Ibid., Vol. 15, Ramat Rachel, pp. 31–32.
19. Feinstein, M. *Responsa Iggrot Moshe.* Choshen Mishpat 2:73.
20. Ibid., Choshen Mishpat 2:18.
21. Waldenberg, E.Y. *Assia*, 1983; 9:10–15.
22. Maimonides, M. *Mishneh Torah*, Rotzeach 1: 14
23. Zilberstein, Y. *Halachah Urefuah*, 1983; 3:91–101.
24. Feinstein, M. *Responsa Iggrot Moshe*, Choshen Mishpat 2:73.
25. Waldenberg, E.Y. *Responsa Tzitz Eliezer.* Vol. 9, no. 28, p. 3.
26. Oshry, E. *Responsa from the Holocaust.* New York: Judaica Press, 1983.
27. Tendler, M.D. Rabbinic comment on triage of resources. *Mount Sinai Journal of Medicine*, 1984; 51:106–109.

Chapter 24

1. Rosner, F. The spleen in the Talmud and other early Jewish writings. *Bulletin of the History of Medicine*, 1972; 46:82–85.
2. Williams, H. Humor and healing: Therapeutic effects in geriatrics, *Gerontion*, 1986; 1:14–17.
3. Evans, W. Ottawa lodges add humour to armamentarium in fight against cancer. *Canadian Medical Association Journal*, 1990; 142:163–165.
4. Erdman, L. Laughter therapy for patients with cancer. *Oncology Nursing Forum*, 1991; 18:1359–1363.
5. Bellert, J.L. Humor, a therapeutic approach in oncology nursing. *Cancer Nursing*, 1989; 12:65–70.
6. Leiber, D.B. Laughter and humor in critical care: Dimensions of critical care. *Nursing*, 1976; 5:162–170.

7. Saper, B. The therapeutic use of humor for psychiatric disturbances of adolescents and adults. *Psychiatric Quarterly,* 1990; 61:261–272.

8. Gelkopf, M., Kreitler, S., and Sigal, M. Laughter in a psychiatric ward: Somatic, emotional, social, and clinical influences on schizophrenic patients. *Journal of Nervous and Mental Disease,* 1993; 181:283–289.

9. Basmajian, J.V. The elixir of laughter in rehabilitation. *Archives of Physical Medicine Rehabilitation,* 1998; 79:1597.

10. Cousins, N. Anatomy of an illness as perceived by the patient. *New England Journal of Medicine,* 1976; 295:1458–1463.

11. Hunter, P. Humor therapy in home care. *Caring Magazine,* 1997; Sept.:56–57.

12. Dean, R.A. Humor and laughter in palliative care. *Journal of Palliative Care,* 1997; 13:34–39.

13. Balzer, J.W. Humor—a missing ingredient in collaborative practice. *Holistic Nursing Practice,* 1993; 7:28–35.

14. Herth, K. Contributions of humor as perceived by the terminally ill. *American Journal of Hospice Care,* 1990; 7:36–40.

15. Mallett, J. Use of humour and laughter in patient care. *British Journal of Nursing,* 1993; 2:172–175.

16. Fry, W.F., Jr. The physiologic effects of humor, mirth and laughter. *Journal of the American Medical Association,* 1992; 207:1857–1858.

17. Dillon, K., Minchoff, B., and Baker, K. Positive emotional states and enhancement of the immune system. *International Journal of Psychiatric Medicine,* 1985; 15:13–18.

18. Cox, S.V., Eisenhauer, A.C., and Hreib, K. Seinfeld syncope: Catheter. *Cardiovascular Diagnosis,* 1997; 42:242.

19. Elliott-Binns, C.P. Laughter and medicine. *Journal of the Royal College of General Practitioners,* 1985; 35:364–365.

20. Van Zandt, S., and LaFont, C. Can a laugh a day keep the doctor away? *Journal of Practice Nursing,* 1985; 35:32–35.

21. Flotz-Gray, D. Make 'em laugh: Humor programs can help residents heal—Seriously. *Contemporary Longterm Care,* 1998; 21:44–46.

22. Richman, J. The lifesaving function of humor with the depressed and suicidal elderly. *Gerontologist,* 1995; 35:271–273.

23. Brown, L. Laughter: The best medicine. *Canadian Journal of Medical Radiation Technology,* 1991; 22: 127–129.

24. Strickland, D. Overcome terminal seriousness: Let go, laugh, and lighten up. *Seminars in Perioperative Nursing*, 1999; 8:53–59.
25. Robinson, V. The purpose and function of humor in OR nursing. *Today's Operating Room Nurse*, 1993; 15:7–12.
26. Berk, L.S., Tan, S.A., Fry, W.F., Jr., Napier, B.J., Lee, J.W., Hubbard, R.W., et al. Neuroendocrine and stress hormone changes during mirthful laughter. *American Journal of Medical Science*, 1989; 298, 390–396.
27. Wooten, P. Humor: An antidote for stress. *Holistic Nursing Practice*, 1996; 10:49–56.
28. Dugan, D.O. Laughter and medicine: Best medicine for stress. *Nursing Forum*, 1989; 24:18–26.
29. Luke, B. Humor's healing potential. *Health Progress*, 1992; 73:66–70.
30. Hung, A.H. Humor as a nursing intervention. *Cancer Nursing*, 1993; 16:34–39.
31. Rosner, F. Therapeutic efficacy of prayer. In *Medicine in the Bible and the Talmud*; 2nd ed. Hoboken, NJ: Ktav and Yeshiva University Press, 1995, pp. 204–210.
32. Rosner, F. Therapeutic efficacy of chicken soup. *Chest*, 1980; 78:672–674.

Chapter 26

1. Bloche, M.G. The Supreme Court and the purpose of medicine. *New England Journal of Medicine*, 2006; 454 (10):993–995.
2. Gostin, L.O. The Supreme Court's influence on medicine and health. The Rehnquist Court, 1986–2005. *Journal of the American Medical Association*, 2005; 294 (13).
3. Curran, W.J. Court-ordered caesarian section received judicial defeat. *New England Journal of Medicine*, 1990; 323:489–492.
4. Annas, G.J. Conjoined twins: The limits of law and the limits of life. *New England Journal of Medicine*, 2001; 344 (14):1104–1108.

Chapter 28

1. Meyer, H.S. Book review. *Journal of the American Medical Association*, 2005; 294(22);2913–2914.
2. Pilch, R.F, and Zilinskas, R.A. *Encyclopedia of Bio-terrorism Defense*. Hoboken, NJ: Wiley-Liss.

3. Relman, D.A. Bioterrorism: Preparing to fight the next war. *New England Journal of Medicine*, 2006; 534(2):113–115.

4. Lo, B., and Katz, M.H. Clinical decision making during public health emergencies: Ethical considerations. *Annals of Internal Medicine*, 2005; 143(7):493–498.

5. Kennedy, J., and Klafter, A. When a patient threatens terrorism. *Current Psychiatry*, 2004; 3(l):80–84, 86–87.

6. Steinbrook, R. Research in the hot zone. *New England Journal of Medicine*, 2006; 354(2): 109.

7. Okie, S. Glimpses of Guantanamo: Medical ethics and the war on terror. *New England Journal of Medicine*, 2005; 353(24):2529–2534.

8. Annas, G.J. Unspeakably cruel: Torture, medical ethics, and the law. *New England Journal of Medicine*, 2005; 352(20):2127–2136.

Index